International Perspectives on Education Reform
Gita Steiner-Khamsi, Editor

Education and the Reverse Gender Divide in the Gulf States:
Embracing the Global, Ignoring the Local
NATASHA RIDGE

Educating Children in Conflict Zones: Research, Policy, and Practice
for Systemic Change—A Tribute to Jackie Kirk
KAREN MUNDY AND SARAH DRYDEN-PETERSON, EDS.

Challenges to Japanese Education:
Economics, Reform, and Human Rights
JUNE A. GORDON, HIDENORI FUJITA, TAKEHIKO KARIYA,
AND GERALD LETENDRE, EDS.

South–South Cooperation in Education and Development
LINDA CHISHOLM AND GITA STEINER-KHAMSI, EDS.

Comparative and International Education:
Issues for Teachers
KAREN MUNDY, KATHY BICKMORE, RUTH HAYHOE,
MEGGAN MADDEN, AND KATHERINE MADJIDI, EDS.

Education and the Reverse Gender Divide in the Gulf States
Embracing the Global, Ignoring the Local

Natasha Ridge

Teachers College, Columbia University
New York and London

Published by Teachers College Press, 1234 Amsterdam Avenue, New York, NY 10027

Copyright © 2014 by Teachers College, Columbia University

All rights reserved. No part of this publication may be reproduced or transmitted in any form or by any means, electronic or mechanical, including photocopy, or any information storage and retrieval system, without permission from the publisher.

Cataloging-in-Publication Data is available from the Library of Congress

ISBN 978-0-8077-5561-7 (paper)
eISBN 978-0-8077-7304-8

Printed on acid-free paper
Manufactured in the United States of America

21 20 19 18 17 16 15 14   8 7 6 5 4 3 2 1

Contents

Preface	vii
Introduction	1
1. Oil and the Expansion of Education in the Gulf	9
Education as a Development Priority in Kuwait	10
Development of a Formal Schooling System in the Trucial States of the Lower Arabian Gulf	16
An Education Mission in Bahrain	24
Islam as a Driving Force for Education in Saudi Arabia	28
Striving for Education Quality in the Sultanate of Oman	32
Qatar's Progressive Reform Efforts: Education for a New Era	36
Moving Forward	40
2. The Rise of Women in the Gulf	41
Expansion of Schooling Opportunities for Girls	46
Better Educational Outcomes for Girls	49
Rapidly Expanding Female Participation in Tertiary Education	54
Conclusion	59
3. The Quest for Modernity: Gender, Education, and Development	61
Constructing a Discourse Linking Gender, Education, and Modernity in the Middle East	64
The History and Trajectory of the Modernization Project in Education in the Gulf	68
Current Gender, Modernity, and Education Discourses	70
Casualties of the Gender, Education, and Modernity Discourse	77

4. Leaving the Boys Behind — 80
- Boys Falling Behind in GCC Schools — 82
- Teachers, Gender, and Nationality in Boys' Schools in the GCC — 88
- Expatriate Teachers and Boys' Education — 91
- Conclusion — 103

5. Placating the Populace: Nationalization, Gender, and the Threat to Education — 105
- The Rentier State and the Rise of Nationalization Initiatives — 106
- The Issue of Nationalization and Implications for the Education Sector — 110
- Common Characteristics and Challenges of GCC Nationalization Policies — 113
- Nationalization, Education, and Gender Policies at the State Level — 116
- Unintended Outcomes — 125

6. The Value of Education Beyond Work: Implications for Gender — 129
- Returns to Education — 130
- Returns to Education in the GCC — 139
- The Value of Education Beyond the Labor Market and the Implications for Gender — 150

7. The Future of Gender, Education, and Development in the Gulf — 152
- The Gender Gap in the GCC — 155
- Barriers to Change — 159
- The Potential of Gulf Education Systems to Ensure Opportunity for All Students — 161
- Reimagining Gender and Education in the Gulf States — 166

Notes — 169

References — 171

Index — 204

About the Author — 216

Preface

I first moved to the United Arab Emirates (UAE) in September 2001; only 2 weeks later, the events of what is now commonly referred to as "9/11" unfolded. The region was thrust into the spotlight and, in particular, its education sector came under intense scrutiny for the first time. As I worked with Emirati students and read Western newspaper reports about the Gulf, I could not help but notice the vast gap between daily realities lived out by the people of the region and the way they were portrayed by Western academics and the foreign press. In particular, the narrative of the oppressed Gulf female and the corresponding oppressive Gulf male rang increasingly hollow. This observation became the impetus behind my dissertation and, later, further research looking at boys and education in the United Arab Emirates and now the Gulf Cooperation Council (GCC). This book is thus the culmination of 5 years of research and experience living in the region, and if nothing else, it aims to give the reader a more nuanced view of gender and education in the Gulf.

This book could not have been completed without the help of several wonderful people with whom I have been fortunate to work over the past few years. First, Professor Gita Steiner-Khamsi, who has never tired of supporting and encouraging me since we met at Teachers College in 2005. This book was her idea and I am so grateful for that. Soha Shami was not only my greatest help on this project, but also my biggest encourager. She worked tirelessly, supporting me with research, writing, editing, and referencing. Soha will one day be writing her own books, and so I am deeply indebted to her for helping me to produce my first one. Samar Farah has been a wonderful support on various chapters, and I thank her for sharing her own work on the United Arab Emirates, from which I drew throughout the volume. I was also blessed to have two wonderful interns from NYU Abu Dhabi: Leah Reynolds, who worked wonders with NVivo, and Petrus Layarda, who read through countless articles on returns to education. At the end of the project, Susan Kippels and Fiona Crookshank helped greatly to bring the book to its finished state. I also thank my wonderful team at the Sheikh Saud Bin Saqr Al Qasimi Foundation for Policy Research; they supported and helped me so I could focus on finishing this book. I could not have done it without them and I am grateful for every one of them. Finally and most importantly, I acknowledge Jesus, in whom all things hold together; it is He who gave me the ability to write and wonder in the first place.

Introduction

Gender as a unit of analysis seems to be of less and less interest to the West. In universities across the United States, Australasia, and Europe, women's studies courses are in decline (Barback, 2011; Osell, 2008). In education policy circles, discussions about the performance of women and girls have become passé as girls continue to surpass boys in both persistence and performance (Autor & Wasserman, 2013; DiPrete & Buchmann, 2013). However, despite this growing marginalization of gender in education and academia, I argue that gender has never been a more relevant lens through which to examine education than in today's world. The challenge now facing the wider field of gender studies, however, is to expand the definition of gender to encompass both men and women. The current framing of gender, as limited to women, obscures big-picture trends in gender dynamics and prevents both policymakers and educationalists from being able to examine the wider range of issues now relating to gender.

Although the academic rise of females, vis-à-vis males, in the West[1] is now common knowledge, what is less well known is that this rise is no longer confined only to those countries. Women and girls are outperforming their male counterparts in academic achievement and attainment across the globe, from Latin America to China to Eastern Europe, but nowhere do gender gaps more greatly favor females than in the resource-rich economies of the Arabian Gulf (Fryer & Levitt, 2010; World Bank, 2013). The rise of female attainment in the Gulf is a reality that does not resonate well with the Western narrative of the oppressed and disadvantaged Arab female. As such, this phenomenon is scarcely mentioned in academic articles or in local policy documents. This book aims to explore the new paradigm of gender and education in the Gulf, to shed light on the development and reasons behind the existing gender gap, and, further, to explore why it goes unmentioned and unaddressed even by local Ministries of Education (MOEs).

The current international discourse of gender in education, in particular relating to girls, has its roots in 1990, when a number of international gatherings placed girls' education firmly at the forefront of the global policy stage. The first of these were UNICEF's World Summit on Children and United Nations Educational, Scientific, and Cultural Organization's (UNESCO) World Conference on Education for All (EFA), held together in Jomtien, Thailand. Both gatherings highlighted the education of girls as an explicit focus for education and development. Subsequently, in 1995, the United Nations Development Program's (UNDP) *Human Development Report* developed two new gender measures: the gender-related development index (GDI) and the gender empowerment measure (GEM). The core message of the *Human Development Report* in 1995 was "Human development, if not engendered, is endangered" (p. 1). In 2000, the United Nations launched the Millennium Development Goals (MDGs), of which Goal 3 is to "promote gender equality and empower women" by eliminating "gender disparity in primary and secondary education, preferably by 2005, and in all levels of education, no later than 2015" (United Nations [UN], 2013). Also in 2000, UNESCO launched the Dakar Framework for Action goals for the EFA, which consisted of six explicit goals for countries to focus on when addressing education and development. Three of the six goals specifically mention and prioritize the education of women and girls. The combination of the EFA Framework for Action goals and the MDGs positioned girls' education as a nonnegotiable international development priority. Chabbott (2003) argues that this is also evidenced by the fact that gender goals are embedded in at least a dozen other world-level declarations, including declarations on population and social development.

At the country level, the strength of girls' education discourse lay precisely in the fact that it was a cause on which liberals and conservatives could both agree. In the United States there had been greater attention given to girls' education since the 1992 publication of the American Association of University Women report *How Schools Shortchange Girls*. In 1994, Dr. Mary Pipher also caught the American public's attention with her book, *Reviving Ophelia: Saving the Selves of Adolescent Girls*. These calls-to-arms for girls' education were strengthened by growing press coverage in the 1990s of American girls not doing well in mathematics and science or continuing on to college, and not having the same access to higher education courses and jobs that men had (DiPrete & Buchmann, 2013; Else-Quest, Hyde, & Linn, 2010; Grasgreen, 2013). Prior to this more populist-driven concern about the state of girls' education, human capital theory was developed in the 1960s by Theodore Schultz and Howard Becker. The theory argued that education and training needed to be accrued equally to both genders for nations to achieve sustainable economic development. As a result, as recently as 2013, organizations such as the World Bank have emphasized the benefits of gender equality. A 2013 report by the World Bank, *Opening Doors: Gender Equality and Development in the Middle East and North Africa [(MENA)]*, states that "gender equality is smart economics" (World Bank, 2013, p. 2), and the same organization's *World Development Report 2012: Gender Equality and Development* emphasizes this on a global scale. The issue of girls' education therefore went beyond questions of equity and fundamental human rights and became additionally linked to notions of efficiency and economic growth. Academics and feminist writers argued for the rights of a woman to do anything and everything, within a social justice framework (Reynolds, 1991), while economists, right-wing think tanks, and politicians argued that it was necessary for women to be educated to achieve national economic prosperity (Schultz, 1993). It was this bipartisan support for girls' education that propelled countries across Europe, North America, and Australasia to roll out policies and programs designed to empower and engage women and girls in education and beyond.

The combination of national interest in the West and the enshrinement of girls' education within international development goals meant that by the early 2000s most countries had education policies that contained a specific focus on girls' education. In addition, policymakers around the world who sought international recognition made sure to mention the achievements of women and girls in as many international press conferences as possible (Hasib, 2013). Representatives of governments who were aid recipients in Africa and Latin America began to speak regularly about girls' education in order to convey larger messages of modernity and success and position their countries to receive future aid (Dennis, 2008; Global Campaign for Education, 2011; Mettle-Nunoo & Hilditch, 2000). Even in countries where boys had trailed girls on several academic indicators for years, policymakers continued to speak exclusively about the progress of girls (Ridge, 2009).

Since 2000 there has been a steady rise in the number of girls and boys enrolled in school worldwide. Table I.1 shows the gross enrollment ratio for males and females by region and by GCC country in 2000, 2005, and 2010. Some regions remain problematic in terms of low female enrollment, particularly sub-Saharan Africa, but the global push to increase female literacy and education levels has been highly successful overall. At the tertiary level, women are now more likely than men to continue their education and more likely to earn a postgraduate degree (Callister, Newell, Perry, & Scott, 2006; DiPrete & Buchmann, 2006). Males continue to show a trend away from education, and low numbers of men entering tertiary studies is a concern in Western countries (Cappon, 2011).

In terms of gender differences in achievement, the Organisation for Economic Co-operation and Development (OECD) Program on International Student Achievement (PISA) and Trends in International Mathematics and Science Study (TIMSS) both show girls outperforming boys across subjects in the majority of countries. Even in math, which in the West was traditionally dominated by males, girls are starting to perform equal to or better than boys in many OECD countries (Autor, 2010; Bannon & Correia, 2006). Girls also perform better than boys on many national examinations across the world, in countries like Australia, the

Table 1.1. Gross Enrollment Ratios by Gender, Year, and Region

REGION/COUNTRY	GENDER	YEAR 2000	YEAR 2005	YEAR 2010
ARAB STATES (INCLUDING GCC)	Female	56.8	62.2	64.5
	Male	65.1	68.1	68.7
GCC ARAB STATES[a]				
Bahrain	Female	—	90	95.3
	Male	—	82	85.8
Kuwait	Female	—	79	77.8
	Male	—	71	67.8
Oman	Female	—	67	68.3
	Male	—	67	68.1
Qatar	Female	—	85	87.7
	Male	—	71	74.2
Saudi Arabia	Female	—	76	78
	Male	—	76	79.1
United Arab Emirates[b]	Female	—	68	78.7
	Male	—	54	65.4
CENTRAL AND EASTERN EUROPE	Female	78.2	81.8	85.3
	Male	78.2	79.3	81.0
CENTRAL ASIA	Female	72.0	76.3	74.2
	Male	72.9	77.5	75.2
EAST ASIA AND THE PACIFIC	Female	65.7	68.5	73.0
	Male	68.0	69.4	71.6
LATIN AMERICA AND THE CARIBBEAN	Female	79.3	82.5	85.4
	Male	77.7	79.9	81.4
NORTH AMERICA AND WESTERN EUROPE	Female	93.1	96.3	98.6
	Male	88.9	90.4	92.3
SOUTH AND WEST ASIA	Female	44.6	53.9	59.6
	Male	56.0	60.6	64.0
SUB-SAHARAN AFRICA	Female	40.6	48.0	53.9
	Male	48.6	56.3	60.8
WORLD	Female	60.3	65.3	69.3
	Male	65.2	68.1	70.5

Source: UIS, 2013.
Notes: (a) The data on the GCC are for the years 2005 and 2007 (not 2010), as no data were available from 2010 for all GCC countries.
(b) The source for UAE (United Arab Emirates) data is UNDP (2013). Gross enrollment ratios refer to the number of students enrolled, regardless of age, divided by the population of the age group that officially corresponds to that level. The data for these gross enrollment ratios are for all levels combined, except preprimary.

United Kingdom, and the United States, and also in the Middle East, the Caribbean, and Southeast Asia (OECD, 2009). Over the past 13 years the MDG of universal access to primary education for girls and boys has now been achieved in 20 countries (World Bank, 2013a). However, as nations tick off gender equality on the MDGs or on their national goals, this very narrow measure of equality (one limited to girls' enrollment levels) fails to capture issues with what Bannon and Correia (2006) call "the other half of gender." They argue that when the term *gender* is used to refer exclusively to females, it allows for discussion only of girls. As we see girls becoming increasingly educated across the globe, we are also seeing stagnation, and in some countries a decline, in both relative and real terms, in boys' educational attainment and employment figures (Autor & Wasserman, 2013; Baker & LeTendre, 2005).

The relative global decline in males' academic retention and achievement has, in some ways, heralded what Weaver-Hightower (2003) refers to as a "boy-turn" in educational research and policymaking. This turn, as Weaver-Hightower conceives it, could be thought of as a turn away from girls, a turn toward boys, or the boys' turn to receive attention. Globally, however, although some countries, such as Australia and the United Kingdom, have launched initiatives targeting males for intervention and assistance (Cuttance et al., 2006; National Literacy Trust, 2012), the attention paid to addressing the male deficit in education has nowhere been near that paid when there had been a female deficit (Lewis & Lockheed, 2007). There is little discussion about the potential impact of a feminized workforce, of the presence of a large mass of undereducated males and how these new trends will, if nothing else, affect the quality of life of women and children. Currently, the prevailing discourse surrounding gender remains focused on girls (UNDP, 2006; USAID, 2008), and focusing on boys is often miscast as somehow misogynistic or patriarchal (Sommers, 2013). This negative association with programs that focus explicitly on improving boys' achievement or engagement (Whitmire, 2010) may be deterring nations from introducing programs that address the growing gender gap for males. There needs to be a shift in the way we conceptualize such programs and realize that assisting boys does not necessarily result in disadvantage to girls—rather, helping boys gain a good education advantages both males and females alike.

The continued focus by international development agencies and national policymakers on women and girls continues to be much needed in some parts of the world, but the most recent figures from organizations such as the OECD (2009, 2012a) demonstrate that girls' education is no longer a universal policy issue. Even recent international reports, such as the *2012 EFA Global Monitoring Report* (UNESCO, 2012), acknowledge that there are now gender imbalances negatively affecting males. World Bank reports from 2012 and 2013 also openly state that gender inequality, in particular related to enrollment, is no longer an issue in education in some regions. However, if gender issues are concerned with both males and females, rapidly increasing gender divides disadvantaging males also necessitate a focus on gender in policymaking.

In the countries of the Arabian Gulf, with the exception of Yemen, the gap between male and female enrollment and achievement continues to widen. However, nowhere in government policies or public discourse is this topic discussed beyond dismissive comments to the effect that boys these days are lazy and unmotivated and they need to fix themselves (Al Munajjed & Sabbagh, 2011; Young, 2013). There is little acknowledgment that gender disparities, relating to both males and females, are typically a result of structural issues connected to political, economic, and social factors (Stromquist, 2012), and are thus unlikely to be happening because boys who do not do well are simply no good or lazy. Recent research conducted in the UAE by Ridge, Farah, and Shami (2013) found that schools and teachers play a significant role in the retention and achievement of national males, and boys who reported positive relationships with their teachers were significantly more likely to stay in school.

Western coverage of males in the Gulf also does little to facilitate addressing male disadvantage. One-sided literature and media coverage typically stereotype Gulf males as potential terrorists, abusers of women, or spoiled rich kids (Abdulla & Ridge, 2011; Sabbagh, 2003). If masculinity is explored in the region, it is usually explored in terms of alternate masculinities that do not reflect the way masculinity is understood and lived by the majority of men in the region (Peterson, 1989; Sabbagh, 2003). Western academics, the national and international media, and many leaders in the region regularly attribute male educational underachievement to the easy availability of public-sector jobs that pay high salaries and demand very little education (Randeree, 2012; Young, 2013). Alternatively, governments blame families and parents for spoiling their male children. These arguments may sound logical, but they are being made without any empirical evidence to support them. This discourse, though, allows GCC governments to avoid having their policies examined as part of the cause of the current situation. The end result is that educational structures and state education and labor policies escape attention that is well overdue.

Governments in the region have spent millions to improve the quality of education, in particular on curriculum reforms (Brewer et al., 2007; Maroun, Samman, Moujaes, & Abouchakra, 2008), and developing leadership (Maroun et al., 2008; MOE, Oman, & World Bank, 2012), but they are doing very little to address the growing male gender gap.

The specific reference to girls in three of the six MDGs (UNESCO, 2000) requires that signatory Gulf States work toward those goals, not only to signal their progress and compliance but also to signal their embracing of modernity (Qatar Statistics Authority [QSA] & Diplomatic Institute [DI], 2012). Global gender goals merely reinforce the reverse gender gap in the Gulf by compelling countries in the region to continue addressing only females and incentivizing a focus on girls that leads to the further academic marginalization of boys.

This book aims to address the issue of gender and education in the context of resource-rich monarchies of the Arabian Gulf. The book focuses on Saudi Arabia, Oman, Qatar, the UAE, Bahrain, and Kuwait. Yemen is excluded because of a number of factors that make it an outlier in the region, including its system of government, history of civil war, and lack of natural resources. The remaining Arabian Gulf States, while having different levels and types of natural resources, have all built impressive physical and social infrastructure using revenue derived from natural resources. All of the countries examined in this volume are monarchies and, as such, the policy environment is markedly different from Western-style democracies or military regimes. All, to varying degrees, rely on imported labor for low-wage jobs such as construction and domestic work (Randeree, 2012). All of these countries also currently struggle with the issue of low male participation in higher education and poor performance of national males on international and national assessments (Martin, Mullis, Foy, & Stanco, 2012; Mullis, Martin, Foy, & Arora, 2012a; OECD, 2009; UIS, 2012).

The book begins, in Chapter 1, with an overview of the development of mass education in each of the Gulf countries under consideration. This provides important historical, political, and cultural context for making sense of education and gender in the present. Chapter 2 examines the rise of girls in the region as a result of the rapid and widespread expansion of opportunities for education and learning made available to them. Following the discussion of girls and their quantitative and qualitative successes, Chapter 3 considers the role that the pursuit of modernity played and continues to play in perpetuating the current gender divide. Chapter 4 then considers boys and their very different educational journey since the discovery of oil. Complicating both the modernization and gender agendas, however, is the nationalization agenda that has come into greater force in the past 10 years (Hertog, 2012; Randeree, 2012). Chapter 5 therefore examines how efforts to create jobs for nationals across the workforce in the majority of these countries have created a further disincentive for males in education. This chapter describes the aggressive nationalization agendas currently under way in the Arabian Gulf countries, amidst private-sector employers' complaints and grave concerns about an undereducated pool of male nationals from which to draw. Boys' education in this situation of a shortage of national labor becomes even more relevant than it was before. Chapter 6 turns to the question of the purpose of education when the labor market and—to a certain degree—society signal it is not worth the time or the effort. This chapter examines the private pecuniary, nonpecuniary, and social returns to education and explores how there are very real returns to education at all levels that make a strong case for males (and females) to continue their education. Chapter 7 concludes with a discussion about the continuing relevance of gender in the region, for the education and labor markets in particular. The importance of seeing gender in a more nuanced way is stressed, as are the dangers of being distracted from the fact that if one half of society is facing obstacles to educational success and longevity, then there are likely to be costs not only for the individual but also for society. By taking an inclusive yet critical look at gender, it is possible to reimagine the Gulf as a place where both men and women can enjoy unique comparative advantages.

Oil and the Expansion of Education in the Gulf

The discovery of oil in the Arabian Gulf in the 1930s transformed the political and economic fortunes of the people of the region. As they envisioned and embarked on forming modern nation states, leaders used their new oil wealth to create or re-create various institutions commonly associated with development and modernity, including schools and universities.

Schools for boys in the Gulf had been established during the pearling boom of the late 1800s and early 1900s. Following the discovery of oil and the creation of nation states, numerous schools opened for both boys and girls, with a remarkably egalitarian balance. Table 1.1 outlines the timing of oil discoveries and when the first formal schools opened in the countries of the Gulf Cooperation Council (GCC).[1]

As Kuwait was one of the first Gulf States to make significant oil profits, after investing in creating its own schools, it subsequently supported the establishment of schools throughout the Gulf. Kuwait provided

Table 1.1. Oil Discoveries and the First Formal Schools in the GCC

Country	Oil Discovery	Source	First Formal School	Source
Kuwait	1937	British Broadcasting Corporation (BBC) (2012)	1911	MOE, Kuwait (2012)
United Arab Emirates	1958	Aldosari (2007)	1912	Davidson (2008a); MOE, UAE (2013a)
Bahrain	1931	Aldosari (2007)	1919	MOE, Bahrain (2013)
Saudi Arabia	1938	Aldosari (2007)	1925	MOE, Saudi Arabia (2011)
Oman	1964	Aldosari (2007)	1930	MOE, Oman (2011)
Qatar	1939	Aldosari (2007)	1952	Brewer et al. (2006)

neighboring sheikhdoms with buildings, curricula, teachers (typically sourced from other Middle Eastern countries, such as Egypt, but paid for by Kuwait), and, in some cases, even school uniforms (Davidson, 2008a). Ironically, Western-style mass schooling became a reality only after the British departure, which left behind an independent Bahrain and Qatar and the newly created United Arab Emirates in the early 1970s. The advent of mass schooling had the unintended consequence of creating equal educational access for both males and females, something that had not been the case in earlier, informal educational efforts.

The historical context of education in each of the oil-rich states of the GCC, Kuwait, the United Arab Emirates (UAE, formerly the Trucial States), Bahrain, Saudi Arabia, Oman, and Qatar, is crucial to understanding the nuanced complexities of gender relations in the region, which are not as they might first appear. This chapter sets the scene for subsequent chapters with an overview of the development of education in each of these states.

EDUCATION AS A DEVELOPMENT PRIORITY IN KUWAIT

Before oil was discovered, numerous invasions and attempted appropriation by the Ottoman Turks had pushed the Kuwaiti Sheikh Mubarak Al Sabah to seek the same type of naval protection agreement that Britain had signed with the neighboring Trucial States (BBC, 2012; MSU, 2012). Kuwait thereby became a formal protectorate of Britain in 1899, with Britain serving as its foreign affairs administrator (BBC, 2012). Despite the presence of the British in Kuwait, education in this era consisted of traditional al katateeb schools that were held in neighborhood mosques and focused on rote memorization of the Quran and its teachings, as well as arithmetic and basic literacy. By the end of 1910, Sheikh Yousef Bin Essa Al-Kinaei, a member of the ruling family, decided after hearing educational stories about key Islamic figures in his Diwan (Ruler's Court) that it was important to educate the masses. In 1911, he opened the first formal school for boys, the Mubarakiya School, with the help of the Kuwaiti people, who donated 78,000 rupees to the cause (MOE, Kuwait, 2012), making Kuwait the first country in the Arab Gulf to introduce formal schooling.

When large oil reserves were discovered by the U.S.–British Kuwait Oil Company in 1937, Kuwait experienced tremendous economic and social transformation (BBC, 2012). Education quickly became a national priority, and the traditional school model shifted to a modern three-level education system. Initially, the Education Council set up a few private, fee-charging schools to serve the sons of well-to-do merchants who could afford the cost of private schooling (Metz, 1993). In 1936, education was provided by the government (MOE, Kuwait, 2012), and by 1945, the government continued with the construction of 17 public schools to expand the schooling system (Kuwait Cultural Office [KCO], 2006). This significant achievement resulted in serious debate on two fronts: which subjects would be taught and their content, and whether to include girls. Controversy arose around some subjects such as geography, which was considered sinful by some as it proposed what were considered radical ideas about the Earth being round and evaporation being caused by the sun as opposed to the sky (Al-Awadi, 1957). Although such subjects as geography, history, physics, and chemistry were to be introduced, no local teachers were qualified to teach them (Al-Awadi, 1957). Therefore, expatriate Arab teachers from Syria and Palestine were brought in (Al-Awadi, 1957). Girls who attended school in the past had been criticized, and there was widespread general criticism to exposing girls to ideas on the opposite sex and teachings rooted outside the Quran (Al-Awadi, 1957). With respect to the curriculum, Al-Awadi (1957), however, describes how, over time, concerns regarding the education of girls and the curriculum waned and the new formal schooling system became more accepted by the general public. This shift in public opinion accompanied an overall surge in interest in schooling and education, as economic returns emerged in the form of better positions and higher salaries in government and private companies (Al-Awadi, 1957).

Kuwait's first national education system consisted of three levels: primary, preparatory, and secondary. At the primary level, students developed basic reading and writing skills. At the preparatory level, these skills were further developed, and students were introduced to drawing, arithmetic, geography, history, biology, health, chemistry, physics, and Arabic and English language studies. Students could choose to continue to secondary schooling for more advanced study of these subjects, though young men were often lured into the labor market after completing the preparatory stage. The Petroleum Company was gaining economic momentum at the time, and there was high demand for male Kuwaitis with at least primary-level education. Students who completed secondary education could then choose to enroll in the Technical College, which was founded in 1955 and became the Middle East's best vocational higher education institution. Modeled after a similar 5-year curriculum in Egypt, the Technical College devoted 70% of learning time to practical work and only 30% of learning time to theoretical work. The development of vocational education to smooth the school-to-work transition for young Kuwaiti men and women was, according to Al-Awadi (1957), revolutionary for the Gulf at that time.

By 1957, Kuwait had become one of the strongest regional competitors in education, joining Egypt as a powerful supporter and contributor to regional education and development. Students represented 9% of the population, with 11,225 boys and 6,300 girls enrolled in school (Al-Awadi, 1957). More developed than its regional counterparts, the Kuwaiti general education system, an adaptation of the Egyptian education system as described in

Box 1.1, was soon exported to and adopted by other countries in the Gulf region, namely, the UAE. In addition to providing general education, Kuwait's Education Department provided special needs institutions, adult education centers, and professional training for technical work. Foreigners, primarily Arab expatriates, provided professional training to Kuwaiti nationals who had become unemployed due to a decline in the pearling industry, which had previously provided significant employment opportunities. Kuwaiti students were also given incentives to continue their education by means of a monthly financial assistance allowance for students enrolled in local colleges and study-abroad programs for Kuwaiti students interested in gaining international experience (Al-Awadi, 1957).

> **Box 1.1. Egypt as an Education Aid Donor to the Gulf States**
>
> Since the 1940s, Egypt has been the primary curriculum provider for schools across the GCC (Al-Awadi, 1957). The first Egyptian education mission arrived in Kuwait in 1944 with the aim of simply transferring an identical education system from Egypt to Kuwait without accounting for differences in culture, nationality, or teacher experience or quality (Al-Awadi, 1957). Since then, hundreds of thousands of Egyptian teachers were "seconded," or formally transferred by the Ministry of Education (MOE) in Cairo, often with a reduction in travel cost, to serve as teachers in the GCC countries (Engman, 2009). In a sense, the exporting of teachers and educational services from Egypt to the GCC was considered an investment for the Egyptian MOE, and, thus, it was carried on for at least four decades following the initial mission and is still going on today. The MOE in Cairo has been directly involved in the process of negotiating teacher contracts in the Gulf countries and has thus been able to reap the benefits of the bargain. Moreover, the number of teachers who were seconded to GCC countries has been found to be very responsive to oil price fluctuations, as shown in Figure 1.1, suggesting a correlation between investment in Egyptian teachers and national revenue from oil in the GCC (Engman, 2009).
>
> Along with the transfer of educational systems and teachers came a transfer of approaches to teaching and learning. Having no locally trained teaching staff, GCC states had no option but to adopt and replicate a teacher-centered approach to teaching and learning that was marked by an emphasis on hard skills such as memorization and repetition (Al Munajjed & Sabbagh, 2011; Davidson, 2008a). Curricula were outdated and failed to take into account pedagogical and technological advancements (Engman, 2009). Ayntrazi (2012) also suggested that until the

Figure 1.1. Total Number of Seconded Egyptian Schoolteachers and Oil Price Fluctuations, 1952–2003

Sources: Ministry of Education (2008) and Financial Trend Forecaster (2008) as cited in Engman (2009).

1980s, many of the Egyptian teachers who taught in public schools across the GCC were politically oriented toward the Muslim Brotherhood and had been expelled from Egypt. According to Ayntrazi, "The outcome [produced] an imbalanced curriculum; focusing on religion to the detriment of basic skills in language, science and math."

However, by the 1990s, the declining quality of Egyptian educators and curricula became apparent and resulted in an almost equal reduction in demand for Egyptian teachers in the GCC. The UAE and Saudi Arabia, for instance, cut recruitment of new Egyptian teachers by 90% and 67% respectively, every year from 1992 (Engman, 2009). At the same time, GCC states began to invest heavily in training local staff at newly opened teacher education colleges (Engman, 2009).

Despite the growing quantity of locally trained educators, particularly females, quality continues to be an issue (Engman, 2009). The effects of a largely Egyptian-based education system are very much present. In 2011–2012, an Abu Dhabi Education Council (ADEC) survey of public schoolteachers in Abu Dhabi found that 49% of teachers are dissatisfied with the public school curriculum and did not believe that it prepared students for tertiary education or the labor market (Zaman, 2013b). Ironically, today, GCC secondary certificates are not recognized by Egyptian universities, and students graduating from GCC curricula are required to sit through a secondary school examination before being admitted (Fakkar, 2011).

In 1965, a new law made basic education free and compulsory for national students, boys and girls, between the ages of 6 and 14 (Metz, 1993). The same law covered the costs of transportation, uniforms, meals, and books for national students (Metz, 1993). One year later, the country's first and only public higher education institution, Kuwait University, was established, making way for further developments in the education sector (Metz, 1993). However, in 1990 the invasion of Kuwait by Iraq and the Gulf War had a profound impact, not only on Kuwaiti society but also on the education sector (see Box 1.2).

Box 1.2. Kuwait University: Rebuilding from Nothing

The Gulf War of 1990 marked a critical stage in the development of education in Kuwait. Like much of the rest of the economy, the education sector was devastated by the Iraqi occupation. With over $20 billion paid out by Kuwait's rulers in war costs and billions of revenue dollars lost from destroyed oil wells and reserves, reconstruction efforts following the war were severely hampered (Crystal, 1990).

Postwar reconstruction of Kuwait University faced several obstacles along the way. The war severely damaged the university's facilities, resources, and equipment. Administrative computer systems, student records, and a priceless collection of Arabic manuscripts had been lost in the war, and the university retained only 10% of its students and faculty members after the war. Many faculty members had been forced to leave for neighboring countries, where they found temporary jobs at other institutions. Students and faculty from countries that had sided with Iraq or remained neutral, particularly Palestine and Iraq, were not allowed to return to the university. A rising student population that now consisted primarily of Kuwaiti nationals thus came to be taught by a much smaller faculty, resulting in a less favorable student-to-faculty ratio. Distrust of foreigners intensified, and tensions between Islamists and secularists transferred to the university in the form of bans on veils and co-ed clashes (Bollag,1994).

Nevertheless, several positive changes came out of the war-ravaged university. In trying to prove that the world was right to have supported Kuwait in the invasion, Kuwaitis became more determined to demonstrate their self-sufficiency and productivity. This intent resulted in more research, much of which focused on the effects of the war on public health, society, and the economy (Bollag, 1994). The appointment of

> Faizah M. Al-Kharafi, the first Arab woman to head a national university, was a step to reducing gender inequalities in education leadership. On the security side, Kuwait University now has dedicated strategies and facilities inside and outside the country to back up computer systems and library and research records. In stark contrast to conditions during and immediately after the 1990 Gulf War, the university now ranks in the top 10 universities in the Arab world (Abdullah, 2012).

Today, Kuwait has a literacy rate of over 93% for those aged 15 and above. Women are also actively engaged in higher education—women comprised over 67% of Kuwait University graduates in 2006 (Krause, 2009). There is considerable government support for education, with 3.8% of GDP allocated to the education budget. Kuwait's MOE is currently prioritizing the modernization of public schools, upgrading facilities, improving the quality and curricular relevancy of 344 primary and secondary schools, and building up to 182 new schools and an institution for training and applied education. Competitive salaries to attract highly qualified teachers from across the region and efforts to improve the quality of existing teachers through comprehensive teacher-training programs have been another core element of the most recent national development strategy, Vision 2030 (OBG, 2012).

Despite these many advances in the education sector in Kuwait, the public school system still faces many challenges (Al-Shehab, 2010). It is reported that public schools are in danger of losing international accreditation and recognition because average teaching hours do not satisfy international standards. In the academic year 2006–2007, average teaching hours in Kuwait fell to 528 hours per year, significantly below the international average of 800 (OBG, 2012). There is also an acute shortage of local teachers; over 90% of Kuwait's teachers were non-Kuwaiti in 1990 (Metz, 1993). Although this figure has decreased, and it has been reported anecdotally that almost 100% of primary teachers are now Kuwaiti, challenges persist in attracting nationals to the profession. Dissatisfied Kuwaitis are moving away from the teaching profession and seeking higher-status jobs. Rather than encouraging and incentivizing Kuwaitis, the MOE has taken on a project to hire more foreign teachers by academic year 2013–2014 (MOE opens door, 2013). The education system also suffers from an inability to meet the needs of the labor market. As Al-Shehab (2010) suggests, there is a "mismatch between the educational agenda and the labor market['s] real needs" (p. 181). Although vocational education and technical training may be a perceived solution to this problem, perceptions of such programs as inferior to academic education present a serious obstacle to investment in this strategy.

With respect to gender, there are also significant challenges arising from the Islamist-dominated parliament. Most recently, in 2003 university classes became gender segregated (Calderwood, 2011) in response to a bill that was passed in 1996 calling for the segregation of men and women in higher education (Del Castillo, 2003). This not only forced the universities to spend an enormous amount of money to revamp facilities and buildings to accommodate segregation by sex (over $150 million in the case of Kuwait University), but there have also been functional and practical implications for the universities. In Del Castillo's (2003) article "Kuwaiti Universities Return to Separating Men and Women" in *The Chronicle of Higher Education*, the Dean of the College of Social Sciences remarks, "With a college like mine, where 90% of the students are women, it's effectively already segregated.... What should I do about the 10% of men? It's not practical for me to open a new course for just three or four men." The new policy has further exacerbated the shortage of qualified professors because segregation has required additional sections of many classes. In 2011, 2,095 qualified Kuwait University applicants were denied acceptance, largely due to the lack of capacity that resulted from segregating classes (Calderwood, 2011). This poses a serious problem to the education system as a whole as well as to both men and women for at least the foreseeable future.

In summary, despite having the oldest education system in the region, Kuwait faces many challenges similar to those happening across the Gulf and the Middle East at large. Poor education quality, a shortage of national teachers, and a disconnect between education and the labor market are issues that hinder efforts to move the system forward. More interestingly, however, gender-related issues, including sex-segregation and female dominance in higher education, are areas of concern that have received little attention. The next chapter will venture deeper into some of these issues.

DEVELOPMENT OF A FORMAL SCHOOLING SYSTEM IN THE TRUCIAL STATES OF THE LOWER ARABIAN GULF

Prior to the discovery of oil in the Arabian Gulf, the British were particularly concerned with the sheikhdoms that lay on the edge of the peninsula (Davidson, 2008a; Peterson, 2008) because vessels from these states had a history of threatening their maritime trade route from India to England. Hoping to reduce trade disruptions from marine warfare and piracy, Britain instituted a system of maritime truces to encourage cooperation between the sheikhdoms, which became known as the Trucial States and comprised the emirates of Abu Dhabi, Dubai, Sharjah, Ajman, Umm

Al Quwain, Ras Al Khaimah, and Fujairah. During that time, schooling was offered by the local mutawa'a, or religious preacher, in the form of Islamic studies based on rote learning and memorization of the Quran. This approach was later extended to include more advanced Islamic legal and science education (Davidson, 2008a). At the end of the 19th century, the Trucial States experienced a massive boom in the pearling industry as global demand for pearl and pearl-based luxuries grew (Davidson, 2008a). The influx of wealth and greater power for merchant families made way for local philanthropic efforts to build the first formal private schools in Dubai and Sharjah in 1912 (Davidson, 2008a; MOE, UAE, 2013a).

By the 1920s, many of the sheikhdoms had established their own educational institutions and schools using imported curricula and teachers from neighboring Arab countries (MOE, UAE, 2013a). The shift from traditional Islamic *al-katateeb* education to more secular and vocational education for both boys and girls was the first step toward the establishment of mass schooling that we see today (Davidson, 2008a; MOE, UAE, 2013a). These early private educational successes were crippled, however, when the pearling industry collapsed as a result of a combination of factors beginning with the global stock market crash that originated in the United States in 1929 (Davidson, 2008a). Other external factors that undermined the Trucial States' pearling industry included the "exclusive agreements" with Britain that restricted all trade outside the Britain–India network, and launched Japanese patents for a new technology to cultivate cultured pearls (Davidson, 2008a). With less support from merchant patrons, salaries for teachers and maintenance of schools became unsustainable, and students were forced to leave school, some returning to the *al-katateeb* system (Davidson, 2008a).

After several failed attempts to revive the education system between 1938 and the 1940s, the Trucial States secured financial support from Kuwait's Sheikh Abdullah Salem al-Sabah, who channeled enormous funds to Dubai's Education Department in the 1950s (Davidson, 2008a). This patronage financed salaries; trained teachers; built schools for boys and girls; established trade, vocational, and agricultural schools; opened the first adult education centers; and offered overseas scholarship programs for high-performing students (Davidson, 2008a; Engman, 2009). It was also channeled into developing the UAE's first modern public school in 1953, the Al Qassemia School in Sharjah (MOE, UAE, 2013a). Along with this financial support came curricular support, which allowed Dubai to adapt Kuwait's school curriculum (Engman, 2009). Benefactors from Iran, Saudi Arabia, and India offered further assistance and built Iranian, Islamic, and Indian schools, respectively (Davidson, 2008a). The foreign providers and imported teachers soon began to pose a serious concern to Emirati sheikhs who distrusted foreign involvement and to British administrators who feared the importation of the Arab nationalist movement to the Trucial States (Davidson, 2008a). Shortly after, in 1958, oil was discovered in Abu Dhabi, and oil-generated revenue underpinned the rapid development of a Western-style schooling system in the UAE (Davidson, 2008a; Gardner, 1995).

In 1971, the Trucial States gained independence and became known as the United Arab Emirates (UAE). The development of a national education system now became a national priority. The intention was to develop the national workforce to undertake new economic activities related to the oil boom, and to simultaneously support efforts to diversify the heavily oil-dependent economy (Gardner, 1995). The first president of the UAE, Sheikh Zayed Bin Sultan Al Nahyan, articulated his vision to prioritize human resource development through youth education: "Youth are the real wealth of the nation.... The real asset of any advanced nation is its people, especially the educated ones, and the prosperity and success of the people are measured by the standard of their education" (MOE, UAE, 2013a; National Qualifications Authority [NQA], 2013). In order to achieve Sheikh Zayed's aims, the federal government established the Ministry of Education in 1972 to be responsible for the development and management of all government schools throughout the seven emirates (Farah & Ridge, 2009; MOE, UAE, 2013a).

The newly established MOE encountered two main challenges in its early years: an extreme shortage of schools and a nonexistent national curriculum (Davidson, 2008a; Gardner, 1995; Suliman, 2000). To address the first challenge, the UAE embarked on a massive construction project between 1971 and 1982, building 254 schools and hiring four times more teachers, many of whom were local women (Davidson, 2008a). With the establishment of mass formal schooling, rapid progress was made in the education system, especially in terms of access. In 1971, student enrollment rate was just over 28,000, but education was accessible only in the cities and higher education was nonexistent (MOE, UAE, 2013a; NQA, 2013). Educational services were still immature and remained inaccessible to many smaller towns and villages. Federal Law No. 11 of 1972 made basic education compulsory and free, and brought dramatic changes to the system (NQA, 2013). In 1975, literacy rates were only 54% among men and 31% among women (NQA, 2013).

Developing a national curriculum proved much more difficult because it required more than just financial injections (Davidson, 2008a). The UAE's education system in the 1970s was a near replica of the Kuwaiti curriculum, which was largely an adoption of Egypt's national curriculum at the primary, preparatory, and secondary levels (Davidson, 2008a; Farah & Ridge, 2009). It was not until 1979 that the UAE's MOE launched the National Curriculum Project to develop a comprehensive Emirati curriculum, and only in 1985 was it fully implemented in all government schools (Farah & Ridge, 2009). A slightly adapted version of the Emirati curriculum was employed in technical and trade schools, as well as in oil and manufacturing company training programs (Davidson, 2008a; Suliman, 2000). However, to a large extent, the new curriculum only served the purpose of developing national textbooks and did not establish a set of educational standards to work toward for certain grades and subjects (Farah & Ridge, 2009). Private education, as described in Box 1.3, was increasingly becoming an alternative for nationals and an only option for expatriates.

Box. 1.3. Private Education as an Alternative or Only Option

With close to 88% of the UAE population coming from abroad and public options unavailable to non-Emiratis (HSBC, 2012), demand for private schooling is growing exponentially and far outpacing supply. In Dubai and Abu Dhabi, for instance, 87.8% and 58% of the total student populations respectively attend private schools (Moujaes, Hoteit, & Hiltunen, 2011). At the Abu Dhabi Indian School, 4,500 students applied but only 75 were admitted for the 2012–2013 academic year (Francis, 2013). With the absence of a public alternative, most students who are not admitted have no other suitable options within their financial range; these students are forced out of the education system or into schools with poorer standards and lower rankings (Dhal, 2013). A growing desire for high-quality education by Emiratis has also meant that an increasing share of Emirati students is enrolling in the private sector (Moujaes et al., 2011). The excess demand presents a challenge to both education providers and families who seek to enroll their children in private schools. For instance, more than 15,000 students are on the 2013–2014 waiting lists for private school admission in Dubai and Abu Dhabi alone ("Waiting List for Admission Crosses 15,000," 2013). Along with the growing demand, a lack of government regulation of private schools poses serious questions around issues of access and equity that must be investigated.

In higher education, regulation is more transparent. Privately operated higher education institutions (HEIs) in the UAE fall into two groups: HEIs licensed by the Commission for Academic Accreditation (CAA) of the MOHESR, and HEIs not federally licensed, operating under the free zones in Dubai and Ras Al Khaimah (CHEDS, 2012). CAA-licensed HEIs are regulated by the MOHESR and include semi government institutions, independent private institutions, and branch campuses of international institutions (CHEDS, 2012).

CAA-licensed HEIs saw student population grow 31% from 2008 to 2011; by 2012, 69,509 students were enrolled in 74 licensed HEI institutions (CHEDS, 2012). Nonlicensed institutions are independent of the MOHESR and offer degrees from the home countries of the branch campuses (CHEDS, 2012). Nonlicensed institutions currently serve more than 13,000 students and are spread over 28 campuses across Dubai and Ras Al Khaimah (CHEDS, 2012). Success rates across the different institution types differ slightly, with federal institutions achieving 95% success rates and CAA-licensed institutions achieving 90% success rates (CHEDS, 2012). Success rates are defined by CHEDS (2012) as "the percentage of credits passed (including D grades) during the previous semester" (CHEDS, 2012, p. 46). With such rapid progress and growth among private institutions across the UAE, it will be interesting to see what the future holds in terms of challenges and opportunities in this sector.

Across the UAE, increasing access to education over time, whether through public or private institutions, has led to marked increases in adult literacy rates. In the period 1984–1994, adult literacy was 72% for males and 69% for females; in the years 2005–2010, adult literacy had risen to 89% for males and 91% for females (NQA, 2013). Not only does this highlight improvements in the provision of education, it also shows a move toward gender equality in the distribution of education. Table 1.2 presents a snapshot of the current schooling system across the UAE.

Table 1.2. Snapshot of the UAE's Education System (2010)

INDICATOR	TOTAL	PERCENT FEMALE
Preprimary student enrollment	125,000	49
Primary student enrollment	327,000	49
Secondary student enrollment	337,000	50
Tertiary student enrollment	87,000	60
Number of private schools[a]	483	NA
Number of public schools	721	NA
Number of teachers (preprimary)	7,000	98
Number of teachers (primary)	19,000	86
Number of teachers (secondary)	27,000	65

Sources: The Global Gender Gap Report 2012 (Hausmann, Tyson, & Zahidi, 2012); (*a*) Private Schools Landscape in Dubai, 2012–2013 (Knowledge and Human Development Authority [KHDA], 2013); "Private Schools" (ADEC, 2013); "43 Private Schools in Sharjah Seek Hike in Tuition Fees" (Jamal, 2013); "Schools and Skills in RAK" (RAKFTZ, 2013); Dubai FAQs (2010a, b).

With regard to higher education, the first university, the United Arab Emirates University (UAEU), was established in 1977 (NQA, 2013). Since then, the number of higher education institutions in the UAE has grown to a total of 116 (KHDA, 2012b), with participation rates increasing from 2% in 1980 to 25% in 2008 (NQA, 2013). The Higher Colleges of Technology (HCT), formed in 1988 (HCT, 2012), Zayed University (ZU), established in 1998 (ZU, 2013), and UAEU account for 37% of total HEI student enrollment, according to the MOHESR. The three institutions form the federal higher education system. Enrollment rates at these three federal institutions grew 22% between 2008–2009 and 2010–2011 (CHEDS, 2012). Examining the tertiary education system as a whole in 2012, we can see that 39% of Emirati women and 12% Emirati men were enrolled, giving the UAE the second-highest global female-to-male tertiary enrollment ratio in the 2012 World Economic Forum's Global Gender Gap Report (Hausmann et al., 2012).

In higher education, additional challenges exist. Burgeoning academic offerings in the areas of business and engineering attracted approximately 50% of students enrolled in higher education in the UAE to pursue degrees in these areas, despite growing labor market demand for more technical areas of study, such as math, sciences, and computer literacy (NQA, 2013). Moreover, research capacities remain undeveloped and only 0.01% of the national budget is devoted to research, in contrast to Japan's and Finland's budget of around 3% (Swan, 2013). Finally, while tertiary enrollment rates have steadily risen since 1980, when there was only a 2% participation rate, UAE's current 25% enrollment rates are still low by international standards (NQA, 2013).

As depicted in Figure 1.2, the UAE education expenditure, as a percentage of government spending, has on average been the highest in the region, between 1999 and 2004 (World Bank, 2013b). At nearly 25% of total government expenditure, the UAE's government invested significantly more in the education sector as a percentage of government spending than the global average, which was consistently around 15% (World Bank, 2013b). This is promising for the future of the UAE's education system, as it suggests that improving the education sector is a major focus of the government going forward. However, it is important to note that in terms of percentage of GDP, other GCC countries spend more in total than the UAE. In fact, as of 2009, the UAE spent approximately only 1% of its total GDP on education, one of the lowest rates in the world (UNDP, 2013).

Beginning in the early 2000s, a trend toward decentralization of the education sector emerged in the UAE. In 2005, the emirate of Abu Dhabi established the Abu Dhabi Education Council (ADEC), which now operates all public and private schools in Abu Dhabi. Following this, in 2006, the government of Dubai made the decision to establish the Knowledge and

Figure 1.2. Public Spending on Education as a Percentage of Total Government Expenditure

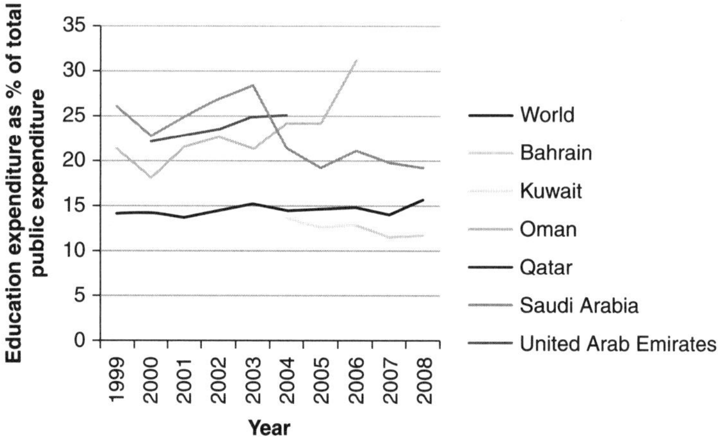

```
                    World
                    Bahrain
                    Kuwait
                    Oman
                    Qatar
                    Saudi Arabia
                    United Arab Emirates
```
(Education expenditure as % of total public expenditure, 1999–2008)

Source: World Bank (2013b).

Human Development Authority to oversee the administration of all public and private schools in the emirate, effectively separating Dubai schools from the authority of the MOE. However, in 2008, the global economic downturn heavily impacted Dubai, forcing the government of Dubai to hand the administration and financing of public schools back to the MOE. As a result, the KHDA currently has regulatory authority only over private schools in Dubai. ADEC, on the other hand, has strengthened its role in the education sector of Abu Dhabi and has embarked on a number of ambitious reform programs such as the New School Model (NSM).[2] The government in Sharjah also established the Sharjah Educational Council, which offers input on matters affecting schools in Sharjah and oversees the regulations for private schools, though public schools in Sharjah remain under the jurisdiction of the MOE. As of 2013, the MOE is responsible for public schools in all emirates except Abu Dhabi and is responsible for all private schools except in Abu Dhabi, Dubai, and Sharjah. It has extended compulsory education from primary to secondary school, with a total of 9 years required for students (MOE, UAE, 2013a). Public schools are gender segregated. Women teach at girls' schools and, increasingly, at boys' schools at the preprimary and primary levels. Men teach at boys' schools at the preparatory and secondary levels (Dixon & Le Roux, 2012).

As the UAE has developed and the government has sought to encourage young people to take up employment in the private sector in order to alleviate pressure within the growing and unsustainable public sector, there has been concern about the type and quality of education provided in public schools. As a result a number of efforts have been made to address quality at both the country and the emirate levels. At the country level, the MOE embarked on a 2-year principal training program with Pearson Education in an effort to improve leadership across the UAE ("Pearson Helping UAE," 2013). The KHDA in Dubai has been conducting school inspections for the past 5 years, not only in private schools but also in public schools (KHDA, 2013). Similarly, ADEC is now conducting school inspections in Abu Dhabi to help schools identify and then address deficiencies (ADEC, n.d.). More recently, ADEC has also partnered with Pearson Education to develop an inspections bureau that will function independently of ADEC's larger school operations in an effort to relegate some of the inconsistencies that exist within the system (ADEC, 2013). Other fledgling efforts to address issues of quality include the Sheikh Saud bin Saqr Al Qasimi Foundation for Policy Research in Ras Al Khaimah, which offers demand-driven, free, professional development workshops for all teachers in the emirate. To engage teachers, the Al Qasimi Foundation has also established the RAK Teachers' Network portal. To date, over 400 teachers have received training and 650 teachers from the UAE, Egypt, England, India, Morocco, Oman, and Switzerland are members of the growing local online educators' community (Sheikh Saud bin Saqr Al Qasimi Foundation for Policy Research, 2013).

Despite these efforts to improve quality at the local level, serious concerns remain about the quality as measured through performance in international assessments such as the Program on International Student Achievement (PISA), Trends in International Mathematics and Science Study (TIMSS), and Progress in International Reading Literacy Study (PIRLS). Test results from the 2012 PISA assessment reveal that the UAE, though ranked higher than its only other participating regional counterpart, Qatar, ranked 48th out of 65 countries tested in reading, science, and math, with girls outperforming boys in all three subjects (Organisation for Economic Co-operation and Development [OECD], 2013). In the 2011 TIMSS assessment, grade 8 students performed better on average than grade 4 students in both math and science; however, overall, the UAE often ranked far below the TIMSS scale average and performed within the low international benchmark range of the performance spectrum (IEA, 2011). Similarly, in the 2011 PIRLS assessment, the UAE's 4th-grade students ranked below the international average, placing 39th out of 44 participating countries (Mullis, Martin, Foy, & Drucker, 2011). Table 1.3 presents the UAE's results in these assessments.

The UAE has made significant advances in both the provision and quality of education across the country. Citizens and residents went from having little to no access to education in the 1950s and 1960s to complete coverage by the mid-1970s. This expansion catered equally to boys and girls and allowed for all children in the country to attend school, irrespective of gender or geographical location. The creation of higher education

Table 1.3. UAE Performance in International Assessments

	2009						Ranking	Source
	F	M	D	F	M	D		
PISA (Reading)	469	413	55	—	—	—	48/65	(OECD, 2013)
PISA (Math)	436	432	5	—	—	—	48/65	(OECD, 2013)
PISA (Science)	462	434	28	—	—	—	48/65	(OECD, 2013)
	2011 Grade 4			2011 Grade 8				
TIMSS (Math)	438	430	8	464	447	17	42/53; 23/45	(IEA, 2011)
TIMSS (Science)	437	419	18	477	452	25	45/55; 25/46	(IEA, 2011)
PIRLS	452	425	27	—	—	—	39/44	(Mullis et al., 2011)

Notes: F, female; M, male; D, gender differential in favor of females.
In the ranking column, the ranking before the semicolon for the TIMSS assessments is for grade 4 and the ranking after the semicolon is for grade 8.

institutions also allowed citizens to continue their education without leaving home. This opportunity made higher education much more accessible for women and gave them new professional opportunities in the labor market. The development of education in the UAE has overall benefited both men and women, but has given women particularly important advantages, which we will discuss in the next chapter.

AN EDUCATION MISSION IN BAHRAIN

In the 19th century, Bahrain was the main pearl hub in the Arab Gulf, with pearl beds surrounding the entire island and a trade route linked to the Indian Ocean. During this period, the British signed the first of several agreements with Bahrain to establish naval bases around the island, enabling the British India Navigation Company to control trade between India and the Gulf. Britain gained further control following the collapse of the pearl industry in the early 1920s. The economy began to recover after 1931, when Bahrain made its first oil discovery and successfully transformed and rebuilt its society using the newly discovered resource wealth (Gardner, 2010). Mosques were built across the country, and public hospitals and universities were opened (Gardner, 2010). New oil wealth also financed the construction of suburbs in Manama, where schools were built for both males and females.

Although oil discoveries played a big role in the mass construction of schools, education had already long been well regarded in Bahrain. In 1893, an American mission launched the first formal semiprivate school to teach English and Arabic (Bahrain News Agency [BNA], 2011). Twenty-six years later, in 1919, Bahrain inaugurated its first public school, Al-Hidaya Al-Khalifia Boys School, with generous funding from the community of Muharraq and the support of the Bahraini royal family (BNA, 2011). This marked the beginning of Bahrain's formal public education system. Amidst growing awareness of the value of education for society, formal schooling opportunities were soon extended to girls. The first public school for girls opened in Muharraq in 1928, also making it the first girls' public school in the GCC region as a whole (United Nations Commission on Sustainable Development [UNCSD], 1997). In these early days, schools needed to maintain a delicate balance between religion and modern science in order to ease Bahrain's transition to a Western-style education system (Madany, Ali, & Akhter, 1988).

Initially, schools in Bahrain were governed by the Education Committee, which pooled resources from public donations and contributions from the royal family. By 1929, it had become evident that a new regulatory and funding body was needed to take on these responsibilities; so Bahrain's Ministry of Education (MOE) was formed that year under the direct sponsorship of the government (UNCSD, 1997). As with the majority of the Arab Gulf countries, Bahrain's education system consists of 9 years of basic/general education and 3 years of secondary education. The first 6 years of the basic education portion form the primary school stage and the subsequent 3 years form the preparatory stage. In 2005, education law no. 27 made the primary and preparatory stages compulsory for all children in Bahrain between the ages of 6 and 14.

Despite many similarities between the education systems of Bahrain and the other countries of the Arab Gulf, significant differences make Bahrain unique. For instance, unlike many other monarchs in the region, Bahrain's king has long been personally interested and invested in learning about successful education models and global education systems. According to the BNA (2011), "[Sheikh Khalifa] went to Britain in 1956 where he spent five months examining teaching methods and recent programmes as well as administrative systems in schools. He came back home in 1957 with new ideas to improve education in his homeland." In addition, unlike Qatar and the UAE, which have only recently experimented with decentralization, Bahrain has been promoting decentralization since the 1980s. Bahrain was the first country to divide its MOE into autonomous units with horizontal patterns of interaction, as opposed to traditional vertical units. The horizontal structure provided for more flexible and democratic decisionmaking, which proved to be successful in terms of reducing execution time and problems related to miscommunication. Schools also gained autonomy under ministerial decision no. 375/168/90 of 1990, which made the school principal the overarching administrator of the school. Bahrain also features a system of educational districts that is not present in other GCC countries. The system is a part of the greater decentralization plan to enhance efficiency of schools through coordination among the school districts, rather than directly through the MOE. Every educational district consists of 20 primary schools and receives resources equal to its counterparts. In 2006–2007, the district system was extended to include intermediate and secondary schools. Today the district system functions almost independently to best meet the needs of the students in each district (UNESCO & IBE, 2011).

With respect to women's education, Bahrain has made remarkable progress since the opening of its first girls' school in 1928 (Al-Zuhayyan, 2012). In 2001, 103 out of 203 schools were girls' schools, and girls accounted for 50% of the student population in public schools and 44.5% of the population in private schools (Al Gharaibeh, 2011). By 2012, 97% of girls and 92% of boys were enrolled in secondary schooling (Hausmann et al., 2012). Women are enrolled at a rate 12% higher than men at the tertiary level (Hausmann et al., 2012). In terms of performance at school, evidence suggests that girls have been more successful than boys at every educational level and in every subject, and that the gender differential in favor of girls increases at every stage (UNESCO & IBE, 2011). For example, the difference in the average national assessment scores for math between girls and boys in grade 3 in 2010–2011 was 0.83; by grade 6, the difference jumped to 1.44 in favor of girls (UNESCO & IBE, 2011).

By 2010, Bahrain was among the top-performing Arab states in terms of educational development. According to UNESCO statistics from 2005 to 2010, Bahrain was the only country in the region to achieve a 100% youth literacy rate, far surpassing the regional average of 86% (UNESCO, 2010). Bahrain also ranked 51st in the world in the 2008 Education for All Development Index (EDI), second in the region after 46th-ranked UAE (UNESCO, 2011). Bahrain's dedication to inclusive education has marked the education system as progressive. In 2006, Bahrain adopted a full-fledged inclusive education program governed largely by the MOE and the newly founded Directorate of Special Education. The program was committed to educating children with special needs and providing equal opportunities for girls, expatriates, and children who study "without walls." As a part of this program, a Gifted Students Centre was also established to identify, track, and invest in gifted children. Early childhood care was provided and educational sponsorship for orphans was endorsed by the Royal Charitable Foundation. Though most kindergartens are not yet accommodating children with special needs, significant progress in this area has also been made.

Higher education functions somewhat more independently within the MOE and is governed by the Higher Education Council, formed in 2005 under Higher Education Law No. 3 (MOE, Bahrain, 2008). The council oversees all administrative, regulative, financial, contractual, and academic matters related to higher education institutions in Bahrain (MOE, Bahrain, 2008). The first public higher education institutions to be established were the Gulf Technical College, the College of Health Sciences, the University College of Arts, Science and Education, and the Arabian Gulf University (AGU), founded in 1968, 1976, 1979, and 1980, respectively (Madany et al., 1988; Karolak, 2012). In 1986, the Gulf Technical College, later renamed Bahrain Polytechnic, and the University College of Arts, Science, and Education merged together to form the University of Bahrain (UoB), Bahrain's best-known public university today (Madany et al., 1988; Karolak, 2012). Each of these institutions was set up with the aim of meeting the need for qualified professionals in the labor market and the country's fast-paced, oil-fueled economic development efforts (Madany et al., 1988). In 2000, a new wave of private tertiary institutions, including New York Institute of Technology, Ahlia University, and Gulf University, entered the stage (Karolak, 2012). UoB nevertheless remains the most-attended university, with over 12,000 students enrolled in 2010 (UoB, 2013).

In line with Bahrain's Vision 2030, one of UoB's top priorities became training and educating the country's future schoolteachers and administrators (MOE, Bahrain 2008; UNESCO & IBE, 2011). UoB opened the Bahrain Teachers College (BTC) in 2008 as an instrument to pursue this vision. Since its establishment, the university has not only helped to develop the professional skills and knowledge of current and future teachers but also played a vital role in changing the perception of teaching as a low-grade profession, making it a more viable option for Bahrainis (UNESCO & IBE, 2011). Today, the MOE offers attractive incentives for students to join BTC, including full financial grants, a guaranteed teaching job after successful completion of coursework and graduation, a bilingual learning experience, and international education standards incomparable to those offered by other local institutions (UNESCO & IBE, 2011).

However, despite UoB's efforts to train teachers, the existing education system continues to face challenges relating to teaching and learning. Teachers, reportedly disgruntled by unmet promises of salary increases and improved working conditions in difficult economic times, lack the motivation to continue in their profession and are increasingly quitting their jobs (Toumi, 2008). The quality of education also remains an issue, as with most countries in the Arabian Gulf, despite the existence of the Quality Assurance Authority for Education and Training (UNESCO & IBE, 2011). This is demonstrated by the low performance of Bahraini students in international assessments such as the TIMSS as compared with the global average (UNESCO & IBE, 2011). Finally, a tradition of rote learning carries on at some level, with very little time in the curricula dedicated to developing students' analytical and critical thinking skills (UNESCO & IBE, 2011).

ISLAM AS A DRIVING FORCE FOR EDUCATION IN SAUDI ARABIA

In the middle of the 18th century, the Saud family based in Al Nejd, central Saudi Arabia, sought to create a state based on Islamic principles, and by 1902, they had, under King Abdulaziz Ibn Saud, made Riyadh their capital (Aldosari, 2007). However, it was not until 1932 and the capture of the Al Hasa and Hijaz that what we know today as the Kingdom of Saudi Arabia was established (Aldosari, 2007; Al-Rasheed, 2003). Just 6 years later, in 1938 oil was discovered in Saudi Arabia and the American-owned oil company ARAMCO initiated production. By 1960, the Kingdom became the world's largest single oil exporter, with oil reserves accounting for 25% of the global market. It was by this economic power that Saudi Arabia was able to become the founding member of the Organization of Petroleum Exporting Countries (OPEC) (British Broadcasting Corporation, 2013), which would eventually allow the country to push for the development of a formal education system, among other capacities.

Years before the oil discovery, however, in the early 19th century, education was composed largely of classes for religious studies and recitation taught in or near mosques. Boys were typically enrolled in these public classes, while girls received private tutoring at home by Quran teachers or *kuttab* (Metz, 1992). At the basic level, education comprised religious teachings, elementary arithmetic, and Arabic language studies (Metz, 1992). Nevertheless, illiteracy remained high due in part to a focus on memorization over reading and writing (Metz, 1992).

The drive for formal education began with the establishment of a number of private schools, established in 1919 under the supervision of the Ottoman rulers, who hoped to build an internal support system that would ease the Ottoman conquest (Al-Abdulkareem, n.d.). According to Metz (1992), these schools "offered limited secular education for boys," and were often politically inclined, and thus, were seen as a threat to the Hashemite ruling power at the time. Most of them were closed down by Sharif Hussein Bin Ali, Hashemite ruler of Mecca, in his Great Arab Revolt against the

Ottoman Turks in which he broke away from Ottoman influences, including those in education (Al-Abdulkareem, n.d.).

A transfer of power from him to King Abdulaziz, however, resulted in a move back to formal education. As an educated man himself, King Abdulaziz understood the importance of education and ordered the formation of a new education system, the Directorate of Education, beginning in 1925 (Al-Abdulkareem, n.d.). In the same year, the first curriculum was established by a Syrian academic and modeled after the Egyptian curriculum (Alromi, 2000). Supplemental aid and teaching resources were also provided and subsidized by Egypt to help build the first formal public school in the country (Alromi, 2000).

However, it was not until 1936 that public education began to flourish beyond the first public school, which was initially met with challenges that took a decade to counteract (Alromi, 2000). A newfound wealth from oil prompted the growth in attendance of public schools to 2% for girls and 22% for boys by 1938 (Aldosari, 2007). It also enabled the financing of 182 primary schools by 1949, giving the primary schooling sector a total enrollment rate of 21,409 pupils (Al-Abdulkareem, n.d.). The push for primary education was then complemented by an initiative to begin public funding of secondary schools from 1951. By 1954, the Saudi Ministry of Education (MOE) was established to oversee a new schooling system that would cover primary, secondary, and tertiary education for all provinces all over the country under the Crown Prince Fahad (later King Fahad) (Al-Abdulkareem, n.d.; Metz, 1992). Only 3 years later, King Saud University, the first nonspecifically religious university, was opened for men (Metz, 1992).

Public, nonreligious education for women remained highly controversial, with religious leaders pronouncing education for women a danger to society (Abdulkareem, n.d.; Metz, 1992). Nevertheless, public schooling for girls was introduced to the Kingdom in 1956 and met with some support as people began to recognize a woman's right to education as described in Islamic teachings that called for equity in education (Metz, 1992). With the expansion of public education in Saudi Arabia and the growing recognition of the benefits of education for women, demand for girls' schooling rose. In order to simultaneously cater to the growing demand for girls' education and to placate religious elements, the *ulama*, or body of religious scholars, was tasked to form the General Directorate of Girls' Education in 1960, specifically to oversee and provide girls' education from kindergarten to higher education (Abdulkareem, n.d.; Metz, 1992). By 1981, enrollment rates had increased to 43% of girls and 81% of boys, illustrating growing awareness of the value of education over the years.

In 1989, Saudi Arabia's schooling system had expanded to include 950 new schools, 7 universities, and 11 technical colleges, giving it a total of 14,000 education institutions with 400,000 students (Metz, 1992). General education was structured as elsewhere in the Gulf with 6 years of primary schooling, 3 years of intermediate schooling, and 3 years of secondary schooling, including kindergarten available as an option (Metz, 1992). Between 1985 and 1990, the government funded all levels of education, in addition to providing books and health services for students (Metz, 1992). Education accounted for a massive 20% of the government's total expenditures (Metz, 1992). In later years, expenditure increased to become the highest in the world, reaching 28% in 2003. Between 1980 and 2005, average expenditure on education as a share of GDP in the Kingdom was 6.9%, 1.3% higher than that of the United States and 5.1% higher than that of the UAE, two other OECD countries (Maroun, Samman, Moujaes, & Abouchakra, 2008).

However, despite the government's financial support for education, the system continues to lag behind in terms of international and regional standards. Low returns to education were demonstrated by a low ranking in the Education Development Index (EDI), 97 out of 125 in 2004, lower than all other Arab Gulf countries with the exception of Yemen (Maroun et al., 2008). Similarly, the 86% average adult literacy rate between 2005 and 2010 was significantly below all other countries in the region, especially Qatar, which had an adult literacy rate of 96% (UNESCO, 2010). Again with the exception of Yemen, Saudi Arabia had the lowest gross enrollment ratios (for all levels of education) in the region in 2005, at 57% in contrast to the regional average of 74% (Benard, 2006).

On the curriculum side, a heavy focus on Islamic studies, with an average of nine periods a week dedicated to religious studies, reduces the amount of time spent on subjects such as math, science, and history (Metz, 1992). No material that conflicts with the strict Wahhabi Islamic movement's beliefs is allowed to be taught in schools, and this has in many cases limited what students are able to learn from school (Aldosari, 2007). A fear of exposing children to different ideas and cultures that may not align with Islamic teachings has also limited the education system's ability to integrate technology and media in classrooms and provide students with the complete learning experiences of their counterparts in other parts of the world (Center for Religious Freedom of the Hudson Institute, 2008; MOE, Saudi Arabia, 2005). At the tertiary level, the range of degrees offered in Saudi Arabian institutions is also limited (Alamri, 2011). Furthermore, the lack of focus on research has hampered several government efforts to gain international accreditation (Alkhazim, 2003).

A demographic shift marked by a growing youth population has led to a rapidly expanding demand for schooling at all stages of education (MOE, Saudi Arabia, 2005). Growing demand has been met with a shortage of accessible quality education, posing serious challenges to the system

(Courington & Zuabi, 2011; MOE, Saudi Arabia, 2005). It has been difficult to finance the establishment of new schools from an already overstretched education budget (Ten-Year Plan, 2005). Courington and Zuabi (2011) emphasize the existence of academic specializations that are not aligned with labor market needs. This situation has created an excess of unemployed youth within certain specializations, especially in religious studies and literature, and a shortage of employees in more highly demanded specializations related to science, information technology, business, and math (Courington & Zuabi, 2011).

Like its Gulf neighbors, Saudi Arabia has also struggled to build and maintain a high-quality, local teaching force. Although Saudi Arabia's teaching force grew dramatically from 330,000 teachers in 1999 (Hussain, 2007) to 642,704 teachers in 2009 (World Bank, 2013c), a shortage of qualified teachers persists. Male nationals are opting out of the teaching profession, and as a result there is a heavy reliance on expatriate Arab teachers for boys' schools (Hussain, 2007). Also, Saudi nationals who become teachers are largely theoretically trained and their low levels of practical training hampers student learning, according to Courington and Zuabi (2011). A rigid, centralized curriculum requires teachers to focus on preparing students for examinations at the end of each term; so teachers are further limited in the level of creativity they can bring to their teaching (Hussain, 2007).

Higher education suffers from similar issues. Rising demand for higher education meant that an estimated 62.5% of high school applicants were not able to secure a spot in higher education institutions in Saudi Arabia in the academic year 2009–2010 (Jamjoom, 2012). The gap between supply and demand of higher education continues to grow and, according to Jamjoom (2012), is expected to grow to 67.2% by 2030–2031. With the current population growth rates and the capacity of available institutions, it is expected there will be an even larger number of nonadmitted students in the coming years. This situation, coupled with Saudi Arabia's already high 13–15% unemployment rate, points to an unhappy future for many young Saudi nationals (Alkhazim, 2003). In addition, the lack of financial resources has limited opportunities to fund the development of new institutions or expand existing ones (Alkhazim, 2003). The government's educational budget is not only stretched among educational programs, but also distributed directly to students in the form of a $200 to $300 monthly stipend per student enrolled in any higher education institution.

In 2004, Saudi Arabia's MOE launched a comprehensive 10-year educational development plan to identify specific challenges to the system and devise programs to resolve them with an eye to demographic and economic trends (MOE, Saudi Arabia, 2005). One such program was the school building project that began in 2004 and aimed to have finished building 2,731 new schools by 2014 (Kingdom of Saudi Arabia Ministry of Education, 2008). As of 2012, news reports highlighted the fact that 580 new schools were built in Al Madinah alone ("SR5 Billion Spent," 2012). A second program is the curriculum development program. The program seeks to address students' learning needs by hiring international experts and creating national expertise to provide qualitative improvements in the school textbooks and curricula, with greater emphasis on critical thinking. To address the issue of teacher quality, the MOE established professional development and training programs in the areas of curriculum and teaching techniques, evaluations, professional growth, classroom environment, learning technology, and student activities (Australian Council for Educational Research [ACER], 2013; UNESCO, 2008). The Ministry of Higher Education undertook an expansion project, increasing the number of government universities to 23 and public colleges to 147 (Alamri, 2011). A postsecondary medium-level diploma through the community college system is now available to students who want to pursue tertiary education in select areas for 1 to 2 years (Alkhazim, 2003). In an effort to promote research, King Abdullah University of Science and Technology set up a research center to attract students who wish to pursue graduate studies in a diverse selection of fields (Alpen Capital, 2010). These are all steps forward, but there is still much room for growth.

STRIVING FOR EDUCATION QUALITY IN THE SULTANATE OF OMAN[3]

Like its GCC counterparts, earliest forms of education in Oman were rooted in Islam. The kuttab method of teaching took place in mosques or houses, or outdoors under trees, and its primary aim was to teach boys and girls to memorize and interpret the only textbook available at the time, the Quran (Goveas & Aslam, 2011). In 1964, oil discoveries in Oman prompted a new era of social and economic change that triggered developments in the education system. According to Rassekh (2004), the first stage of these developments was marked by the establishment of Oman's MOE in 1970, under His Majesty Sultan Qaboos bin Said's guidance (Al Nabhani, 2007). The MOE oversaw and initiated rapid growth in the number of schools, students, and educational institutions in Oman between the early 1970s and 1980. Within the span of 10 years, between 1970 and 1980, the number of schools in Oman jumped from 3 to 3,894 and the number of students from 909 to 106,032 (Rassekh, 2004). Public schools were open to girls, and girls' enrollment rates grew from zero to 35,190 in the same 10 years (Rassekh, 2004). Three schools were also set up to provide evening school for adults. Table 1.4 shows the number of schools and enrollment figures between 1980 and 2003 in

Table 1.4. Oman's Number of Schools and Enrollment Figures (1980–2003)

Year	No. of Schools	No. of Students	No. of Girls	Proportion of Girls (%)
1980–1981	373	106,032	35,190	33
1995–1996	953	488,797	236,331	48
2003	1,022	576,472	279,180	48

Source: Rassekh (2004, p. 7).

Oman. While these developments were remarkable, the rapid pace of change did not provide enough time for the construction of appropriate facilities to ease the learning process, and many students and administrators in schools throughout Oman suffered the consequences of poor construction such as poor-quality facilities and haphazardly selected teachers (Rassekh, 2004).

The second stage of the development of the education system began in the early 1980s (Rassekh, 2004). The MOE sought to address the primary issue that had arisen as a result of the fast pace of development in the education system in the previous period, which was quality (Rassekh, 2004). The MOE hired local and international education experts to review the education sector and work toward revising policies on teacher education, teacher methods and materials, and national curricula (Al Nabhani, 2007; Rassekh, 2004). Other measures taken toward the goal of Total Quality Management (TQM) (Al Nabhani, 2007) included renewing school buildings, training and developing teachers professionally, and providing laboratory resources for teaching science (Rassekh, 2004). Quantitative developments continued between 1981 and 1985; the number of schools rose from 408 to 588, students increased from 120,718 to 218,914, and teachers increased from 5,874 to 9,793 (MOE, Oman, 2011). Adult literacy rates jumped progressively from 33% to 55% in the span of 20 years (1970–1990) (MOE, Oman, & World Bank, 2012).

Strategic reforms associated with Oman's Vision 2020 initiative marked the third stage of educational development in the country, between 1995 and 2003 (Rassekh, 2004). To keep up with the rapid pace of globalization and technological advancements, there was a growing need for stronger math and science education (Rassekh, 2004). Strategic reforms in these areas included introducing computer classes into the schools as required subjects, establishing stricter entry requirements for teachers, paying more attention to science subjects, and improving the status of the teaching profession. In the academic year 1996–1997, after coming to the realization that secondary school graduates in Oman did not have the English language skills required to enter higher education, the MOE introduced English as a primary subject from grade 1 (Al Shmeli, 2009). What followed this third phase of the reforms was an unexpected rise in the percentage of female students and teachers, which marked the beginning of a female-dominated education sector in Oman (MOE, Oman, & World Bank, 2012; Rassekh, 2004).

With regard to higher education in Oman, the first university, Sultan Qaboos University, was established in 1986 (Al Shmeli, 2009). Starting with a few hundred students that year, enrollment has since grown to more than 17,000 students as of 2009 (Al Shmeli, 2009). Gradually, Oman's tertiary system has grown to 36 government or quasi-government higher education institutions and 25 private institutions (Al Shmeli, 2009). Enrollment rates have risen from around 300 in 1986 to 80,000 studying locally and over 12,000 studying abroad in 2009 (Al Shmeli, 2009). In response to the growing demand for higher education, the Higher Education Council was established in 1998 (Rassekh, 2004). Since then, the Higher Education Council has focused on diversifying program offerings to reach a wider audience and also meet the needs of the highly globalized economy. To do this, the Council introduced specialized tertiary institutions, such as the Oman College of Tourism, and called for new program offerings in existing universities (Al Shmeli, 2009). The Council was also responsible for establishing an academic accreditation council that would identify areas of weakness in tertiary institutions and find solutions to these problems (Rassekh, 2004). Lastly, the Council responded to student demand by making career guidance services available at the universities (Rassekh, 2004). Looking forward, the MOE aims to introduce further policies and programs to help address existing challenges in the tertiary education system (Rassekh, 2004).

Today, however, several challenges still persist. First, while a number of steps have been taken to advance the quality of students' learning outcomes, evidence from national and international learning assessments reveal that students continue to lag behind international academic standards and national expectations. In the 2007 TIMSS examinations, Omani students performed significantly below the international math section average and closer to the international average in the sciences section. In both areas, they scored significantly higher than their GCC counterparts, with the exception of Bahrain. Nevertheless, the assessment scores demonstrated that nearly 60% of Omani students scored below "low" (i.e., fewer than 400 points) in math and nearly 50% scored below "low" in sciences. Similarly, the MOE found that students in government schools performed below national expectations in all subjects, particularly in math (MOE, Oman, & World Bank, 2012). A second ongoing challenge is teacher quality. Specifically, teacher education in Oman is largely traditional, with less emphasis on practical training and pedagogy than on theory and content. Teacher-training programs are also not aligned with school curricula, and this contributes to teacher-to-student knowledge transfer barriers. In addition, extensive administrative tasks affect teachers' performance and ability to take on teacher-training courses to improve their skills. A teacher transfer system that allows teachers with more than 1 year of teaching experience to request a locational transfer leaves remote areas such as Al Wusta with disproportionately inexperienced teachers and contributes to high turnover rates overall (MOE, Oman, & World Bank, 2012).

Finally, boys' disengagement at school is reflected in their consistent underperformance compared to girls. A joint report by Oman's MOE and the World Bank entitled *Education in Oman: The Drive for Quality* (2012) finds that Omani boys' choices with respect to how they decide to distribute their time between leisure and studying have negatively impacted boys' academic performance. Compared to the rest of the world and the region, Oman also has the highest education gender gap in favor of girls. In Chapter 2 we will delve deeper into the reasons for and consequences of this gender gap, but it is important to note that this is one of the primary challenges to the schooling system in Oman.

Today education is a growing priority area for the Omani government. Aware of the need to diversify the economy and focus on developing the country's human capital, Oman has recently taken several measures to reform the education sector (Rassekh, 2004). The structure of the schooling system was changed from the typical 6 years of primary, 3 years of preparatory, and 3 years of secondary schooling to a system of 10 years of compulsory basic education featuring two cycles of 4 and then 6 years, respectively, and a final stage of 2 years of secondary schooling (Rassekh, 2004). The new structure aims to reduce the number of students who leave school at an early age (Rassekh, 2004). Similarly, school days were increased from 160 to 180 days a year, with five class hours per day, up from four, to give students more learning time at school (Rassekh, 2004; MOE, Oman, & World Bank, 2012). Schools are also attempting to become more democratic and less centralized with the establishment of formal stakeholder groups that include a school board, student council, and parent–teacher association (MOE, Oman, & World Bank, 2012).

In working toward achieving further progress in Oman's education system, a 2012 report published jointly by the MOE, Oman, and World Bank outlines several recommendations for future actions. First, it recommends increasing the time students spend in productive schoolwork annually to a full 180 days, which was done. The recommendations also suggest that schools and teachers place heavier emphasis on the development of higher-order thinking skills that can be used to solve problems in international and national assessments. According to the report, results from these assessments can then be used to identify areas of difficulty for various subjects and teacher-training programs can be developed to target common concerns that are well-matched to the curriculum. Finally, the report recommends thorough and systematic examination of the gender gap in achievement, particularly the underachievement of boys.

QATAR'S PROGRESSIVE REFORM EFFORTS: EDUCATION FOR A NEW ERA

Only 32 years prior to the discovery of oil and gas, Qatar's resources were limited to 1,430 camels, 250 horses, and 817 pearl boats, a striking contrast to today's 25.7 billion barrels of oil and natural gas deposits of over 900 trillion cubic feet (Brewer et al., 2007; Ministry of Business and Trade, n.d.). After World War II, oil and gas became the main source of livelihood in Qatar, replacing fishing, pearling, and trade. In the 1950s, oil revenues drove modernization, and expansion was facilitated by British influence and a new wave of immigrants from beyond the Gulf. Early plans for modernization began with the establishment of new schools, the first being Qatar Elementary School for boys, which opened in 1952. The school hosted 190 students studying four different subjects outside of traditional Islamic studies (Qatar News Agency, n.d.). Not long after, in 1956, the first public school for girls opened. The school was socially accepted due to a fatwa, or religious proclamation, issued by one of the country's most prominent religious sheikhs, claiming that girls' education was in line with the teachings of the Quran (Brewer et al., 2007).

In the following year, a regulatory and administrative mechanism was set up to oversee the new education system that was being put into place; it was called Wizarat Al-Maarfa and was a precursor to the present-day MOE (Brewer et al., 2006; Qatar News Agency, n.d.). Curricula were also imported from Egypt and other Arab countries (Qatar News Agency, n.d.), with some curricular differences between boys' and girls' schools (Brewer et al., 2007). For instance, girls were expected to get one hour of physical education per week compared to boys, who got two, and they were also required to take a subject called "home economics, needlework, and childcare for girls" (Harby, 1966). However, by 1965 the first Qatari curriculum was rolled out, along with textbooks specifically geared toward Qatari students. Within 5 years after the introduction of national Qatari textbooks into schools, near gender equity was achieved in the Qatari schooling system. This was in contrast to other countries in the Gulf that took longer to fully involve females (Brewer et al., 2007). However, the overall schooling system structure was the same as the rest of the GCC, with 6 years of elementary (or primary), 3 years of preparatory, and 3 years of secondary schooling. In addition to public schooling, the system also offered three types of private schooling. Community schools hosted children of non-Arab nationalities and were often sponsored by foreign embassies. "International" schools were not sponsored by embassies and enrolled children from different nationalities, including Qatari children. Their curricula were often American- or British-based; so the main language of instruction was English. Finally, "private Arabic" schools were established for Qataris and other Arab nationals who preferred Arabic language instruction but also more advanced versions of the curricula, as well as better resources and facilities (Brewer et al., 2007).

With an increasingly educated population came growing demand for higher education institutions in Qatar by the mid-1970s. To meet this demand, Qatar University was established in 1977 and became the first public university in the country (Stasz, Eide, & Martorell, 2007). Qatar University initially offered bachelor's programs in education, science, humanities, and social sciences, and Sharia and Islamic studies (Brewer et al., 2007). The university was later extended to include engineering and administration and economics departments (Brewer et al., 2007). All programs are provided free of cost for Qataris and GCC nationals who meet the entry requirements and maintain a minimum grade point average (GPA) of 2.0 throughout their years of study (Stasz et al., 2007). Qatar University is now one of the primary options for tertiary education for Qataris; the university enrolled 65.4% of all Qatari tertiary students in the academic year 2009–2010 (General Secretariat for Development Planning [GSDP], 2012). However, having recently shifted from English to Arabic language instruction (Fenton, 2012; Lindsey, 2012) and denied entry to over 1,800 applicants in the past few years (Khatri, 2012b), Qatar University has been the subject of serious concern among educational practitioners and policymakers.

In addition to Qatar University, there are a range of private universities, most of which are situated in Education City. Under an initiative by Qatar Foundation for Education, Science, and Community Development, Education City was developed in 1997. In addition to one Qatari university, Education City currently hosts eight international branch campuses based in America, the United Kingdom, and France. Among the branch campuses are world-class universities Virginia Commonwealth University School of the Arts, Weill Cornell Medical College, Texas A&M University, Carnegie Mellon University, and Georgetown University (Stasz et al., 2007). The College of the North Atlantic, CHN University, Stenden University Qatar, and University of Calgary–Qatar are four other private options located outside Education City.

Enrollment rates differ between the universities, but there is a stark contrast in enrollment rates between the private and public sectors. Whereas 91% of all Qatari students attending 4-year tertiary programs were enrolled in Qatar University in 2005–2006, only 9% were enrolled in all of the private universities inside and outside Education City. Of the total number of Qatari students in 4-year programs in 2005–2006, 23% were male and 77% were female (Stasz et al., 2007). Currently, most degree offerings are established in relation to employers' needs; however, some gaps still need to be filled (Stasz et al., 2007).

Additional options for postsecondary degrees in Qatar include a professional diploma or professional degree from one of the following colleges: Community College of Qatar, Qatar Aeronautical College, Qatar Finance and Business Academy, and the Ahmed Bin Mohamed Military College. Study-abroad programs are also very common and often offer attractive alternatives to locally based universities. In the academic year 2010–2011, a total of 126 Qatari secondary-school graduates obtained scholarships for undergraduate and postgraduate studies overseas, with 32% more males than females (GSDP, 2012). Nevertheless, it should be noted that a large percentage of these students, 45% in 2000–2005, drop out before completing their 4-year programs abroad and many of these students end up coming back to Qatar to complete their education (GSDP, 2012).

There have been rapid developments in the education system in Qatar since the first public school opened in 1952. In 2003, the Qatari government partnered with RAND Corporation to oversee a massive overhaul of the entire public education system. With the help of RAND, a voucher system was implemented and all schools became autonomous entities that report only loosely to the MOE. However, by 2012 RAND was no longer working with the education authorities and there was much criticism about the new system, especially the new emphasis on English. As a result, there has been a recent recentralization of the system and the MOE has resumed authority over schools in Qatar. In 2012, literacy rates were among the highest in the region at over 99%, and educational attainment rates were growing every year. Education accounted for 4.1% of government expenditure in Qatar, with only Oman and Saudi Arabia spending more (GSDP, 2012). The country also has ambitions to become a leading research hub in the region, with a dedicated Qatar National Research Fund awarding grants worth over $53 million a year to scientists, researchers, and students (GSDP, 2012).

An ongoing challenge facing the development of education in Qatar, like elsewhere in the GCC, is teacher quality, which is hindered by the high turnover rates of non-Qatari teachers, who make up 70% of the total teacher population (GSDP, 2012). Annual renewal of contracts, low salaries compared with other GCC countries (excluding Saudi Arabia), transfers from school to school without advance notice, and general job insecurity all contribute to teachers' low personal investment in their students and their jobs (Brewer et al., 2006). In trying to resolve some of these issues, the

MOE developed a system of "model schools," in which boys from grades 1 to 4 were taught by female teachers who were largely Qatari nationals (Brewer et al., 2006). However, in January 2013, female teachers were banned from teaching boys due to concerns about boys adopting feminine behaviors incompatible with Islamic religious beliefs (Toumi, 2013a). Qatari female teachers were transferred to girls' schools and non-Qatari female teachers were left without jobs and no right to a new position.

In addition to teachers, students in Qatar have been found to lack motivation (GSDP, 2012). They spend approximately 50% fewer hours doing homework than the international average and are also absent from school 11% to 12% more than their American counterparts (GSDP, 2012). Contrary to Ridge et al.'s (2013) findings in the UAE, the Qatari National Human Development Report (GSDP, 2012) states that one of the primary reasons for students' lack of motivation to learn and pursue higher levels of education is the pull of the labor market. The availability of high-paying jobs for high school graduates, and sometimes even dropouts, constitutes a large opportunity, which undermines continuing education. Furthermore, Qatarization policies that mandate that Qataris comprise a minimum percentage of any company reduces the incentive for males to continue their education, with many reportedly paid salaries in order to demonstrate compliance to the law but never actually have to report to work (GSDP, 2012). The implications of these policies are covered in more detail in Chapter 6. However, despite high expected economic returns to education in Qatar, many male students choose to leave school at an early age, either during or immediately after secondary school. In addition, among the students in Qatar who continue in secondary school, many choose the "arts" stream as opposed to the "science" stream. In fact, between the academic years 2000–2001 and 2009–2010, the segment of students opting for the sciences declined by 20%, from 28% to 8% (GSDP, 2012). The low numbers of Qataris pursuing the sciences leaves Qatari capacity in the scientific sectors highly depleted and could pose a threat in terms of sustainability in the workforce.

Another challenge is that although 4.1% of Qatar's total income is channeled into the education sector, resources largely support the MOE's large staff rather than the schools themselves. With over 17,000 personnel in the MOE in 2000, it is no surprise that there was a shortage of funds dedicated to maintaining and improving school facilities. In some schools, this also meant that between 40 and 50 students were crowded into one small room, with almost negligible one-on-one attention (Brewer et al., 2006).

While Qatar's education system has come a long way since the initial reform plans in 2001, a number of challenges still need to be addressed in the coming years. The rapid pace of reform has also denied key stakeholders, such as teachers, the chance to learn to navigate the new system and, in some cases, accept it (Brewer et al., 2006). Limited local expertise and capacity also constrain further developments (Brewer et al., 2006). International assessment results from PISA, PIRLS, and TIMSS indicate that Qatari students lag far behind students from other countries in performance (GSDP, 2012). Of particular concern is the education of males, who are significantly underperforming on international assessments and seek higher education in very small numbers.

MOVING FORWARD

Holding 45% of proven global oil reserves and 20% of proven global gas reserves, the GCC region has no shortage of resource wealth (Abu Dhabi National Oil Company, 2013). Since the discovery of oil in the early 1900s, the region's education sector has experienced tremendous growth and transformation, which is evident to both nationals and expatriates. Provision of and access to public schooling has reached levels unmatched by other countries in the Arab world or the developing world at large. Literacy rates in most GCC countries are above 87%, with countries such as Bahrain and Qatar achieving nearly 100% youth literacy. In the quest to build knowledge-based societies, Kuwait, the UAE, Bahrain, Saudi Arabia, Oman, and Qatar have undertaken education reform projects that have, for the most part, produced satisfactory results in terms of improving educational accessibility. Reforms designed to improve quality have entailed curriculum modernization, teacher training, regulatory efforts making education compulsory, awareness-raising, and overall prioritization of education. However, reforms have often been hindered by inefficient administrative practices and politics, overly bureaucratic governing bodies, and slow acceptance or, at times, opposition to change.

Subsequent chapters explore the unique intersection of education and gender in the oil-rich countries of the Arabian Gulf. To date, the rapid expansion of educational opportunities have empowered women and created a system wherein females are well educated but face barriers in the labor market. The reverse is true for males; men have relatively easy access to employment but often receive substandard education, especially in the public systems. How these outcomes will play out is yet to be seen, but early signs point to unsettling social upheaval that may have unanticipated and profound consequences for local communities. In Chapter 2 we look more closely at the patterns affecting girls and women in the GCC region, and examine how females have taken advantage of the many opportunities and choices available to them.

2 The Rise of Women in the Gulf

> It is ironic that as women gain a greater role in Gulf life in coming years, they will attain a position that will be much closer to that of their great-grandmothers and grandmothers in the 1920s than to that of their mothers in the 1970s and 1980s. (Foley, 2010, p. 169)

Before moving on to examine the rise of women on the Arabian Peninsula, it is important to examine the broader context in which the Arabian woman is understood. Historically, the earliest depictions of women stated that "the Arab woman is portrayed as a belly dancer or whore, a veiled submissive member of a luxurious harem or a speechless oppressed character with no identity" (Sidani, 2005, p. 498). In more recent times, Arab women have been portrayed more as veiled, powerless victims of repressive patriarchal societies as evidenced by an array of media reports (AbuKhalil, 2005; Sabbagh, 2003; Sonbol, 2006) and assorted biographies and autobiographies relating stories of the oppressive treatment of women in the Middle East (Mahmoody, 1991; Sasson, 1992; Souad, 2003). Academia has not been immune to stereotyping either, with some academics (Doumato & Posusney, 2003; Moghadam, 2003) subscribing to and perpetuating the narrative of the oppressed Muslim Arab woman and thus portraying her, according to Abu-Lughod (2002), as in need of "saving." The conflation of Muslim and Arab also presents a problematic construct as often the experiences or behaviors of diaspora can lead Western audiences to believe that Muslim women everywhere are similar (Ali, 1998). This failure to distinguish between Muslim Arabs and non-Arab Muslims and then again to be able to distinguish between Muslim Arab groups can result in the creation of either dangerously inaccurate stereotypes (Bullock, 2002) or cultural relativism (Afkhami, n.d.), wherein human rights violations are ignored in the name of culture and religion. Some of this is evidenced in the recently established Shariah courts of the United Kingdom (Waters, 2013).

Contesting both these views of the Muslim Arab woman, Sidani (2005) goes to great lengths to point out that Islam's first convert was a business woman, and in the early years of Islam, women had an active "visible role." He concedes that, as time passed, their involvement in the public sphere declined and, by the early 1900s, Arab women were excluded from the rights to education and involvement in public life (Al-Faruqi, 1987). However, Foley (2010, p. 171) writes that in the Gulf "women operated businesses...in Dubai, Jeddah and other coastal communities" and that women were active in the public sphere up until the collapse of the pearling industry in the 1930s, when the men no longer had work on the boats and returned to take over the shopkeeper and merchant roles that women had been occupying. Foley (2010) describes how in 1931 the Dubai government tried to ban women from selling fish, but to their surprise, male fishermen called for the law to be repealed. By the 1950s and 1960s in the Middle East at large, Sidani (2005) notes that social revolution and the awakening of Arab nationalism created changes that empowered women socially and economically. Citing Haddad (1984), Sidani (2005) says that in this era the Arab woman was able to become "the lawyer, the doctor, the engineer, the cabinet minister, the ambassador, the judge, the police officer, the paratrooper as well as the nurse, the teacher and the social worker." Middle Eastern women's access to education, in particular, expanded exponentially. Indeed, female literacy rates across the Gulf States, Levant, and most of North Africa increased threefold in the past 30 years (Sidani, 2005). While these new opportunities for women were not equally spread across all countries in the Middle East, access to mass education dramatically changed the aspirations and ambitions of many Arab women, who, in turn, made increasing demands for equal participation in both the public and private spheres. Western literature and the Western media, however, have tended to dwell on the comfortable stereotypes of either the oppressed Arab Muslim woman confined to a domestic role or the Arab Muslim woman who is not oppressed but rather chooses a life of confinement that is ironically identical to the oppressed woman. There is very little room in Western imagination to envisage Arab Muslim women with lives as complex and varied as women the world over. While culture and religion create similarities of experiences in the region, other factors such as type of government and level of income lead to enormous variations in the lives of women in the Middle East. In all cases of Western thought, nonetheless, Arab women are always regarded as worse off compared to Arab men (Sabbagh, 2003), no matter what measure is used.

The narrative of the oppressed Arab woman, coupled with the rise and spread of global ideologies about girls' education and its benefits for national development, has led to a slew of development reports on gender in the Middle East. Reports such as the *Arab Human Development Report (AHDR)* (UNDP, 2006), *Gender and Development in the Middle East and North Africa (MENA)* (World Bank, 2004), *Status and Progress of Women in the Middle East and North Africa* (World Bank, 2009), and the *EFA Arab States Regional Report* (UNESCO, 2002) all present the same story of marginalized girls and oppressed women. Assumptions that Arab women have little power to make choices as a result of cultural, religious, and family restrictions are emphasized in much of the existing human development literature, a pattern that Adely (2009) highlights in her article "Educating Women for Development: The Arab Human Development Report 2005 and the Problem with Women's Choices." Expanding choice through education is a priority for human development because exposure to education typically results in greater desire to participate in the labor market and in better health. In other words, women's development is typically represented as a function of education and other factors. However, in the Arab world, these "predictable" patterns do not always exist. Instead, a gender paradox exists whereby despite high rates of educational attainment, women have low levels of economic participation. Adely (2009) notes that "Arab women's choices have not always fit the patterns and correlations that development researchers have come to assume and assert in their educational policies and programs" (p. 107). The 2005 *AHDR* report, Adely argues, misrepresents the gender paradox by tracing the failure of women to participate in and benefit from the economy to their educational "denial" and "deprivation."

In Freedomhouse's *Women's Rights in the Middle East and North Africa: Progress Amid Resistance* (Kelly & Breslin, 2010), Arab women are framed as being oppressed by male-dominated societies with religious laws and values that position them as less than "full persons," unable to make decisions about anything from marriage to public participation. However, conservative interpretations of Islam within the traditional *ulama* discourse reflect only one interpretation of Islam and its views on women. Different interpretations of Islam are not accounted for in many international development reports, nor do these documents present the possibility that, given the choice, some women may not desire a life aligned with Western-projected preferences for female development (Sidani, 2005). The generalization of the Arab family unit, as restricting female education, is fairly inconsistent with the findings from Adely's (2009) research. She reveals that many Arab families go to great lengths to educate their daughters even to the degree of incurring serious debt. Ironically, while critical Western commentators call for more Gulf women in politics and public life, women in the West are less represented in the sciences than women from the GCC. Adely (2009, p. 112) points out that "if one accepts a standard of educational progress for women that accords greater value to male-dominated fields, many women in the Arab world are actually doing better than women in the United States." Table 2.1 shows the reality of women's representation in politics, the workforce, and academia in the Arab world, compared to the West. It shows that the Arab and the Gulf regions graduate higher proportions of women in the sciences (51% and 57%, respectively) than the

Table 2.1. Women in the Labor Force, Government, and Academia

	ARAB REGION (%)	GULF REGION (%)	OECD (%)	WORLD (%)
Labor force participation rate, female for 1990–2011 (% of female population ages 15+)[a,b]	25	32.4	49.3	52
Proportion of seats held by women in national parliaments for 1990–2012 (%)[b]	7.4	4.3	20.02	16.11
Proportion of women studying science in 2010[b,c]	65	N/A	N/A	N/A
Proportion of female science graduates in 2010[d]	51	57	40	46
Female-to-male university enrollment ratio[b]	98.01	173	117.5	106.98

Sources and notes: (a) Economist Intelligence Unit (2012); (b) World Bank (2013g); (c) in Saudi Arabia, women make up 65% of total students enrolled in the science fields. These include life sciences, physical sciences, mathematics and statistics, and computing (Economist Intelligence Unit, 2012); (d) UIS (2012); no data are available on the United Arab Emirates and Bahrain for the Gulf region.

Organisation for Economic Co-operation and Development (OECD) region (40%) and the world average (46%). According to the Economist Intelligence Unit (2012), 73% of all science graduates in Saudi Arabia were women in 2010, which is an even more extreme example of what is common throughout the Gulf region.

In 2006, the National Science Board of the United States also acknowledged that in some Arab countries a higher percentage of females were studying the sciences than in the United States. Data from the *EFA Global Monitoring Report* (UNESCO, 2008), displayed in Table 2.2, also show higher science enrollment rates for females in Arab countries than for females in the United States and the United Kingdom. However, nowhere in the *AHDR* (UNDP, 2006) is this stated; rather, that report makes it appear as if the percentages of women studying science are low compared to worldwide averages, and the report holds the Arab world to standards that have not actually been attained anywhere else.

A 2004 World Bank report, *Gender and Development in the Middle East and North Africa*, also focuses exclusively on the problems of girls (despite the word *gender* in the title). The report problematizes girls' education in the region and focuses on those countries where there are fewer girls enrolled than boys in school. Countries that appear in statistical tables as having more girls enrolled than boys are not discussed at any length in

Table 2.2. Percentage of Women in the Science and Engineering Fields in Selected Countries (2008)

Country	Women in Science (%)	Women in Engineering, Manufacturing, and Construction (%)
Algeria	54	31
Bahrain	75	23
Qatar	75	16
Kuwait	60	50
Lebanon	46	20
Palestinian A. T.	50	31
United Kingdom	36	19
United States	38	16

Source: EFA Global Monitoring Report (UNESCO, 2008).

the report. Other reports from the World Bank have also persisted with the narrative of the oppressed Arab woman. The fact that boys are not discussed anywhere in the World Bank (2004) or UNDP (2006) documents is revealing of prevailing beliefs about gender in the region. These reports are, it appears, intent on showing two problems only: the accepted, defined, and institutionalized problem of girls in education and the equally accepted problem of the misogynistic, traditional, culture-bound Arab male (Ali, 2002). The 2008 MENA Development Report *The Road Not Traveled: Education Reform in the Middle East and Africa* (World Bank, 2008) was one of the first reports to acknowledge that "the region no longer has severe gender disparities in secondary and tertiary education" (p. xvi). It also stated that at the secondary level almost all countries have obtained gender parity and that out of the 19 countries included in the report, 13 have more females than males enrolled in tertiary education. While the 2008 *EFA Global Monitoring Report* (UNESCO, 2008) acknowledged gender disparities in favor of both girls and boys, the MENA report (World Bank, 2008) did not go this far. There was no mention of disparities for boys at any stage in the 2008 MENA report, despite 8 countries having a gender parity index (GPI) over 1.03 for secondary education and 11 countries having a GPI over 1.03 at the tertiary level. In the *EFA Global Monitoring Report* (UNESCO, 2008), on the other hand, any figure below 0.97 or above 1.03 indicates a disparity. While the UNESCO (2008) report acknowledges that the region has made significant strides in the education of girls, it unfortunately fails to identify any inequalities affecting boys.

EXPANSION OF SCHOOLING OPPORTUNITIES FOR GIRLS

In all of the resource-rich Gulf States, the earliest public schools catered to males. However, in the GCC countries the first public schools for girls generally opened soon after the first public schools for boys. Table 2.3 shows when the GCC countries opened both the first boys' and girls' schools.

Some of these schools opened before the area's oil industry, but the discovery of oil in all of these countries enabled rapid expansion of the education system so that by the 1990s all of the Gulf States had achieved close to full enrollment of both boys and girls in primary education and in preparatory education (which together typically comprise the duration of compulsory education). In Qatar, the first public school for girls opened in 1956 (5 years after the first public school for boys), and boys' and girls' attendance at school was nearly equal by the 1970s (Brewer et al., 2006). As of 2010, Qatar had close to 100% net enrollment of both girls and boys at the primary level, but at the (lower and upper) secondary level girls started to pull ahead, with the enrollment rate for girls at 93%, while for boys it is only 76% (UIS, 2011, 2012). Qatari youth (boys and girls) aged 25–29 had only 9.3 average years of education in 2001, but 11.5 average years of education in 2010 (UIS, 2011). On the basis of data from the same year but disaggregating by gender, it can be seen that Qatari girls have a longer average school life expectancy of 13.6 years (in contrast to 11.6 years for boys [UIS, 2012]).

Table 2.3. Timeline of First Girls' and Boys' Schools in the GCC

Year First Girls' School Opened	Year First Boys' School Opened	Country
1928	1919	Bahrain[a]
1937–1938	1936	Kuwait[b]
1955	1953	Sharjah (became the United Arab Emirates in 1971)[c]
1956[d]	1925[e]	Saudi Arabia
1956	1951	Qatar[f]
1935	1930	Oman[g]

Sources and notes: (a) Ministry of Education (MOE), Bahrain (2013); (b) MOE, Kuwait (2012). An American missionary established the first boys' school (Al-Diwan Al-Amiri, n.d.); (c) United Arab Emirates index: Education (n.d.); (d) El-Sanabary in Sabbagh (2003); (e) Akeel (2005); (f) Brewer et al. (2006); (g) Sultanate of Oman MOE (n.d.); Al Khaduri (2007). Public schools were established much later by the government.

In Saudi Arabia, the wife of King Fasial, Iffat A. Thunayan, established the first girls' school in 1956 (El-Sanabary in Sabbagh, 2003). By 1981, the number of girls enrolled in schools in Saudi Arabia was almost equal to the number of boys (Hamdan, 2005). The percentage of female students at all school levels increased from 33% in 1974–1975 to 48% in 2004–2005. Concurrently, the number of female schools in Saudi Arabia increased from 26% of all schools in 1974–1975 to 49% of schools in 2004–2005 (Al Munajjed, 2009). In 2010, females accounted for 49% of the total student population, with net enrollment rates of 89% (compared to 90% for boys) at the primary level and 83% (compared to 78% for boys) at the secondary level. Females and males in Saudi Arabia are expected to stay in school for 15 years, on average (CIA, 2011).

Bahrain, the first GCC country to open a formal school for girls in 1928, rapidly expanded education opportunities for girls after the discovery of oil. By 2001, 103 of the 203 schools in Bahrain were for girls (Al Gharaibeh, 2011). In terms of enrollment, 87% of girls and 77% of boys in Bahrain were enrolled in secondary education in the same year (Al Gharaibeh, 2011). UNESCO (UIS, 2012) data found close to 100% literacy rates for males and females and close to full primary school enrollment for both males and females in 2009. At the secondary level, girls' net enrollment in the same year was around 91%, while boys had 87% net enrollment (UIS, 2011). In addition, girls represent 49% of the total student population at the primary level in Bahrain and are achieving a 100% effective transition rate from primary to secondary education (UIS, 2011).

The first government girls' school was established in Kuwait in 1937–1938, only one year after the establishment of the first government boys' school (Meleis, El Sanabary, & Beeson, 1979). In 1946, when oil was discovered, there were fewer than 1,000 female students in Kuwait; by 1951, more than 3,500 girls were attending primary school (Meleis et al., 1979). By 1960, there were about 45,000 students enrolled in the Kuwaiti educational system, including 18,000 girls (Kuwait Cultural Office, 2006). In 1975, females comprised 50% of secondary school students in Kuwait and 49% of graduating secondary school students (Meleis et al., 1979). As of 2010, 100% of Kuwaiti girls were enrolled in primary school, which ranked the country 27th globally in the primary school female enrollment share indicator (NationMaster, 2013). In Kuwait, the gender parity indices of primary and secondary gross enrollment in 2009 were 0.98 and 1.03, respectively, indicating near equity at the primary and secondary levels (UIS, 2011).

In the United Arab Emirates, the first Western-style schools were built by the Kuwaiti government in Sharjah in 1953, and in Dubai and other emirates in 1963 (all before the creation of what is now the United Arab Emirates). Girls were enrolled in the first schools built for them in Sharjah by 1955 (Soffan, 1980). After 1971 and the creation of the United Arab

Emirates, mass schooling began in earnest with the provision of schools for boys and girls in every emirate. Girls' education was encouraged and promoted throughout the country by the first president, Sheikh Zayed Al Nahayan, and his wife Sheikha Fatima. Data from the United Arab Emirates paint a vivid picture of how females thrived amidst expanded educational opportunities. In 1999, the illiteracy rate for males aged 15 and over in the United Arab Emirates was 26%; for females it was 22%. Also in 1999, 63% of boys and 72% of girls in the United Arab Emirates were enrolled in secondary school. In 2000, the United Arab Emirates had equal enrollment rates for boys and girls in primary education, although girls have since surpassed the boys in net enrollment rates at the secondary level, with a rate of 84% compared to 82% in 2009 (UIS, 2011; UNESCO, 2000). In tertiary education, girls made up 60% of all students in 2010 (UIS, 2012).

Mass education took off much later in Oman than in other GCC countries. In 1969–1970, there were no schools for girls (Al Khaduri, 2007) and there were only three boys' schools serving 909 students in all of Oman at the time (Rassekh, 2004). By 1980–1981, this had increased to 389 schools educating around 70,000 boys and 35,000 girls. By 2003, there were more than 1,000 schools catering to approximately 575,000 students, of whom 48% were girls. As late as 1984, female illiteracy rates were at 84%. By 1997–1998, girls represented 50% of students enrolled in schools in Oman, but enrollment rates for both boys and girls at the primary level were still low. Even in 2000, only 64% of girls and 65% of boys in Oman were enrolled in school (Al Khaduri, 2007). These rates have risen significantly in recent years, however, to almost 100% net enrollment rates at the primary level and approximately 90% for both boys and girls at the secondary level in 2010 (UIS, 2012).

To summarize, after the individual GCC states committed to mass education, both girls and boys benefited tremendously from expanded schooling opportunities. Enrollment rates in 2010, shown in Table 2.4, underscore the commitment of GCC governments to girls' education.

Table 2.4. Secondary School Net Enrollment Rates by Gender and Country (2010)

Country	Females (%)	Males (%)
Saudi Arabia	83	78
Oman	90	89
Qatar	93	76
United Arab Emirates[a]	84	82
Bahrain[a]	91	87
Kuwait	93	86

Source and note: Global Education Digest 2011 (UIS, 2012); (a) rates for United Arab Emirates and Bahrain reflect data for the year 2009 (UIS, 2011).

As schooling opportunities for girls expanded, girls also began to excel in their studies. One argument as to why this has been the case is that they realized that education was the key to challenging cultural norms that had previously restricted women to the house (Raanan, 2009). The next section looks first at how girls' education was transformed by the establishment of local colleges of education and then examines how girls took advantage of expanded and improved educational opportunities to remain in school longer than boys and outperform boys across all subjects and grades.

BETTER EDUCATIONAL OUTCOMES FOR GIRLS

As schooling expanded and colleges of education were established at national universities in the GCC, local women began training as teachers. Kuwait and Bahrain established the earliest teacher-training centers in the 1960s (University of Bahrain, 2009; Vreede-de Stuers, 1974); in the 1980s, other GCC countries followed, and large numbers of national women entered the teaching workforce, replacing female expatriate teachers who had been staffing girls' schools until this time. For example, in 1986 more than 44,000 Saudi women were employed as teachers and administrators in girls' schools, replacing the expatriate Arab teaching staff (El-Sanabary as cited in Sabbagh, 2003). As employment opportunities for Gulf women at the time were limited, teaching was a highly sought-after career and attracted highly intelligent and passionate young women (Abdulla, 2005). The entry of national female teachers to Gulf schools had a significant impact on the education of girls. Instead of being taught by expatriate Arab teachers who reportedly felt some superiority over the Gulf Arabs (Ridge, 2009), girls in the GCC were now taught by teachers from their own societies who had a vested interest in seeing these young women succeed (Al Masah Capital Limited, 2012). In addition to these changes in the culture of girls' schools, girls themselves took advantage of the opportunities that expanded access to both school and higher education offered them. This is consistent with a growing body of literature on girls' education that finds that once girls have access to school, they tend to remain in school longer and perform better (Grant & Behrman, 2010).

School Life Expectancy

With regard to school life expectancy, Table 2.5 shows that females had more years of schooling in 2009 and 2010 than their male counterparts in two of the four GCC states for which data on school life expectancy are available, and in the United Arab Emirates, boys and girls had attained equal years of schooling. In Qatar, 2012 data find that female educational attainment in terms of number of years of education exceeds that of males for all ages under 40 (GSDP, 2012).

Table 2.5. Net Years of Schooling by Gender (2010)

Country/Region[a]	School Life Expectancy (Years)[b]	
	Female	Male
Oman	14.1	13.6
Qatar	14.2	12.3
Saudi Arabia	14.6	15.2
United Arab Emirates	11.8[c]	11.8[d]
World	11.6[c]	11.3[c]

Sources and notes: (*a*) no data are available on Bahrain and Kuwait for the Gulf region; (*b*) UIS (2011); (*c*) Global Education Digest 2012 (UIS, 2012). These rates reflect data for both lower and upper secondary school for the year 2010; (*d*) this datum is for the year 2009 (UIS, 2011).

These patterns of girls' achieving greater years of education and lower grade repetition point to the high value that girls, and their families, appear to accord to education. The reasons for this may be linked to girls' ambitions to have greater life choices and opportunities in the future, as well as families wanting to keep girls "safe" and occupied before marriage (Abudabbeh, 1996). In the United Arab Emirates, data from the MOE about the reasons why a student had dropped out of school found that the only reason given for girls dropping out of school before completing grade 12 was marriage (as opposed to extended absences or being excluded, which were reasons more common for boys). These figures were also extremely low (at no more than 2%) (Ridge, 2009).

Attainment

Moving on to attainment, we can see similar patterns with girls outperforming boys overall on both international and national assessments. The involvement of the GCC states in international educational assessments such as PISA, TIMSS, and PIRLS has been sporadic for the most part, with countries only recently choosing to take part, and thus there are often no data over time. However, what is consistent in these assessments is that there are frequent, dramatic gender differentials in favor of girls, which are presented in Tables 2.6–2.9.

Table 2.6 presents the results of the 2009 PISA assessments for Qatar and the United Arab Emirates, the only two Gulf States that participated in that particular round of the assessment. It shows that girls outperformed boys in all three PISA areas of focus (reading, math, and science) at a statistically significant rate. The largest gender gap was in reading,

Table 2.6. PISA Mean Scores in Reading, Math, and Science for Qatar and the United Arab Emirates (2009)

	READING		MATH		SCIENCE	
	F	M	F	M	F	M
Qatar[a]	397	347	371	366	393	366
United Arab Emirates[b]	460	402	424	418	454	422
OECD[a]	513	474	490	501	501	501

Sources: (a) OECD (2010); (b) Walker (2011).

Table 2.7. TIMSS Mean Scores in Math by Gender, Grade, and Year

	2003		2007				2011			
	GRADE 8		GRADE 4		GRADE 8		GRADE 4		GRADE 8	
	F	M	F	M	F	M	F	M	F	M
Saudi Arabia	326	336	—	—	341	319	418	402	401	387
Oman	417	385	—	—	**399**	**344**	398	372	**397**	**334**
Qatar	—	—	307	285	325	288	420	407	415	404
United Arab Emirates	—	—	452	438	461	461	438	430	464	447
Bahrain	—	—	—	—	414	382	440	432	**431**	**388**
Kuwait	—	297	**333**	**297**	364	342	**358**	**323**	—	—

Source: TIMSS International Student Achievement in Mathematics Reports (2003, 2007, 2011).

with a staggering 58-point difference in UAE scores and a 50-point gap for Qatar. While this trend is consistent with OECD averages that show a large gender gap favoring females, the size of the gap is far greater and there were also significantly large gender gaps in science. Qatar and the United Arab Emirates had wider gender gaps in science scores than any other participating country, with mean score differences of 26 and 31 points, respectively.

Tables 2.7 and 2.8 present the mean scores for mathematics and science in the TIMSS assessment for participating GCC countries between 2003 and 2011. The findings shown are consistent with findings from the PISA assessment. With the exception of grade 8 math scores for Saudi Arabia in 2003, girls outperformed boys at every level (grades 4 and 8), in both math and science, in all three years of the assessment. The gender differential is statistically significant almost across the board; the bolded values in Tables 2.7 and 2.8 point to the largest differences in performance between girls and boys.

Table 2.8. TIMSS Mean Scores in Science by Gender, Grade, and Year

	2003		2007				2011			
	GRADE 8		GRADE 4		GRADE 8		GRADE 4		GRADE 8	
	F	M	F	M	F	M	F	M	F	M
Saudi Arabia	407	391	—	—	426	383	453	405	450	424
Oman	—	—	—	—	452	391	394	360	458	380
Qatar	—	—	307	281	354	284	408	382	432	406
United Arab Emirates	—	—	473^a	448^a	495^a	483^a	437	419	477	452
Bahrain	453	423	—	—	499	437	461	438	482	423
Kuwait	—	—	379	315	441	391	371	319	—	—

Source and note: TIMSS International Student Achievement in Science Reports (2001, 2007, 2011); (*a*) United Arab Emirates is represented by Dubai.

The math results show that in Oman, for example, girls in grade 8 outperformed boys by 55 points in math, the largest gender difference in math scores among the 48 countries that participated in the 2007 TIMSS assessment. A few years later, Oman's girls outperformed boys to an even greater extent, with girls achieving 63 points higher in math and 78 points higher in science. In Kuwait, the gap between boys and girls for grade 4 math has remained at over 35 points from 2007 to 2011. In Bahrain, there is a 43-point gap favoring females in grade 8 math. This phenomenon of girls in the Gulf significantly outperforming boys has received considerable attention, as it does not fit global patterns on attainment in math, in which boys still tend to outperform girls. Fryer and Levitt (2010) have dubbed the Muslim Culture Hypothesis as a potential explanation of the occurrence. Acknowledging it as speculative, Fryer and Levitt (2010) propose that one reason for the varying achievement between the sexes may be the popularity of single-gender schools in Islamic countries.

Expanding on science results, there are similar patterns but larger gaps. Kuwait showed a 64-point gap favoring females for grade 4 students in 2007. All Gulf participating countries had a significant gap favoring grade 8 females in 2007, with differences of up to 70 points (Qatar). The 2011 results show equally large gaps in achievement.

Table 2.9 presents the mean scores for boys and girls in the PIRLS assessment for 2011. The findings again reflect girls' dominance vis-à-vis boys at both the grade 4 and 6 levels. At the 4th grade, the global average for girls was 520 as compared to 504 for boys, a gap of 16 points. In the Gulf States, these scores were at best 27 points apart in the United Arab Emirates, and at worst 54 points apart in Saudi Arabia and 53 in Kuwait (Mullis, Martin, Foy, & Drucker, 2011). Kuwait also had one of the highest gender

Table 2.9. PIRLS Mean Scores for Grade 4 Students by Country and Gender (2011)

	F	M
Saudi Arabia	**456**	**402**
Oman	411	371
Qatar	441	411
United Arab Emirates	452	425
Dubai	483	470
Abu Dhabi	442	406
Kuwait	**443**	**391**

Source: PIRLS International Student Achievement in Reading Report (2011).

differences in reading achievement of all the countries who participated in PIRLS worldwide in the previous two assessments (Kennedy, 2007; Mullis, Martin, Gonzalez, & Kennedy, 2003).

In terms of national examinations also, girls, unsurprisingly, outperform boys. On the Qatar Senior School certificate for students leaving secondary school in 2010–2011, female scores were 20 points higher than male scores (GSDP, 2012). In Bahrain, girls have outperformed boys on national examinations in all subjects, in all grades, since 2009 (QAAET Annual Report, 2011). Girls outperformed boys, on average, in all 11 regions of Oman in every subject area of the national MOE assessments for grades 4 and 10. Teachers in Oman have also consistently given higher achievement ratings to girls than to boys, even in primary schools where boys and girls are taught together. Teachers in Oman rating grade 1 boys rated them higher than girls only in sports (MOE, Oman, & World Bank, 2012, p. 81). In the United Arab Emirates, a study on gender differences by Al Khateeb (2001) analyzed the performance of 2,000 students on final math examinations over 10 years and demonstrated that, though Western literature suggests boys are inclined to excel at this subject, Emirati girls had performed better than boys in the final examinations for the past 6 years. In fact, the performance gap on this test widened year by year, with girls steadily pulling away from boys. Data from the United Arab Emirates for the 2005 General School Certificate Examinations held at the end of year 12 in the United Arab Emirates found the percentage of girls in the 90–100% bracket was triple that of boys across all subjects (MOE, UAE, 2007). More recently, in 2010, the UAE National Assessment Program (UAENAP) revealed that girls are still preforming better than boys in math, science, English, and Arabic (Egbert, 2012).

Girls in the Gulf States are now attaining greater levels of education and outperforming boys across all subjects and grades in both international and national assessments. While the reasons for this deserve greater attention, it is clear that access to education in the first place played a significant role. In addition to this, the changing nature of the teacher workforce in girls' schools provided national girls with highly talented national teachers and positive role models to aspire to. Girls more than boys have been able to take full advantage of what their education systems have had to offer them. As girls performed better in school, they also demanded continuing education opportunities, which the next section explores more fully.

RAPIDLY EXPANDING FEMALE PARTICIPATION IN TERTIARY EDUCATION

Tertiary studies for women in the Gulf began with the establishment of national universities and the creation of colleges of education. This was largely as teaching was deemed to be an appropriate career for women due to the sex-segregated nature of schools. Table 2.10 shows the years that the university education became available in the GCC countries. Kuwait was the first country to offer full-time programs to women in 1966, the same year the university was opened to men.

As of 2012, women outnumbered men by three to one in some Gulf countries in higher education (UIS, 2012). This is consistent with global

Table 2.10. Timeline of University Education Availability

Country	Year First University Accepted Women[a]	Year First University Opened for Men
Bahrain	—	1968[b]
Kuwait	1966[c]	1966[c]
United Arab Emirates	—	1976[d]
Saudi Arabia	1961 (part-time)[e]	1957[e]
Qatar	1973[f]	1973[f]
Oman	—	1986[g]

Sources and notes: (a) precise years when universities were established for women Kuwait, the United Arab Emirates, and Oman are uncertain; (b) University of Bahrain, 2009; (c) the earliest tertiary option for women was in 1961, when the first of several teacher-training schools opened and offered a 3-year course. However, the first university was opened in 1966 (Vreede-De Stuers, 1974); (d) UAEU, (n.d.); (e) Ghainaa Publications (2008); (f) Qatar University (2013); (g) Sultan Qaboos University (2013).

trends of increased female participation in higher education (Hausmann et al., 2012). In the Gulf, however, these trends are accentuated, with far great numbers of women in the United Arab Emirates, Qatar, and Saudi Arabia, in particular, choosing to continue their studies. Over time the number of offerings available to women has rapidly expanded from education, and countries like the United Arab Emirates and Qatar now proudly announce women's participation in all fields, from engineering and medicine to the arts. Figure 2.1 illustrates the rising ratio of girls to boys in tertiary education across all GCC countries.

The General Secretariat for Development Planning (GSDP) in Qatar states that "in 2010 the ratio of women to men studying mathematics and sciences at Qatar University was six to one" (2012, p. 38). Only 9% of women in higher education in Qatar attend technical colleges, with 81% attending Qatar University. On the other hand, 56% of Qatari men in higher education opt for technical colleges, with only 35% choosing to attend Qatar University (GSDP, 2012). The remaining men and women enrolled at the tertiary level attend private colleges. Despite the greater number of Qatari women undertaking tertiary studies, fewer Qatari women than men are awarded scholarships to study overseas (GSDP, 2012). Whether this is because fewer women are accepted or because fewer women apply due to cultural considerations (or for other reasons) is unclear. In Qatar, private monetary returns to education are larger for men than for women, suggesting a disconnect between education and the labor market, which we will explore later. However, according to the Qatar Statistics Authority, greater

Figure 2.1. Trends in Gender Parity Index in Tertiary Enrollment (1971–2010)

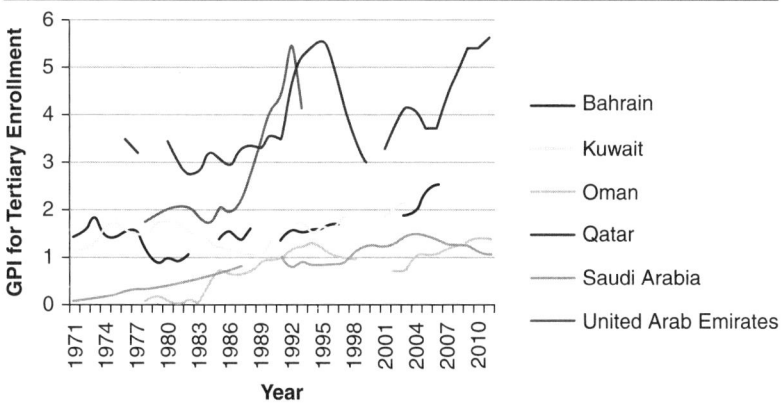

Source and note: World Bank (2013f). GPI is calculated as the ratio of girls to boys.

levels of education raise the probability that Qatari women will work and increase salaries for those who do work (GSDP, 2012). There are still tangible benefits for women who pursue their studies.

In Saudi Arabia, the number of tertiary institutions for women grew from 15 in the 1960s to 155 in the 1970s (Al Mohsen, 2000). Tertiary studies for women began with arts and education, while all other fields were only available to men. The first tertiary institutions to admit women in 1961 were King Saud University, which accepted women as part-time students in the arts and commerce colleges, and the Islamic University in Madinah, which served female students for postgraduate studies only (Ghainaa, 2008). In 1979, King Saud University opened the first women's campus in the country, which offered subjects such as Arabic, English, history, and geography. In the 1980s, opportunities grew as Saudi women were allowed to study more subject areas such as medicine, public administration, and education at new campus branches (Hamdan, 2005). In 2011, women represented more than 58% of Saudi university students, with statistics indicating that the total number of women seeking a bachelor's degree tripled from 1995–1996 to 2005–2006 (Al Banawi & Yusuf, 2011). Of the 106,095 Saudi students studying abroad in 2011, women comprised 31% (Avancena, 2011). The number of female students opting not to continue their studies also decreased from 39% in 1997–1998 to 20% in 2004–2005 (Al Munajjed, 2010b). While there has been an expansion in the number of women attending university and in the type of courses available to women, there is still a lot of work to be done in terms of diversification and on-time graduation. In 2007, 93% of women with degrees in Saudi Arabia still had degrees in education or human sciences (Al Munajjed, 2010b). Many girls, however, still fail to graduate on time, with rates for delayed graduation as high as 60% in 2005–2006 (Al Munajjed, 2010b).

As seen in Table 2.10, Kuwait was one of the first countries in the Gulf to create opportunities for women to attend higher education in country. The earliest tertiary option for women began in 1961, when the first of several teacher-training schools opened and offered a 3-year course (Vreede-De Stuers, 1974). These schools catered to Kuwaiti females who had completed intermediate schooling and trained teachers for kindergarten and primary schools. Once the secondary schools had expanded sufficiently, these teacher-training schools began offering shortened 2-year courses for girls who had completed secondary school (Vreede-De Stuers, 1974). However, it was not until 1966 and the establishment of the University of Kuwait that comprehensive locally based higher education became available for Kuwaiti women. The university attracted large numbers of Kuwaiti women to the arts and education program in particular, and by 1973–1974, nearly three-fifths of Kuwaiti teachers were women (Meleis et al., 1979).

With regard to gender though, only 2% of the first class of 418 students was female, but by 1975–1976, women comprised 61% of all students (Meleis et al., 1979). By 2001, 19% of Kuwaiti women and 15% of Kuwaiti men had attained higher education in Kuwait (Shah, 2004). Kuwait had a tertiary enrollment index of 2.72 in favor of women in 2003 (World Bank, 2008), and Kuwaiti women comprised two-thirds of university students in Kuwait in 2008 (Al-Mughni in Kelly & Breslin, 2010). Kuwait has appointed women to positions of power in education and, in turn, provided its women with important role models; the government has signaled its willingness to not only invest in women's education but also recognize their skills in the workforce. One example of this is Dr. Faiza Al-Kharafi, who served as the director of Kuwait University from 1993 to 2002 ("Middle Eastern Women to Watch," 2005; "Who's Who Among Arab Women," n.d.)

Bahrain also has a long history of higher education for women. As early as the 1950s, the Bahraini government was providing scholarships for women in the country to study abroad in Lebanon (Al Gharaibeh, 2011). Female participation in higher education has continued to spread in Bahrain. In 2004 and 2009, respectively, women outnumbered males in undergraduate programs and represented 66.1% of students at Bahrain University (Al Gharaibeh, 2011) and 72% of the total Bahraini student population at Arabian Gulf University (Krause, 2009; Ahmed, 2010). By 2009, Bahraini women accounted for 70% of university graduates (Karolak, 2012), and the numbers are growing further, as educated females become role models for young women across the nation. Females account for 33% of the total teaching staff at the tertiary level, higher than the GCC average of 32% (Al Masah Capital Limited, 2012). The challenge, however, is to enable equal access for women to all fields of study. Segregation of courses by gender in secondary schools in Bahrain currently removes the option for women to major in technical programs at the university level (Ahmed, 2010). According to Freedomhouse's report by D. A. Ahmed (2010), "This segregation affects future job opportunities.... Although no other subjects are actually restricted, [Bahraini] women remain underrepresented in areas such as engineering and over-represented in education and health care." With regard to postgraduate education in 2001, 190 Bahraini women had obtained PhDs, but males outnumbered females two to one in this area (Al Gharaibeh, 2011). Importantly, not only are more women continuing their studies, they are also being promoted to key positions in higher education. As in Kuwait, Bahrain has also appointed women to positions of power in the local universities. For example, Sheikha Mariam bint Hassan Al Khalifa previously served as president of Bahrain University and currently is vice chairwoman of the Supreme Council for Women (Al Gharaibeh, 2010; "Graduates Honoured," 2013).

In Oman, the gender differences in terms of female participation at the only public university, Sultan Qaboos University (SQU), are not as large as those in other GCC states. In 2002, 54% of students at Sultan Qaboos University SQU were women, but by 2005–2006, this had fallen to 50%. Despite girls outperforming boys on the grade 12 examinations, the Ministry of Higher Education has introduced a quota system to avoid having more girls than boys in university. The quota is announced each year and varies across disciplines; it favors boys by applying a lower selection cutoff point to their grade 12 examinations. For example, in engineering 732 girls who had applied were not accepted and boys with lower grades were accepted in their place. In total 3,624 boys and 887 girls were admitted, though based on grade 12 examination results, the numbers should have been 2,911 boys and 1,599 girls (MOE, Oman, & World Bank, 2012, p. 81). This is creating a situation in which boys are essentially rewarded for poorer grades rather than having an incentive to improve. Table 2.11 outlines the number of qualified females denied acceptance in certain majors due to the selection system in higher education in Oman. It can therefore be seen that the lower figures for female enrollment are largely a result of quotas on women studying at SQU rather than a lack of interest on the part of women.

Across the GCC countries women are taking increasing advantage of local tertiary opportunities in far greater numbers than men, which is fueling increased demand for employment. The opening of local tertiary institutions has allowed women who may not have been able to study abroad

Table 2.11. Number of Females with Adequate Marks Not Offered Places in Major Groups Due to the Selection System

Major Group	Number
Engineering	732
Science	578
Foundation Year	451
Social Sciences/Art	210
Education	208
Information Technology	186
Medicine and Health	140
Business Administration	133
Sharia and Law	60
Agriculture and Marine	22

Source: MOE, Oman, & World Bank (2012).

for a variety of reasons to continue pursuing their education in far greater numbers than before. This trend shows no sign of abating, and as local PhD programs open up, women are at the forefront of enrolling in these new courses. For women, the key challenge that remains is equality of access to the same programs as men, especially in the sciences. While this is changing in some countries such as the United Arab Emirates (Masdar Institute, 2013), it remains a significant issue for women in Saudi Arabia and Oman.

CONCLUSION

Women from the resource-rich GCC countries are increasingly more and better educated than ever before. They not only excel in comparison to males, but in terms of participation in the sciences and nontraditional disciplines they are also better represented than their Western counterparts. The stereotype of the oppressed Arab woman, who is denied opportunities for education and development, that is so popular in the West simply does not hold true in the GCC countries. The expansion of educational opportunities for women at all levels has meant that they are now able to live far more independent lives than their mothers. They are by their own and others' accounts women to be reckoned with. They are ministers (Chatriwala, 2013), lawyers (Toumi, 2012), engineers (Olarte, 2009), teachers (Toumi, 2013b), fighter pilots (Yaqoob, 2008), and mothers (Van Leijen, 2013). They do not fit the commonly held ideal in which Arab Muslim women are so typically cast. They challenge our conceptions of choice and freedom, and in so doing, they defy efforts to make them into what others want or think they should be. In the words of Her Excellency Sheikha Lubna Al Qasimi, Minister of Foreign Affairs in the United Arab Emirates, "Gone are the days when women's role is limited to the home. With world-class education facilities right at our doorsteps, as well as increased political representation, there is now a greater understanding and acceptance of the needs and rights of women in the Arab world" (Al Qasimi, 2007).

None of this is to say that women's rights are without reproach in the Gulf States or that there are no barriers to break through. In terms of employment, women are still overrepresented in the education field across the region and need access to a wider range of programs. Saudi Arabia also remains an outlier in terms of access for women to different fields of study in higher education and then to work, which will be explored in a later chapter. However, the literature for women in Saudi Arabia fails to acknowledge that while there is still discrimination, there have been great achievements for women in terms of education. This tendency in general of the literature on the region to downplay the successes of women and girls in order to play up the discourse of the oppressed Gulf women has had a profound impact. This impact has been not only on the way that the West conceives of gender roles in the region, but also on local policymakers in terms of their perceptions of the policies required for Gulf States to be perceived as modern. This overarching discourse on modernity, gender, and education is examined in more detail in the following chapter.

3

The Quest for Modernity

Gender, Education, and Development

> Among developing country governments, development agencies, and civil society organizations alike, when we talk of gender, we mean women. If men are discussed at all, it is usually in relation to their role in advancing women's equality, rather than men's gender issues in and of themselves. (Bannon & Correia, 2006, p. xviii)

> Women are central to the evolving Qatari family. Even as they maintain an adherence to valuable traditions, women are adapting to the impacts of modernization. (GSDP, 2011, p. 165)

As discussed briefly in the Introduction and in Chapter 2, there is a great deal of international acclaim to be won by countries that choose to focus on issues relating to women and girls in education. In particular, for the countries of the Gulf, there is a strong incentive to focus on women and girls in education as this has become powerfully linked in global discourses to being a modern nation state. As mentioned previously, the year 2000 heralded the launch of the Millennium Development Goals (MDGs) and the release of the Dakar Framework for Action on Education for All (EFA). Both of these global agreements centered on the use of indicators and goals to measure development. The introduction of goals in development meant that certain areas of development were suddenly elevated over others (Jansen, 2005). With regard to education, the new goals meant that girls' education now became an integral and unquestioned part of not only the definition of the modern nation state but also a key prescription for countries eager to be perceived as modern nation states (Chabbott, 2003). Three of the eight MDGs contain specific references to women and girls:

> Goal 2 is to "Achieve Universal Primary Education," which is particularly focused on gender equity in enrollment rates; the target states "Ensure that, by 2015, children everywhere, boys and girls alike, will be able to complete a full course of primary schooling."
> Goal 3 is to "Promote Gender Equality and Empower Women."
> Goal 5 is to "Improve Maternal Health." (United Nations Statistics Division, 2013)

In the multidonor initiative to reach Education for All, led by the United Nations Educational, Scientific and Cultural Organization (UNESCO), four of the six goals set at Dakar target females specifically:

Goal 2 is "Ensuring that by 2015 all children, *particularly girls*, in difficult circumstances and those belonging to ethnic minorities, have access to and complete free and compulsory primary education of good quality."
Goal 3 mentions the importance of helping "adolescent girls."
Goal 4 is "Achieving a 50 per cent improvement in levels of adult literacy by 2015, *especially for women*, and equitable access to basic and continuing education for all adults."
Goal 5 is "Eliminating gender disparities in primary and secondary education by 2005, and achieving gender equality in education by 2015, *with a focus on ensuring girls' full and equal access* to and achievement in basic education of good quality." (UNESCO, 2000, emphasis added)

Goal 2 of the MDGs mentions boys, but nowhere else in the MDGs or in the Dakar Framework for Action are boys or men mentioned. This is despite that, at minimum, research finds not involving men and boys in development creates further inequalities not only for men but also for women and girls (Bannon & Correia, 2006).

Following from the MDGs and the Dakar Framework, setting gender goals for economic development has now become a common trend emulated by other international organizations. Chief among these has been the World Economic Forum (WEF), an increasingly visible business-focused organization started by German businessman Klaus Schwab, famous for annual meetings that gather celebrities, politicians, and CEOs in Davos,[1] Switzerland. The WEF began publishing its *Global Gender Gap Report* in 2006 on the premise that it "provides a framework for capturing the magnitude and scope of gender-based disparities around the world" (WEF, 2013). In essence, the *Global Gender Gap Report* uses league tables to rank countries from most to least gender equitable and to laud countries where women overrepresent men and shame those where men are overrepresented.

In addition to the WEF, the Organisation for Economic Co-operation and Development (OECD) has also become more interested in gender since the millennium and has both a gender initiative and an online portal dedicated to gender equality. Reflective of the economic rationale driving its mission is a 2012 release stating that the OECD believes it is important to "tackle the gender gap to produce growth" and details how "more progress will be essential for countries to benefit from the economic contributions women can make and to not waste the years of investment in the education of girls and young women" (OECD, 2012b). The production of gender reports by organizations such as the WEF and the OECD is relevant to the discussion of global trends linking girls' education and modernity because it demonstrates the broad appeal of a policy focus on women and girls to both ends of the political spectrum, making it a far harder issue for governments outside the West to ignore or take a contrary view. The marriage of the human rights discourse on education for marginalized populations, such as women and girls, to the economic rationale expressed by human capital theory, and the view that women are valuable economic agents who require attention, makes for an enduring policy focus even when it has become irrelevant. Women are thus being co-opted for agendas far larger than improving their access to employment and/or equal pay. They have a symbolic value in any policy discussion that will almost guarantee consensus, no matter who the actors are around the table.

In the face of such widespread support for girls' education, emphasizing a focus on boys' education could be regarded as "illogical at best" (Jansen, 2005). Not only can it be viewed as illogical, it is also almost impossible for a country to focus on boys' education without potentially either jeopardizing aid flows or harming its reputation through appearing misogynistic. In countries that are aid dependent, aid conditionality typically compels them to focus on girls through mandating adherence to the MDGs and the Dakar Framework (Chabbott, 2003). However, for wealthy countries such as the Gulf States, girls become an object of policy interest more through the exercise of "soft power" (Bieber & Martens, 2011). This is the type of power exercised by international organizations like the OECD and the WEF, either through the gender measures reported by the OECD's Program on International Student Assessment or through the use of league tables in the WEF's *Global Gender Gap Report*. Thus, girls' education and not boys', women's rights and not men's have become, at least at the discourse level, nonnegotiable components of the international community's policy prescription for development and modernity.

Scholars such as Steiner-Khamsi (2004), Schriewer and Martinez (2004), Silova (2004), and Spreen (2004) believe global policies (such as those relating to girls' education) become widespread not because of amorphous globalization forces, but as a result of nations seeing compatibility between certain policies and their own interests, whether their interest is to obtain loans or to signal modernity. That is, they take on what they need and discard what they do not. When nations agree to undertake reforms, these scholars argue, it often coincides more with their own internal political situations and needs than with anything external (Phillips, 2004; Schriewer & Martinez, 2004; Steiner-Khamsi, 2004). For example, nations may choose to focus on girls' education to signal alignment with international policies, or to signal modernity to their own people at times when leaders require external justification for particular policy directions. However, whatever the reasons that nations adopt policies, even symbolic borrowing of the discourse gives strength to the "truths" it contains (Escobar, 1994; Parpart, Connelly, & Barriteau, 2000). Not only do these "truths" then become more widely accepted, but they also privilege certain issues over others and create situations whereby leaders, often without realizing it, begin to buy into these ways of thinking—regardless of the realities their nation faces. Whether precipitated by political expediency, external pressure, or belief in aspects of best practice, once a policy becomes disseminated widely, it achieves a life of its own and tends to rise above any type of criticism. In the GCC, it can be argued that states adopted the girls' education discourse due to a desire to be perceived as progressive and modern on the world stage, both in order to counter the negative image of Gulf States as oppressors of women and to be well regarded by leading OECD member states and key trade partners, such as the United States, Germany, and the United Kingdom.

This chapter first situates the construction of modernity, gender, and education discourse in the Middle East through examining reports on education and gender in the Middle East from international organizations (IOs) such as the United Nations (UN) agencies, the World Bank, and the WEF, in addition to reports from management consultants such as Booz & Company. Next, it discusses the history and trajectory of modernization in the GCC countries and how countries moved from constructing schools to constructing curricula and wider educational reforms. The chapter then examines different government strategies and reports from the various GCC states to determine how, in what context, and for what purpose references to gender, education, and modernity are used. Finally, the chapter concludes with a discussion on the co-opting of gender and education in the GCC, such that while men and boys fail to capture the attention of policymakers, girls continue to be praised for educational achievements but can be denied basic rights in other areas. While the greater enrollment of females and various achievements by women are significant achievements, the narrow measures used by international agencies to define empowerment allow countries in the region to cover up other structural and social inequalities for women. This further disadvantages women while simultaneously ignoring and exacerbating educational inequalities for men.

CONSTRUCTING A DISCOURSE LINKING GENDER, EDUCATION, AND MODERNITY IN THE MIDDLE EAST

Key to the construction of a regional discourse linking gender, education, and modernity have been a number of regional reports published in the last decade by the United Nations Development Program (UNDP), the

World Bank, and other IOs. These reports echo the prevailing global discourses relating to gender, education, and modernity and apply them to the Middle East context. Gender, defined as women and girls, is a central concern in many reports on the Middle East and North Africa (MENA) region (Al Munajjed & Sabbagh, 2011; UNDP, 2006; UNESCO, 2011; WEF & European Bank of Reconstruction and Development [EBRD], 2013; World Bank, 2008, 2013) no doubt partly due to the vast amount of literature focusing on the notion of the oppressed Muslim woman, as discussed in Chapter 2. In this section, we examine a sample of four reports written by IOs from 2005 to 2013 with regard to how, or if, they linked gender and education and modernity. The reports are *The 2005 Arab Human Development Report: Towards the Rise of Women in the Arab World;* a 2008 World Bank report on the MENA region, *The Road Not Travelled: Education Reform in the Middle East and North Africa;* a 2011 report from Booz & Company entitled *Youth in the GCC: Meeting the Challenge;* and a 2013 World Bank report, *Opening Doors: Gender Equality and Development in the Middle East and North Africa.* These reports were selected as, first, they focused on more than one country in the region; second, they were concerned with development, education, and gender; and third, we wanted to look at the perspectives of a range of different organizations, and so reports were taken from international development organizations (The UNDP and the World Bank) and the private sector (Booz & Company).

The Arab Human Development Report (AHDR) (UNDP, 2006) titled "Towards the Rise of Women in the Arab World," as indicated by its title, focuses entirely on women and girls. It argues that girls in the Arab world are deprived of education and they are held back by traditional, male-dominated societies. In addition, it states that Arab women have fewer employment opportunities as a result of "conservative authorities, discriminatory laws, chauvinist male peers and tradition-minded kinsfolk watchfully regulating their aspirations, activities and conduct" (p. III). While the focus is firmly on women and girls, the 2005 *AHDR* does acknowledge some of the difficulties men are facing, such as high illiteracy rates and low economic participation rates. However, the report offers only recommendations on how to address these problems with regard to women. Overall, there is a strong sense throughout the report that women are competing with men in a race to succeed and that tradition and culture are preventing them from doing so. In the 2005 AHDR, modernization is seen as the remedy to the current state of affairs and a key part of the modernization prescription is for Arab states to focus more on women and girls.

The *2008 World Bank Middle East and North Africa (MENA) Development Report* titled "The Road Not Traveled: Education Reform in the Middle East and North Africa" (World Bank, 2008) echoes the *AHDR* in its negative portrayal of tradition and the role of tradition in holding the MENA countries back from becoming modern societies. Although the 2008 report presents data illustrating that the MENA countries have "closed the gender gap" in education, the discourse of the report echoes the discourse found in the *AHDR*. In other words, despite the achievement of girls in education, the report continues to emphasize the dangers of the traditional (anti-female) nature of education in the MENA region juxtaposed with modern global education trends (pro-female) that are synonymous with success, equity, and quality in schooling (World Bank, 2008). Both reports discuss the need to move away from traditional teaching methods, traditional industries, and traditional values toward what is new and modern in order to develop and join the global community.

Booz and Company's 2011 report *Youth in the GCC: Meeting the Challenge* continues to promote a largely one-sided discourse on gender and education in the MENA region. Al Munajjed and Sabbagh (2011) argue that girls across the GCC countries are doubly disadvantaged in education, claiming that in addition to being disadvantaged by the traditional teaching methods used in schools, girls are often taught a restricted curriculum (compared to boys) in subjects such as "math, science, foreign languages, and computers" (p. 44). However, results from the 2007 TIMSS and 2009 PISA, as presented in Chapter 2, indicate otherwise; in all resource-rich GCC states, girls fared significantly better than boys across all tested subjects, including science and math. Despite this and in line with other global discourses promulgating a focus on girls' education, the report calls for offering even better educational opportunities for girls (Al Munajjed & Sabbagh, 2011, p. 49). Thus, the report ignores regional realities relating to education and gender and blindly promotes policies that could potentially lead to boys falling even further behind.

In light of the fact that females have surpassed males in terms of enrollment, attainment, and achievement in most GCC countries, the focus of the 2013 World Bank report appears to have shifted away from propounding the expansion of educational opportunities for girls. This has been replaced with a discussion of the lack of opportunities for women in the labor force rather than any discussion on the serious deficiencies in boys' education. Despite "Gender Equality" being the theme of the *2013 MENA Development Report*, the report shows scant interest in examining statistics that reflect the declining enrollment, achievement, and attainment of boys and the ramifications of this for MENA society. Instead, the report largely focuses on the legal, economic, social, and educational barriers facing women's choices and mobility (World Bank, 2013). On a positive note, in contrast to earlier international reports that contained a more competitive portrayal of gender relations, such as the *AHDR* (UNDP, 2006), the *2013 MENA Development Report* does acknowledge that for youth of both genders there need to be reforms in a variety of areas "to secure equal opportunities for women alongside men" (World Bank, 2013, p. xi). However, beyond a few statements like this, any discussion of opportunities and threats for males was largely absent. Had the writers of the report genuinely been interested in gender equality for both men and women, one would expect that the content would address the difficulties faced by each gender. In other words, the report would provide a closer look at the problems boys face in schools and suggest initiatives to improve the quality of schooling for boys, while simultaneously calling for better economic opportunities for women. With regard to modernity, the report spends a chapter carefully discussing whether tradition and linked concepts such as religion and culture are significant barriers to women's participation in the labor market. While it is inconclusive and very carefully worded, the prescriptions for increasing equality in terms of the participation of women at the end of the report are typical policy prescriptions drawn from "evidence and examples from the international arena" (World Bank, 2013, p. 127), that is OECD countries, such as work–life balance, access to child care, and the like. The term *international* (practically synonymous with *modern*) is used in this context to legitimize the prescriptions that follow in much the same way that calling something modern would have in earlier times. The term *modern* is used infrequently and typically used only to describe a desirable workplace. In the final chapter males are not mentioned even once, even though this is the chapter dedicated for policy prescriptions to assist women. We would expect to see discussion in this chapter about the relational nature of gender and, at the very least, what programs could be done with men to assist women.

Despite some shifts in the language used throughout international development reports over the past decade, these reports continue to promulgate essentially the same discourse of women's inequality even in the face of changing realities on the ground. This discourse restricts any discussions of gender to a singular focus on women and girls and as such precludes any real discussion on issues facing men and boys. Simultaneously, the same discourse also links development and modernity in the education sector and now the labor market to a focus on women and girls. These reports and many others like them ignore the relational nature of gender and the fact that inequalities for men and boys will have ramifications for women and girls as well. Rather, these reports consider the current educational inequities facing boys to be of little concern despite acknowledging the highly patriarchal nature of the region. These ramifications are discussed in subsequent chapters but include many social costs that impact families and society at large. Unfortunately, current trends indicate that the discourses put forth in regional reports promoting the cause of girls and women exclusively will likely continue, while the issue of boys' declining performance and poor retention remains unarticulated and unaddressed by policymakers. It is evident that it would be extremely difficult for countries in the region to change the current gender discourse to focus on males, as this would mark a significant break from both global and regional discourses on gender and education. The next section of this chapter looks at the history and trajectory of the modernization project in the Gulf with regard to education. It then examines how the language of these international reports with regard to gender and education has come to be embedded in national-level reports.

THE HISTORY AND TRAJECTORY OF THE MODERNIZATION PROJECT IN EDUCATION IN THE GULF

The impetus for modernization in the Gulf began in the 1960s and 1970s with the discovery of oil (Al Fahim, 2011; Peterson, 2009). At that time, building schools was only one part of the ambitious and rapid modernization programs that the rulers of the resource-rich Gulf States embarked on after realizing their newfound wealth (Al Fahim, 2011). The first phase of modernization programs across the region consisted of the construction of physical infrastructure writ large. Roads were built, buildings constructed, and power plants developed, all to allow for the extraction of massive quantities of oil and gas and to cater to the large numbers of people needed for such an undertaking (Al Fahim, 2011; Davidson, 2008b). Consistent with rentier state theories, Gulf States also constructed the physical infrastructure that the local population required, which included schools and hospitals (Davidson, 2008b; Foley, 2010). Houses for nationals were built, and land that had previously been unclaimed began to be marked out in terms of ownership (Heard-Bey, 2004; Jones, 2010). As the first modernization projects advanced, however, it became clear that the Gulf States also needed to create new bureaucratic structures to support projects and ways of doing things that were previously unknown or had not been required in the pre-oil system.

Education, in the first wave of modernization, was very much about creating infrastructure, both physical and human (Heard-Bey, 2004; Madany et al., 1988). The biggest priorities were the construction of schools and staffing them with teachers (Davidson, 2008a; Madany et al., 1988). By the 1990s, however, with most physical infrastructure in place, the majority of staffing issues addressed, and enrollment rates at close to 100% for primary and preparatory levels, the next wave of modernization programs for education began (Brewer et al., 2007; Davidson, 2008b; Karolak, 2012). These new modernization programs focused much more on the quality of education and the need to reform curriculum and pedagogy as part of a drive to become perceived as knowledge-based economies and, thus, as modern nation states (Brewer et al., 2007; Gardner, 1995; Ridge, 2009). This move coincided with the emergence of the large-scale international assessments such as PISA and TIMSS, alongside the establishment of new global education goals articulated by IOs, such as the EFA initiative and its accompanying Dakar Framework and MDGs in 2000. Gulf States were quick to sign on to the MDGs and EFA, and as a result of the reporting mechanisms required by these agreements, Gulf States began to make references to the international goals of gender equality, as articulated in these declarations, in national-level reports.

A lack of local capacity needed to create widespread education reform meant that governments across the GCC countries looked to global management consultancy firms, such as McKinsey & Company and Booz & Company, to provide new strategies for their education sectors (Barber, Mourshe, & Whelan, 2007; Hoteit, Moujaes, Hiltunen, & Sahlberg, 2012; Moujaes et al., 2011). These new education strategic plans were designed to create "modern" education systems through ostensibly helping Gulf States move from being resource-based economies to knowledge-based economies (Kirk, 2011; Schwalje, 2012). This was of particular concern to countries such as Bahrain and Oman, where oil reserves were in decline and tremors emanating from the Arab Spring were felt (Karolak, 2012; MOE, Oman, & World Bank, 2012). It was also a priority for the other Gulf countries, as a pending youth bulge heralded previously unknown demographic pressures on already saturated public sectors (Al Munajjed & Sabbagh, 2011; Forstenlechner & Rutledge, 2011), which will be discussed more in the next chapter.

With regard to gender, these new strategies were largely silent. This echoed trends in OECD countries in which the achievement of gender equality, at least in terms of enrollment and, increasingly, achievement, had meant that gender no longer featured in education reports of many OECD states or indeed from the OECD itself. Education quality was the main focus of these new plans, and this entailed revising curricula, increasing hours of instruction, and improving teacher quality among other things. While reports generated specifically for the MDGs, EFA, or for external consumption (such as for potential investors) still referred to gender (as in the achievements of women and girls), the new internal education strategic plans for many Gulf States did not. As such, a strategic policy bilingualism (Gallagher, 2011; Silova as cited in Steiner-Khamsi, 2004) has emerged in the Gulf States, whereby for internal purposes, particularly for reports and strategies written in Arabic, gender is completely absent. But for external purposes, such as reports in English, the achievements of women and girls often feature prominently. Consistent with the work of Steiner-Khamsi (2004) and others (Maroun et al., 2008), states in the Gulf are attempting to be what they know their stakeholders want to see. They have taken on

Western discourses of gender, education, and modernity to appease international organizations and Western governments, while at the same time they have completely ignored gender in their own internal strategic plans as they realize that their own constituents are far less concerned with this. The result has been that gender (meaning both boys and girls) has been taken off the local policy table and the situation regarding male underachievement is neither problematized nor addressed.

CURRENT GENDER, MODERNITY, AND EDUCATION DISCOURSES

To evidence their newfound modernity, the Gulf States, with the assistance of an army of consultants,[2] now produce an impressive array of reports to highlight their various successes, including in education, gender, and development. In order to examine the extent to which Gulf States have embedded broader international discourses on gender, education, and modernity into national documents, we analyzed 13 official publications from each of the Gulf States considered in this book. These publications are all at the country level and were produced between 2007 and 2012 either solely in English or in both English and Arabic. They include reports on the MDGs for Bahrain, Kuwait, Qatar, Saudi Arabia, and the United Arab Emirates; National Development Strategies for Bahrain and Qatar; and several others relating to education or competitiveness. For a full list see Table 3.1. While some government departments openly acknowledge the use of a partner organization such as the World Bank in the production of a report, others prefer not to acknowledge consultants in any official report, even though unofficially it is widely known that consultants were used.

All 13 reports were analyzed using NVivo to determine how the term *gender* (and its synonyms) is used in these reports and, more importantly, how it is used in relation to education and conceptions of modernity. Analysis of these policy documents revealed not only how fully and frequently Gulf nations use national development reports and strategies to highlight their own progress, but also how nations use the documents to emphasize their modernity and development vis-à-vis their neighbors. An analysis of the most-used words in all 13 documents can be seen in Figure 3.1. This word frequency cloud depicts the most common words in the combined text of all these publications (when numbers and conjunctions are removed), with the size of each word representing the relative frequency with which it appears in the documents.

Of significance is the fact that the only word mentioned more often than *countries* in these national development and education documents is

Table 3.1. Gulf Policy Documents by Author, Country, and Year

TITLE	AUTHOR	COUNTRY	YEAR
Review of the Progress of the Millennium Development Goals in the Kingdom of Bahrain: A National Perspective	UNDP; Central Informatics Organization	Bahrain	2010
A Future Skills Strategy for Bahrain: 2009–2016	Allen Consulting Group	Bahrain	2009
Vision 2030	Bahrain Economic Development Board, Government of Bahrain	Bahrain	2013
Paving the Way for a Sustainable Future: Millennium Development Goals Kuwait Progress Report 2012	UNDP; State of Kuwait	Kuwait	2012
Kuwait Competitiveness Report	Kuwait University	Kuwait	2006
Oman: The Development Experience and Investment Climate	Ministry of National Economy	Oman	2008
Education in Oman: The Drive for Quality	Ministry of Education; World Bank	Oman	2012
The EFA 2000 Assessment: Country Reports, Oman	UNICEF; Education for All; Ministry of Education	Oman	2000
The Millennium Development Goals for the State of Qatar: 2012	Diplomatic Institute; Qatar Statistics Authority	Qatar	2012
Qatar National Development Strategy, 2011–2016	General Secretariat for Development Planning	Qatar	2011
Kingdom of Saudi Arabia: Millennium Development Goals	UNDP; Ministry of Economy and Planning	Saudi Arabia	2011
Millennium Development Goals: United Arab Emirates Report	UNDP; Ministry of Economy	United Arab Emirates	2007
UAE 2010: United Arab Emirates Yearbook	The National Media Council	United Arab Emirates	2010

the word *women*. The words *status, participation, gender, ratio, female, feminine,* and *girl* also appear in this list of top words, indicating that discussions of gender (defined as women and girls) are central to discourses surrounding development in the GCC countries. Also of note is that the word *male* is significantly smaller than all of these words and many others, indicating that it is mentioned much less often.

Figure 3.1. Word Frequency Cloud for 13 Policy Documents

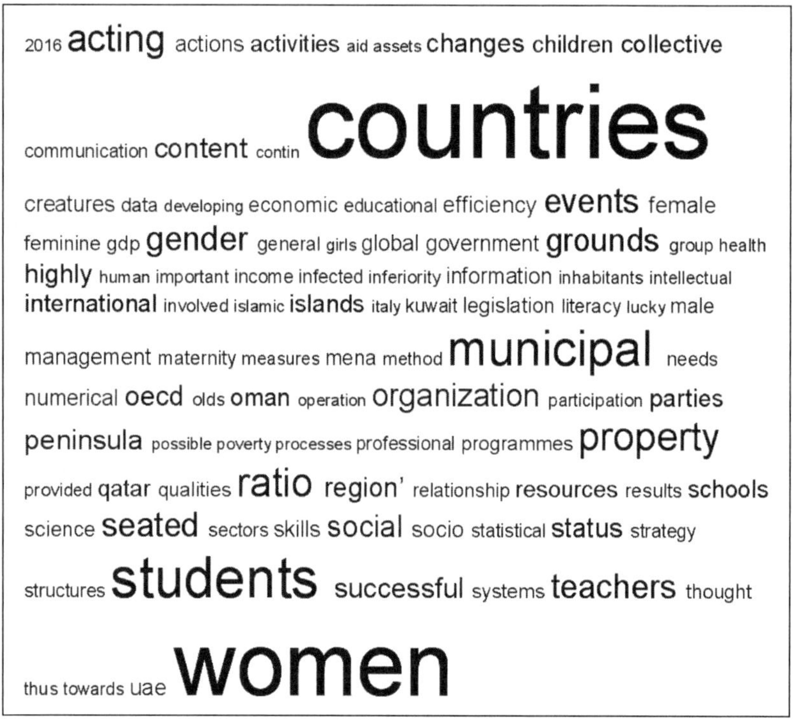

2016 acting actions activities aid assets changes children collective communication content contin **countries** creatures data developing economic educational efficiency events female feminine gdp gender general girls global government grounds group health highly human important income infected inferiority information inhabitants intellectual international involved islamic islands italy kuwait legislation literacy lucky male management maternity measures mena method **municipal** needs numerical oecd olds oman operation organization participation parties peninsula possible poverty processes professional programmes property provided qatar qualities ratio region' relationship resources results schools science seated sectors skills social socio statistical status strategy structures **students** successful systems teachers thought thus towards uae **women**

A text search for "males," "females," "men," and "women" and related synonyms reveals more about the context in which terms related to gender appear. These terms were examined in context to see if they were used in a way that is (1) consistent with prevailing modernization discourses, such as referring to the disadvantage of women, or (2) challenging to prevailing discourses to include issues related to men or boys. In addition, the terms were then analyzed to determine whether they reference development policies that targeted males and females equally. Lastly, the reports were analyzed to determine whether they contained any references or statistics that highlight male disadvantage. Table 3.2 outlines the findings of the text search analysis.

It can be seen that relatively few references challenge prevailing modernization discourses or show the disadvantaged state of males in education. If we look at individual states, we can see that Qatar makes far more references to gender in a way consistent with discourses focused on women. On the other hand, Oman stands out in referencing disadvantages for males, and reports from the country appear to provide more balanced representations. In total, there were 92 references to gender consistent with prevailing modernization discourse and only 23 references to development policies

Table 3.2. References to Modernity and Gender in the GCC Countries

Country	References to Gender That Are Consistent with Prevailing Modernization Discourses	References to Gender That Challenge Prevailing Modernization Discourses	References to Development Policies That Target Males and Females Equally	References and Statistics That Show Males at a Disadvantage	Number of Documents Used for Each Country
Bahrain	25	2	7	4	3
Kuwait	22	—	2	4	2
Saudi Arabia	14	—	1	—	1
Oman	13	6	3	14	3
United Arab Emirates	18	2	1	6	2
Qatar	43	9	9	4	2
TOTAL	92	19	23	32	13

that target males and females equally. In general, however, if a reference is made to males in these reports, it is to demonstrate how many more women there are than men or how much better women are doing. An example of what this looks like in a text can be seen in the following excerpt from the *Millennium Development Goals: United Arab Emirates Report*:

> The proportion of females in higher education [in the United Arab Emirates] has risen remarkably, at a rate that has not been achieved in any other country in the world. During the years 1990 to 2004 the number of female university students has grown to double that of male students. This is the result of the promotion and encouragement of women's education by state and family. In addition, a large percentage of males feel satisfied with secondary education and with what qualifies them to join the labor market at an early age. (UNDP & Ministry of Economy, UAE, 2007, p. 17)

This extract not only highlights the success of the United Arab Emirates in having more women than men in higher education, it also attributes this directly to particular policies, of which there is no evidence. Finally, it completely marginalizes the poor attainment of males by stating that they are "satisfied with a secondary education" without any evidence to support this claim at all.

Linking modernization to a focus on women and girls can be seen in another excerpt from the *Millennium Development Goals: United Arab Emirates Report*. This report, while acknowledging that women still face barriers outside the home, places the blame for women's disempowerment on "cultural legacies and traditions" and advocates changing society's perspective on women. It does not explain how women's roles are exactly limited, compared to what standard, or in what arenas. The report content seems similar to that found in the 2005 *AHDR*, which implicitly assumes that all Arab women must face some barriers:

> The Emirati society, like other Arab societies, has some practices, cultural legacies and prevalent traditions that may lead to limiting women's role in the society. Therefore, the major challenge that faces the State is to change the society's perspective of women's developmental roles. Such an endeavor would necessitate the mobilization of all societal capabilities to ensure the effectiveness of strategies developed for empowering women. (UNDP & Ministry of Economy, UAE, 2007, p. 35)

Thirteen of the 17 sources, including all of the publications discussing the progress of the MDGs, contain more than 100 distinct references that emphasize the achievements of women and girls. The *Review of the Progress of the Millennium Development Goals in the Kingdom of Bahrain* provides an example of how the narrow indicators used for equality by the MDGs can be problematic. The report states that "most ceilings set for quantitative achievement for the MDGs have been achieved, or nearly so, many years ago...particularly as regards Goal 3 (promotion of gender equality)" (UNDP & Central Informatics Organization [CIO], 2010, p. 10).

In a similar vein, the following quote from Kuwait states that in addition to achieving the MDG gender goals in terms of education, Kuwait "could be considered among the world's leaders in promoting gender equity" (UNDP & State of Kuwait, 2012, p. 35). This is a big claim from a nation that recently reverted to sex segregation in its national university (Del Castillo, 2003), gave women the right to vote and hold public office only in 2005 (Rousseau, 2013), and in which Islamist parties advocate against women in politics and the public sphere (Janssen, 2005).

Those sources that strayed from the conventional discourses relating to women highlighted some of the educational disadvantages faced by men and boys. In particular, Oman is unique in the region in its 2012 publication on education. This report, written in conjunction with the World Bank, references the disadvantage of males with roughly the same frequency as it references the need for attention to women and girls. However, often when these references to males are made, closer reading shows that the references were without a detailed discussion of the implications of a reverse gender gap for Oman. The following quote, for example, emphasizes girls' superior performance to boys, but then nothing is said about what the implications of this may be. After discussing the better performance of Omani girls, the report quickly tries to show that some boys are also performing well, but the boys referred to are expatriate males, not Omani, and thus their good performance is not relevant to a comparison with Omani females.

> Girls tend to perform better than boys on public examinations. On the all-important grade 12 General Education Diploma examinations (also addressed in Chapter 4), the results for public school candidates show that the pass rate for Omani females was 9 percentage points higher than for males (Table 3.3). In sharp contrast, males had a marginally higher pass rate than females among the relatively small population of non-Omani students in public schools. (MOE, Oman, & World Bank, 2012, p. 77)

While the majority of the 13 publications refer to gender equality in education as something that has been achieved or soon will be, citing rising female literacy and enrollment rates, there is little acknowledgment that there is now a reverse gender gap that disadvantages males, and therefore there is no discussion of what this might mean for both males and females in the future. The following quote from Bahrain exemplifies the eagerness of these countries to emphasize the achievements of women, with no mention of the underachievement and absence of men.

> Bahrain has succeeded in reducing the human development gap between men and women, for the value of the human development index is equal to the value of the gender-sensitive human development index. Since 2000 the Kingdom has achieved gender equality in all stages of education. In fact, women are more than twice the number of men at the university level. At the same time, there is recorded progress in economic and political participation by women amid a strong and supporting environment to achieve the remaining targets in this goal. (UNDP & CIO, 2010, p. 29)

Finally, countries also use these reports to compare themselves with other countries in the region to show superiority. The following quotes from Qatar and Kuwait both highlight how these countries are performing better in terms of gender equity, defined by the MDGs as enrollment rates, than other Arab countries and countries worldwide. Again, there is no noted concern about low male enrollment rates, and the use of MDG measurement standards allows report writers to ignore areas where there are still real gender inequality.

> Although the gender gap is getting narrower in many countries for primary and secondary education and the postgraduate enrollment rate of females exceeded that of males in some Arab countries, these rates remain higher in Qatar compared to their counterparts in other Arab countries. The current average ratio of females compared to males (at university education) is 132 to 100 respectively. (Qatar Statistics Authority [QSA] & Diplomatic Institute [DI], 2012, p. 22)

Thus, it can be seen that the Gulf States have a clear twofold purpose in adopting conventional gender discourses, first to present themselves as modern to the West and second to enable them to declare superiority regionally and internationally in terms of their path to modernity. The fact that these reports are available in English means they are meant for external consumption and this is the image they want the West to see. This gives strength to arguments by Steiner-Khamsi (2004) and others that nations choose when, where, and how to use particular policies and policy discourses because such discourses align strategically with their internal needs, not because of strong convictions about equity or the global isomorphism, as advocated by Meyer, Boli-Bennett, and Chase-Dunn (1975). In terms of achieving global goals such as the MDGs or with regard to signaling modernity, the majority of the Gulf States have the most to say in the education sector. This is especially true in terms of the measures required, such as enrollment rates; so it is natural that this becomes the sector that is most discussed when highlighting the accomplishments of women and the progressiveness of the Gulf States with regard to women and girls. Discussions relating to boys become marginalized or nonexistent, as boys' education and talk of boys do not mesh well with current development discourses, especially in the realm of education.

CASUALTIES OF THE GENDER, EDUCATION, AND MODERNITY DISCOURSE

To signal their increasing modernity, the Gulf States are now using their resource wealth to not only purchase impressive physical infrastructure but also buy the latest knowledge. This has provided consultants from firms such as McKinsey & Company (Saudi Arabia and the United Arab Emirates), Booz & Company (United Arab Emirates), the Rand Corporation (Qatar), and the World Bank (Kuwait and Oman) to guide the transformation of their public sectors into regional or international models of "best practice." In the education sector all governments in the region have depended heavily on these management consultants to work with the various Ministries of Education to develop comprehensive strategic plans. However, the disconnect between these consultants and the reality of the education sectors in the Gulf has meant that these plans have failed to result in any substantive change in terms of quality of education and, in particular, in terms of student achievement on international assessments (Royston, 2011; Ball, 2007; "Doha Rolls Out Private School Vouchers," 2012; Khatri, 2012c). The use of these consultants has also meant that issues relating to gender go unaddressed as gender is not of interest to either management consultants or governments.

Ironically, despite their own struggling national education systems, governments in the region have sought to position themselves as global knowledge brokers. With the help of yet more consultants, the region has hosted multimillion-dollar education conferences such as the annual WISE conference in Qatar, the short-lived Education Project in Bahrain, and the 2012 Transforming Education Summit conference in Abu Dhabi. These conferences gather experts to share experiences and dispense advice about how to become a top-performing education system. The Gulf States—particularly the United Arab Emirates and Qatar—are determined to present an image of themselves as having modern and developed education sectors that make them credible models for other countries. To that end, the Knowledge and Human Development Authority (KHDA) in Dubai has commissioned the World Bank to write a report detailing how they followed the suggestions of the World Bank 2008 Report *The Road Not Travelled* and should be lauded as a beacon of best practice in the Gulf and the Middle East. This regional and even within-country competitiveness and constant desire to be seen as the biggest or the best is part of what hinders substantive development across the region. The refusal to acknowledge any flaws or weaknesses in their countries prevents nations from addressing real issues such as the poor attainment and persistence of males in education.

Although boys and men are a casualty of international and regional modernity and development discourses, it is important to note that girls and women are also negatively impacted by this same discourse. The neoliberal view of development propagated by IOs such as the OECD, World Bank, and WEF (Scholte, 2005) does not allow for nuanced examinations of issues surrounding gender (Hafner-Burton & Pollack, 2002; Monkman & Hoffman, 2013; Stromquist, 2012). As the chief concern of these organizations is to enhance economic activity and GDP, there is little real concern for the very real structural and social inequalities that women face across the region (Monkman & Hoffman, 2013; Stromquist, 2012). By reducing education to merely an input for growth and by reducing gender equity to enrollment rates or other easily quantifiable measures, governments across the region are empowered to declare great success and gender parity (or greater) for women at all levels of education. GCC countries are incentivized to make much of the fact that women outperform men academically while failing to address legal barriers that prevent a woman from passing on her nationality, working in a mixed-sex environment, studying whatever she qualifies for, traveling alone without a male companion, and inheriting more than an eighth of her husband's estate, as well as many other issues that are deeply embedded in Gulf societal structures (Kelly & Breslin, 2010; Krause, 2009; Rutledge, Al Shamsi, Bassioni, & Al Sheikh, 2011).

The ruling elites of the Gulf are savvy politicians; they know the language that the West wants to hear with regard to women and modernization and they use this to their own advantage. At the 2013 bid in Paris for Dubai to host the World Expo, the committee was surprised by an address given by HRH Princess Haya, the wife of the ruler of Dubai, His Highness Sheikh Mohamed bin Rashid Al Maktoum (Simpson, 2013b). It was a shrewd and calculated move on the part of the government of Dubai designed to send a powerful message of modernity through the use of a woman. An irony was that at the same time Princess Haya was speaking about the virtues of Dubai as a host city and presenting an image of the empowered Arab woman, a Norwegian woman in Dubai was being sentenced to prison for drinking and for having consensual sex after she reported being raped (Goulding & O'Sullivan, 2013). On a different topic but no less revealing about how calculating governments are in the region was an article written by Micheal Janofksy, a *New York Times* reporter for over 24 years who for a time was also the personal blogger for the Crown Prince of one of the emirates in the United Arab Emirates. Janofsky, in his article

"The Sheikh and I: Ghostwriting for a Crown Prince in Exile," states how he was instructed that "the blogs needed to reflect the basic themes of the campaign while pointing out the virtues of modernization and the evils of Iran, both of which the Sheikh knew would appeal to Western governments" (Janofsky, 2013).

Women and girls in the Gulf States have made good use of the advantages that access to education has provided them. Restrictions on women working, especially in the early years after the discovery of oil, meant that many bright and talented national women, who in a different place or time might have been something else, became teachers. This has supported national girls' academic success. A study of student achievement in Israel found that Arab girls performed better than both Jewish girls and Arab boys (Mittleberg & Lev Ari, 1999). Puzzled by the results, the researchers discovered that due to the many restrictions on Arab men working in Israel, some of the best and brightest had become teachers in the absence of other options. Unlike the rest of the Arab world where teaching is a low-status profession, pursued only when one cannot get into something else (Shediac & Samman, 2010), Arab teachers who live in Israel had chosen it as a first option. The result of this was that Arab girls who were desperate to learn were taught by a caliber of teachers they otherwise would not have had. Hannum and Park (2002), in a study on students in rural China, found that students did better when taught by teachers from their own village. It appears that a combination of a lack of other employment opportunities, as was the case in Israel, and the shared cultural connection with their students' national female teachers, especially in the earlier years of the Gulf, seems to have given national girls access to high-quality, passionate teachers from their own communities. These teachers, coupled with the possibilities that girls then saw opening up with more education, seem to have inspired female students to continue their education. The reverse sadly is true for boys. As national men had far more employment options from the beginning, very few went into education in the first place and numbers are on the decline. There are currently very few male national teachers in the United Arab Emirates and Qatar (interestingly, the two Gulf countries where gender gaps are the widest) (Hausmann, Tyson, & Zahidi, 2009; Ridge, 2010). Boys are largely taught by expatriate teachers from other Arab states and have a schooling experience far removed from that of their female counterparts.

The modernization project in the Gulf gave rise to very real advantages for women. In the next chapter we look at the situation of boys throughout the GCC countries and how despite the many advances that have taken place in their societies, they are more likely to drop out of school, to not go to university, to go to jail, and to get poorer grades than girls. The rest of the book then looks at the some of the causes of this situation and the future for males in the Gulf.

4 Leaving the Boys Behind

> Instead of sustained gender-inequality in favor of males, there is growing evidence that females are actually doing better than males in many aspects of attainment of education credentials...the same human capital production and ideological forces that decreased gender differences in earlier stages of schooling seem to now be at work at more advanced levels. (Baker & LeTendre, 2005, p. 30)

Globally, in terms of gender and education, there is a new paradigm at play. Historical advantages enjoyed by males in terms of both access to and quality of schooling have now largely disappeared in the West and increasingly across the rest of the world as access to education for girls increases (UNICEF, 2004). For many this is no surprise and can be attributed to the many advances made by and for women in every sector, including education, over the past 30 to 40 years. Stereotypes about what women can and should study and barriers to their participation have also largely disappeared in conjunction with the creation of equal access to education at all levels. In the West, for the first time in history fewer men than women now attend college and fewer men than women have advanced degrees, as seen in Table 4.1.

In the United States, the African American community feels the gender divide acutely, as African American males are far less likely to complete high school than their female counterparts and are far more likely to be incarcerated than any other race (Levin, Belfield, Muennig, & Rouse, 2007). Not as well studied in the United States, but of equal concern, are White males clustered in low socioeconomic rural communities, such as the Appalachians, who are also less likely to continue school than their female counterparts (Brown, Copeland, Costello, Erkanli, & Worthman, 2009). Elsewhere, such as in Australia and the United Kingdom, the decline in both male retention and achievement has led to various governmental and nongovernmental initiatives designed to re-engage young men back into the education system.[1] However, the steady decline in male achievement and participation has attracted scant attention from academia. Attempts to detail or address boys' educational struggles, in terms of either retention or achievement, are often dismissed as being trivial (Epstein, Elwood, Hey, & Maw, 1998), with critics typically pointing to

Table 4.1. Men in Higher Education in the United States, United Kingdom, Australia, and Other Select Western Countries

Country/Region	College Attendance (% Male)	Master's Degree (% Male)	Doctorate Degree (% Male)
United States[a]	43	40	48
United Kingdom[b]	40	46[c]	
Australia[d]	4	42[e]	
Denmark[f]	42	41	54
France[f]	45	44	53
North America and Western Europe[f]	42	41	51

Sources and notes: National Center for Education Statistics (NCES), 2010; (*a*) Snyder & Dillow, 2012; (*b*) HESA, 2012; (*c*) The percentage of females with either master's or doctorate degrees in the United Kingdom is 54%; (*d*) DEEWR, 2013; (*e*) the percentage of females with either master's or doctorate degrees in Australia is 58%; (*f*) UIS, 2010.

women's lower pay, or higher unemployment levels (Hausmann et al., 2012) as evidence that attention needs to remain firmly on women and girls. While these are valid concerns, however, they do not negate equally valid concerns regarding men and boys in the education sphere in particular.

If the topic of poor male achievement and participation is difficult to discuss in the West, it should be unsurprising that it is even more difficult to discuss in the Middle East, where conceptions of gender are complicated by a strongly dichotomous view of the region by which women are cast as oppressed females and men as oppressive, patriarchal males (Abu-Lughod, 1998, 2002; AbuKhalil, 2005). Far from helping the situation, developmental discourses in the Middle East have historically given little positive attention to males in the region. Kamran Ali (2002) writes that in Egypt, population control programs run by the United States Agency for International Development (USAID) presented men as incompetent, aggressive, lazy, or stupid. Nowhere, Ali stated, were men presented as individuals who could possibly care about their wives, despite widespread anecdotal evidence that they do. Staff at the organization, according to Ali, viewed Egyptian men as incapable of having a positive effect on the lives of the women around them and regard them in a sense as perpetual adolescents. Ali also describes how USAID threatened to cut funding for a particular project if the Egyptian government did not accept its methods of population control, which involved denigrating men in public campaigns and portraying women as needing empowerment and saving. Further, Ali contends that the discourse USAID used in Egypt was framed in terms of "liberating women and educating men to become rational, responsible beings" (p. 121). The continued neglect and marginalization of the issues facing men and boys in the Middle East is not surprising, given that both development agencies and local governments continue to stress the challenges facing women and girls above all else. Boys, regrettably, are primarily portrayed as hindrances and obstacles to be overcome, rather than as people with their own unique set of problems.

In the education sector in the Middle East, very little attention has been paid by either academics or policymakers to regional trends that show a steady decline in the performance and persistence of boys. Instead policymakers have preferred to focus on the increasing numbers of women persisting in their education and doing well at school. This chapter examines the educational achievement and participation of boys in the GCC countries and explores some possible reasons for the current state of affairs. After looking across the GCC countries at trends in boys' education, the chapter focuses in detail on the use and impact of expatriate male teachers on the education of boys in the GCC countries. Subsequent chapters consider the broader environments of family, school, and society and their role in helping or hindering boys and their education.

BOYS FALLING BEHIND IN GCC SCHOOLS

As detailed in Chapters 1 and 2, boys' schools were the first to open in the GCC countries and boys traditionally enjoyed more access to some form of education through the kuttab model in the years before mass schooling. However, it is not inaccurate to say that literacy levels were very low, in general, for both boys and girls in these earlier years. Only wealthy families could afford to educate their sons, and very rarely was there access to any kind of further education outside of the Gulf (Aldosari, 2007). As such, the majority of both males and females in the region were illiterate before the discovery of oil (Aldosari, 2007). With the expansion of education in the GCC countries both boys and girls largely enjoyed equal opportunity to be educated. Currently, as explored in Chapter 2, the gender gaps between boys and girls with regard to education in the GCC countries are some of the largest in the world. In Bahrain, Oman, the United Arab Emirates, Kuwait, Saudi Arabia, and Qatar girls both outperform and outlast boys across all levels of education. Table 4.2 shows the gender gap between boys and girls in the PISA, TIMSS, and PIRLS assessments across the countries of the GCC, the United States, Singapore, Finland, Hong Kong, and the United Kingdom. Positive coefficients indicate a gender differential in favor of girls. It can be seen in Table 4.2 that in the GCC countries boys perform worse than girls in all three international assessments: in reading, math, and science. This is in contrast to the

Table 4.2. Average Gender Differential on PISA, TIMSS, and PIRLS in Select Countries

| | PISA/2012[a] | | | TIMSS/2011 | | | | PIRLS/2011[b] |
| | | | | Math[c] | | Science[d] | | |
Country	Reading	Math	Science	Grade 4	Grade 8	Grade 4	Grade 8	Reading
Bahrain	—	—	—	7	43	23	59	—
Kuwait	—	—	—	35	—	53	—	53[e]
Oman	—	—	—	26	63	34	78	40
Qatar	70	16	35	13	11	26	26	30
Saudi Arabia	—	—	—	16	—	48	26	54
United Arab Emirates	55	5	28	8	17	18	25	27
United States	31	−5	2	−9	−4	−10	−11	10
United Kingdom	25	−12	−13	−3	3	−1	2	23
Singapore	32	3	1	4	9	−4	−1	17
Finland	62	3	16	−7	4	0	5	21
Hong Kong	25	−15	−7	−6	6	−6	2	16

Sources and notes: (*a*) OECD (2013); (*b*) Mullis et al. (2011); + indicates in favor of girls and − indicates in favor of boys; (*c*) Mullis et al. (2012a); (*d*) Martin et al. (2011); (*e*) in Kuwait, grade 6 students (not grade 4 students) were tested for the 2011 PIRLS.

United States and the United Kingdom, in which boys still perform somewhat better in math and science, but not too dissimilar to Finland and Singapore (two of the highest-performing countries), in which the gender gap in science is still primarily in favor of girls and only a small gap exists in mathematics.

Boys in the GCC countries are also outperformed by girls in country-level examinations (Absal, 2011; GSDP, 2012; MOHESR, 2013), as discussed previously in Chapter 2. Figures 4.1–4.3 show a sample of national assessment results for the United Arab Emirates and Qatar for select years. Figure 4.1 presents the National Assessment Program (NAP) results for English (writing section) for both males and females in the United Arab Emirates in 2012, and reveals a clear and growing differential in favor of females across grades 3, 5, 7, and 9 when the exam is administered. Figure 4.2 highlights gender differences in the Qatar Senior School Certificate scores for the 2008–2009 academic year. Not only are females on average doing better than boys in Qatar when the results are broken down, it is also clear that there are fewer girls than boys in the lower score range. A similar gender differential in favor of girls exists in Oman, as indicated in Table 4.3, which shows that the percentage of pass rates in the grade 12 General Education Diploma examinations for both Omani and non-Omani girls was higher than that for boys in the academic year 2008–2009 (Ministry of Education [MOE], Oman, & World Bank, 2012). In Bahrain, girls outperformed boys in all subjects examined in the national examinations in grades 3 and 6 in 2009 (UNESCO & IBE, 2011). The gender gap is greatest in Arabic at both grade levels and widens for all subjects between grades 3 and 6 (UNESCO & IBE, 2011). Interestingly enough, it has been reported in the news that other GCC countries such as Saudi Arabia have used girls' higher performance

Figure 4.1. Average English (Writing) NAP Score in 2012 by Gender (Grades 3, 5, 7, and 9) in the UAE

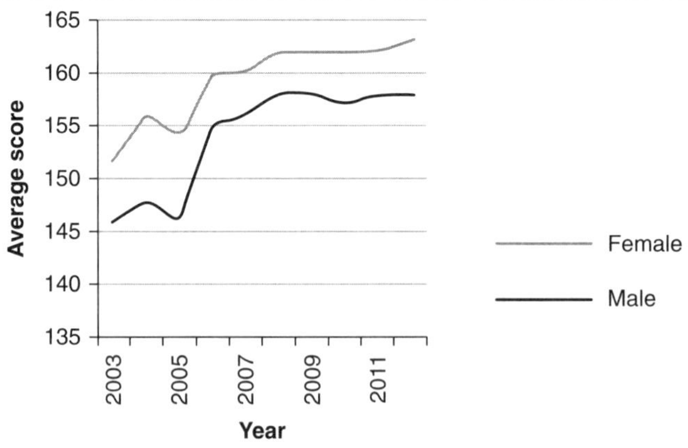

Source: MOE, UAE (2012).

Figure 4.2. Gender Differences in Qatar Senior School Certificate Scores (2008–2009)

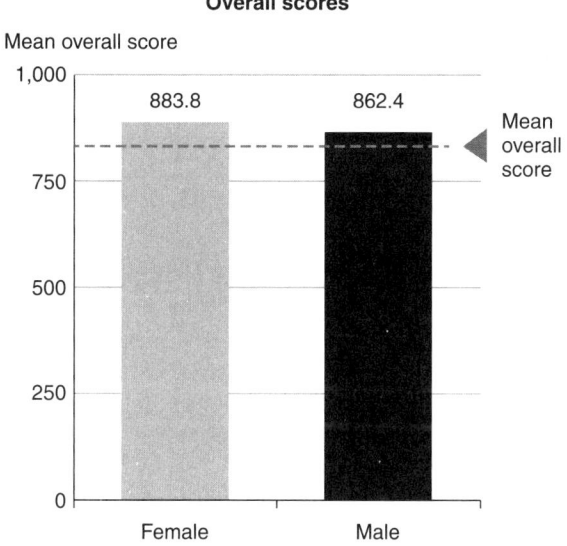

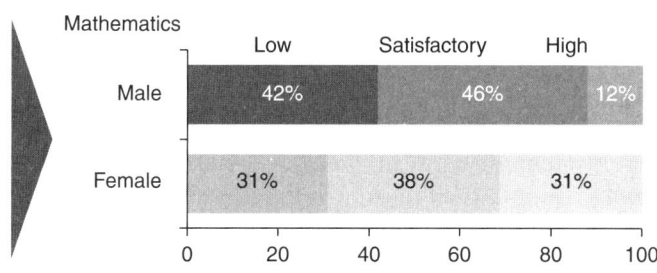

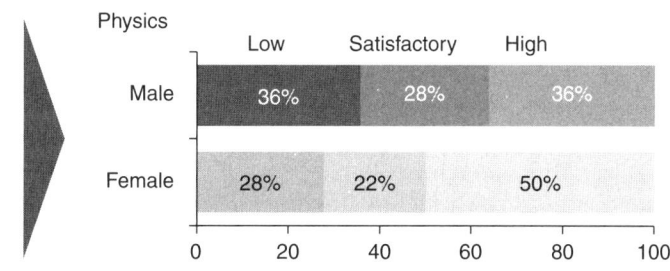

Source: GDSP (2012).

Table 4.3. Oman Grade 12 Examination Results by Gender and Nationality (2009)

	OMANI		NON-OMANI	
	FEMALE	MALE	FEMALE	MALE
Number of entries	21,174	22,451	381	368
Number of passes	19,386	18,648	369	359
Pass rate (%)	92	83	97	98

Source: MOE, Oman, & World Bank (2012).

on standardized tests to "argue that they are championing equality, and it's not a case of boys failing" (Alphonso, 2010). These assessments, in addition to frequent news reports highlighting the academic achievements of girls in all the GCC states ("From Access to Academic," 2013; Malek, 2013), reveal that boys are achieving less than girls across the majority of subjects in all countries, including Saudi Arabia, where one would least expect to find any female advantage.

Not only are boys performing worse than girls in school, they are also less likely to stay in formal education and more likely to repeat grades. Data taken from various UN agencies, shown in Table 4.4, reveal that this trend exists across almost all GCC countries, with the exception of Qatar in 2010, where the percentage of male repeaters is equal to that of female repeaters, and Kuwait in 2010, where the percentage of male dropouts is also equal to the percentage of female dropouts.

However, accuracy with regard to these statistics seems be an issue. Numbers obtained for 2007–2008 from the MOE and the Knowledge and Human Development Authority in the United Arab Emirates revealed much higher rates of dropping out in the United Arab Emirates (see Table 4.5) than was reported in UNESCO reports. Dropout rates for males are also reported to be higher in Oman (MOE, Oman, & World Bank, 2012), Qatar, and Saudi Arabia (Ridge et al., 2013). Many young men from across the region drop out of school toward the end of compulsory schooling, often in the belief that they can find paid employment in the army or police force or elsewhere in the public sector (Shaheen, 2009). Unfortunately, these jobs are no longer easy to find, and many young men who leave school early are struggling to secure a job ("Emiratis Throng Abu Dhabi Job Fair," 2013; Kherfi, 2012).

To date, very little research has attempted to understand why males in the GCC countries are failing to engage or perform in education. The choice to opt out of education is typically attributed to pull factors, such as high-paying public-sector jobs that require little education. However, our research on dropouts has not found the pull of high-paying public-sector jobs to be a

Table 4.4. Percentage of Secondary School Dropouts and Repeaters by Gender in the GCC Countries

COUNTRY	DROPOUTS[a]			REPEATERS[b]		
	MALE (%)	FEMALE (%)	YEAR	MALE (%)	FEMALE (%)	YEAR
Bahrain[c]	1.8	0.3	2000	5.8	2.3	2010
United Arab Emirates	7.7	2.3	2007–2008	4	2	2010
Oman	7	5	2008–2009	5	3	2010
Qatar[b]	9	3	2010	3	3	2010
Kuwait[b]	4	4	2010	6	5	2010
Saudi Arabia[b,d]	9	4	2010	5	3	2010

Sources and note: (*a*) Ridge et al. (2013); (*b*) UIS (2012); (*c*) dropout rates for Bahrain are not available so the rates presented are out-of-school children by gender; (*d*) UNICEF (2008).

Table 4.5. Male Secondary School Dropouts Across Emirates and Grades (2007–2008)

EMIRATE	NUMBER OF DROPOUTS[a]				PERCENTAGE OF DROPOUTS[a]			
	GRADE 10	GRADE 11	GRADE 12	ALL GRADES	GRADE 10	GRADE 11	GRADE 12	ALL GRADES
RAK	230	48	111	389	15.1	5.0	11.3	11.2
Sharjah	318	48	72	438	14.1	4.2	5.4	9.2
Fujairah	137	50	53	240	15.8	7.8	8.6	11.3
UAQ	51	5	21	77	18.3	2.6	9.5	11.2
Ajman	75	28	47	150	10.8	5.1	9.4	8.6
Abu Dhabi	508	118	104	730	9.2	3.0	2.8	5.5
Dubai	133	31	38	202	9.4	3.8	4.4	6.5
All Emirates	1452	328	446	2226	11.6	4	5.4	7.7

Source and note: Ridge et al. (2013). (*a*) Percentage and number of dropouts where dropping out was due to long-term sickness, marriage, exceeding number of leave days, or disciplinary expelling.

deciding factor in male retention. Rather, our research on dropouts in the United Arab Emirates, which will be discussed in more detail in Chapter 6, indicates that the key to this decision lies in push factors, including low socioeconomic background, poorly educated, unsupportive parents, and the quality of teacher engagement. In addition, our research in the United Arab Emirates finds that students who have supportive and caring teachers are statistically less likely to drop out of school than students whose teachers are disengaged and disinterested (Ridge et al., 2013). The next section looks more closely at the teacher workforce in the Gulf and how this has impacted the education of boys.

TEACHERS, GENDER, AND NATIONALITY IN BOYS' SCHOOLS IN THE GCC

As discussed in Chapter 2, with the expansion of access to public schooling in the Gulf, the majority of both boys and girls were able to attend school. In the early years the vast majority of public schoolteachers in Gulf schools were recruited from the wider Arab world, most often from Egypt, Syria, Jordan, and Palestine. It was necessary to hire expatriate teachers because there were not yet universities or teacher education programs in the Gulf, and as such, there were very few national teachers. However, as higher education developed across the Gulf and colleges of education opened, national women in particular started to train as teachers. Over time, the growing pool of national female teachers almost completely replaced expatriate female teachers, whereas due to a much greater variety of employment options for Gulf males, very few went into the teaching profession (this is discussed in more detail in Chapter 6). As a result, public boys' schools, particularly secondary schools, continued to be staffed largely by expatriate Arab male teachers. In addition, due to the highly segregated nature of education in the Gulf, although most states allowed women to teach boys at the primary level (grades 1–5), and some allowed women to teach at the preparatory stage (grades 6–9), once boys entered the secondary stage (grades 10–12), male teachers became mandatory. Over time, there has been a feminization of the teacher workforce in the GCC countries as can be seen in Table 4.6, which presents the percentage of male and female teachers by educational level as defined by UNESCO[2] (Al Masah Capital, 2012).

The increase in the number of national women teachers as compared to national men is the result of a number of factors. While a small number of Gulf males did train as teachers in institutions such as the College of Education in the United Arab Emirates University (Gardner, 1995) and the College of Education in Kuwait University (Al-Sharaf, 2006), national males were typically promoted to leadership positions quickly and few had the chance to remain in the classroom very long (Dickson & Le Roux, 2012). In addition, there was a lack of teacher-training institutes that accepted men, as most were established for women only. Also in the early years, and even today, there was a great demand for national males to work in all sectors. In particular, after independence, national men were needed

Table 4.6. Percentage of Female Teachers at All Education Levels across the GCC

COUNTRY	PRIMARY (%)	SECONDARY (%)	TERTIARY (%)
Bahrain	76	54	33
Kuwait	90	54	27
Oman	64	58	30
Qatar	83	54	38
Saudi Arabia	50	52	35
United Arab Emirates	86	58	31
GCC Average	75	55	32

Source: Al Masah Capital Limited (2012).

for new national defense forces and for the police; so Gulf males had a wide variety of employment opportunities, as compared to women, that both paid more than teaching and required a lot less education. Finally, in the 1970s and 1980s, very few national males had completed their formal schooling; so the pool of available national men capable and qualified to become teachers was very small (Ridge, 2010).

The extent of the shortage of national male teachers varies across the GCC countries and typically reflects larger trends in the percentage of expatriate workers in the labor force. In the United Arab Emirates, Emirati males currently account for roughly 20% of the teaching workforce, and the majority of those are in administration (Ridge, 2010). In a sample of eight boys' schools visited by Ridge (2009) in the United Arab Emirates, there were fewer than five Emirati males actually working as teachers. Similarly, in Qatar and Kuwait, the teaching force in boys' schools is largely made up of expatriate Arabs. In 2011, Qatari teachers accounted for only 30% of the total teacher population in Qatar; expatriate Arabs comprised 53% and expatriate non-Arabs comprised 17% (Toumi, 2011). Boys' schools in Kuwait at the preparatory and secondary levels continue to be dominated by Arab male expatriates; in 2011, jobs were allocated for 4,751 expatriate teachers but only 440 Kuwaitis in boys' schools ("Kuwait to Recruit 4751 Expatriate Teachers," n.d.). In private Arabic schools in Saudi Arabia, Saudization efforts allowed Saudi teachers to fill close to 80% of the teaching positions by 2001 (Al-Asiri, 2001). Information on Saudi teachers in public schools is not publicly available, but reports suggest a large expatriate teacher population of 40% at the secondary level (Zafeirakou, 2007). A large, but unreported, percentage of those teachers are male (Zafeirakou, 2007). In Oman there are far more national male teachers than in the United Arab Emirates, Qatar, and Kuwait (MOE, Oman, & World

Bank, 2012; Rassekh, 2004; Zafeirakou, 2007). However, they are still scarce in certain subjects such as English, of which only 36% of male teachers are Omani, in comparison to 92% of female English teachers who are Omani (MOE, Oman, & World Bank, 2012). Omani male teachers are also scarce in music (3% male, 2% female), fine arts (45% male, 52% female), and biology (56% male, 94% female) (MOE, Oman, & World Bank, 2012). In terms of teacher qualifications, interestingly, Omani female teachers are slightly more educated than Omani male teachers; 84% of Omani female teachers have a university degree or postgraduate diploma, versus 79% of Omani male teachers (MOE, Oman, & World Bank, 2012).

As a result of the shortage of national male teachers across the GCC countries many of the countries have been compelled to rely on expatriate male teachers, in particular in boys' secondary schools. These teachers work under conditions that elsewhere would see them categorized as "contract teachers" (De Laat & Vegas, 2003). While there is some literature on the use of contract teachers in sub-Saharan Africa and elsewhere (De Laat & Vegas, 2003; Engman, 2009; Muralidharan & Sundararaman, 2010), there is currently no literature examining the case of expatriate teachers working in the Gulf. One significant difference between contract teachers working elsewhere and those working in the GCC countries is that typically these teachers are allowed, if they choose, to become citizens of the country to which they have moved. The situation in the GCC countries is unique, in that the countries of the Gulf do not allow expatriate teachers to ever take citizenship, and so even if a teacher spends his or her entire life in the country, as many have done, once they retire they will be required to go back to their country of origin. Furthermore, as they are not citizens, they also do not have the same rights as citizens who are teachers. Thus the zero immigration policies of the Gulf have created a two-tiered workforce in the public education sector, which, I argue, leads to many unintended consequences; we will explore these more fully in the next section.

In summary, as access to education expanded in the Gulf and local colleges of education were created, many more national women than men entered teacher-training courses and became teachers. This created a situation whereby, although boys' and girls' schools received the same financial and curricular inputs, boys' schools remained staffed by predominantly male, expatriate, Arab teachers while girls' schools in the region were almost entirely staffed by national female teachers by the millennium. Although this was not the case for all countries in the GCC, it was very much the case in Kuwait, the United Arab Emirates, Qatar, Bahrain, and, to a lesser degree, Saudi Arabia. In Oman, lower levels of national resources, and therefore income, meant that there were not as many employment opportunities for Omani males as for males from other countries. As a result, Oman was successful in attracting Omani males to the classroom (MOE, Oman, & World Bank, 2012). However, given that everything else is largely equal in the public schools of the Gulf, the impact of having a large number of expatriate teachers in much of the region needs to be more fully explored in the context of the education of boys. The next part of the chapter examines the expatriate teaching workforce in the Gulf's public schools, first with regard to the background of the teachers, and second with regard to their recruitment and conditions.

EXPATRIATE TEACHERS AND BOYS' EDUCATION

There are good empirical reasons to consider the teachers of boys in the Gulf to help us to understand boys' educational outcomes. Ingvarson and Rowe (2007) state that, in general, studies on education consistently indicate that over 40% of the residual variance in measures of student performance (adjusted for students' background and intake characteristics) is at the class/teacher level. Hanushek's (2005) and Hanushek and Rivkin's (2012) works on teacher quality emphasize the importance of well-qualified teachers in improving students' emotional well-being, decisions to stay in school, and academic achievement, and indicate that good teachers can add up to years' worth of learning for a student. A 2007 report by McKinsey and Co., *Improving Education in the Gulf*, states that "boys' schools [in the GCC countries] often employ low-caliber teachers—and, sure enough, the GCC gender gap in student outcomes is among the most extreme in the world" (Barber et al., 2007, p. 43). With many countries in the GCC depending on male, expatriate teachers, who then form the majority of teachers in public boys' schools, it is important to not only understand the impact this has on students, but also recognize that these teachers (who are not all from a single country) not only come from a wide range of backgrounds, but also work under conditions very different from those under which national teachers do.

Background Characteristics

Expatriate teachers working in the Gulf are drawn from the wider Middle East, typically from Egypt, Jordan, Syria, and, to a lesser extent, Palestine and North Africa (Engman, 2009; Khalaf & Alkobaisi, 1999). For example, in the emirate of Ras Al Khaimah (RAK) in the United Arab Emirates, the three main countries from which expatriate teachers originate are Egypt, Jordan, and Syria, as shown in Figure 4.3 (Ridge, 2009 as cited in Ridge, 2010). Similarly, in Qatar, expatriate Arabs from Egypt, Jordan, Palestine, and Syria comprised 14%, 6.2%, 4%, and 3.2%, respectively, of the total secondary schoolteacher population in 2008 (MOE, Qatar, 2009). They are trained in their country of origin and then subsequently hired after gaining some experience to teach in the Gulf.

Figure 4.3. RAK Male Educators by Nationality

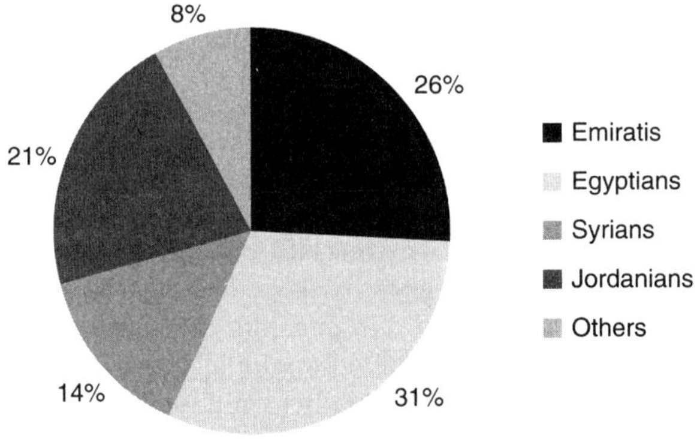

- Emiratis: 26%
- Egyptians: 31%
- Syrians: 14%
- Jordanians: 21%
- Others: 8%

Source: Ridge (2009) as cited in Ridge, 2010.

The fact that expatriate teachers come from a variety of higher education systems all with differing approaches to teacher training creates a problem of consistency in the quality of teaching both within and across schools. Tables 4.7–4.9 show the requirements for becoming a math and science teacher, respectively, in several Arab countries, including the GCC countries, and in a selection of high-performing countries.

In Table 4.7, which shows the requirements for becoming a middle/lower secondary math teacher, it can be seen that while the use of a probationary period is common in the Gulf and top-performing countries on the TIMSS, it is not a feature of the education systems of Egypt, Syria, or Jordan. In addition, neither Egypt nor Jordan requires that trainee teachers complete practicum sessions during training. Syria, on the other hand, requires both a prepracticum and a supervised field practicum for its math teachers.

In Table 4.8, which displays the requirements for science teachers, there is no requirement for a practicum session, either during teacher training or supervised in the field, for any Arab or GCC state except Dubai. With regard to a probationary period, this is required by Oman, Qatar, and Saudi Arabia, but not by Dubai, Egypt, Syria, or Jordan. Dubai also stands alone as the only Arab country to have an induction or mentoring program for its science teachers.

Table 4.9, which examines data from the 2011 TIMSS, shows a move toward more stringent teacher education requirements for both math and science in the TIMSS 2011 in two of the four GCC participants of the TIMSS 2007. Both Oman and Saudi Arabia have now made it a requirement for teachers to go through a prepracticum program during their teacher education. However, the United Arab Emirates (as opposed to Dubai) does not require any practicum component. Jordan also appears to have changed its policy on practicums, now stating it no longer requires one. It is therefore

Table 4.7. Requirements for Becoming a Middle/Lower Secondary-Level Math Teacher (2007)

Country	Rank in TIMSS	Degree from Teacher Ed Program	Prepracticum during Teacher Education	Supervised Practicum in the Field	Passing a Certification Exam	Completion of a Probationary Teaching Period	Completion of Mentoring or Induction Program
Egypt	38	Yes	No	Yes	No	No	No
Syria	37	Yes	Yes	Yes	No	No	Yes
Jordan	31	Yes	No	No	No	No	No
Chinese Taipei	1	Yes	Yes	Yes	Yes	Yes	No
Singapore	3	No	Yes	Yes	Yes	Yes	Yes
England	6	Yes	Yes	Yes	Yes	Yes	No
Australia	14	Yes	Yes	Yes	No	Yes	No
Saudi Arabia	46	No	No	No	Yes	Yes	No
Oman	41	Yes	No	No	No	Yes	No
Qatar	48	No	No	Yes	No	Yes	No
Dubai	28 (est.)	Yes	Yes	Yes	Yes	No	Yes

Source: Mullis, Martin, Olson, Berger, Milne, & Stanco (2008) as cited in Ridge, 2010.

Table 4.8. Requirements for Becoming a Middle/Lower Secondary-Level Science Teacher (2007)

Country	Rank in TIMSS	Degree from Teacher Ed Program	Prepracticum during Teacher Education	Supervised Practicum in the Field	Passing a Certification Exam	Completion of a Probationary Teaching Period	Completion of Mentoring or Induction Program
Egypt	41	Yes	No	No	Yes	No	No
Syria	32	No	No	No	Yes	No	No
Jordan	20	Yes	No	No	No	No	No
Chinese Taipei	2	Yes	Yes	Yes	Yes	Yes	No
Singapore	1	No	Yes	Yes	Yes	Yes	Yes
England	5	Yes	Yes	Yes	Yes	Yes	No
Australia	13	Yes	Yes	Yes	No	Yes	No
Saudi Arabia	44	No	No	No	Yes	Yes	No
Oman	36	Yes	No	No	No	Yes	No
Qatar	47	No	No	Yes	No	Yes	No
Dubai	18 (est.)	No	Yes	Yes	Yes	No	Yes

Source: Mullis et al. (2008).

Table 4.9. Requirements for Becoming a Middle/Lower Secondary-Level Math or Science Teacher (2011)

Country	Rank in TIMSS (Science)	Rank in TIMSS (Math)	Degree from Teacher Ed Program	Prepracticum during Teacher Education	Supervised Practicum in the Field	Passing a Certification Exam	Completion of a Probationary Teaching Period	Completion of Mentoring or Induction Program
Syria	34	39	Yes	Yes	No	Yes	No	No
Jordan	29	35	No	No	No	No	No	No
Chinese Taipei	2	3	Yes	Yes	Yes	Yes	No	No
Singapore	1	2	No	Yes	Yes	Yes	Yes	Yes
England	9	10	Yes	Yes	Yes	Yes	Yes	No
Australia	12	12	Yes	Yes	Yes	No	Yes	No
Oman	37	41	Yes	Yes	No	No	No	No
Qatar	38	33	No	No	No	No	Yes	No
Bahrain	26	34	Yes	No	No	No	No	Yes
Saudi Arabia	32	37	Yes	Yes	No	Yes	Yes	No
UAE	24	23	No	No	No	Yes	Yes	No

Source: Mullis, Martin, Minnich, Stanco, Arora, Centurino, & Castle (2012b).

clear that not only do the requirements to become a teacher vary from country to country, but they also change over time. This makes the issue of hiring teachers with qualifications compatible with local education systems in the GCC countries very challenging. Bahrain, Kuwait, and the United Arab Emirates were newcomers for the TIMSS 2011 and had not participated in the TIMSS 2007.

In addition to differing requirements to become a teacher in these countries, there is also the issue of the quality of teacher education students themselves. Student achievement in math and science is very low across the Middle East. In the 2007 TIMSS at the eighth-grade level, Jordanian students ranked 31st, Syrian students 37th, and Egyptian students 38th out of 47 countries (Bradley, 2010). These rankings indicate that the education systems in these countries, from which the majority of expatriate teachers are drawn, are not producing high-quality graduates in the first place. A recent article on the Egyptian education system described it as failing a whole generation of students, emphasizing the poor quality of the system and the sporadic attendance of teachers, who are more interested in giving private lessons (Bradley, 2010). Those entering the teaching profession in these countries are therefore unlikely to be top students. As in many Arab countries, teaching is a profession of last resort. Teachers tend to be from the lower end of the graduating cohort; top performers enter medicine, engineering, or other more lucrative fields (Hartmann, 2008).

The starting pool of potential male teachers from the wider Middle East is therefore already suffering from some deficiencies. The quality of students entering teacher education programs in these countries is uncertain and is then exacerbated by equally deficient teacher education programs. One area of critical concern is the lack of a practicum component in most teacher-training programs in the Arab world, outside of the Gulf. This lack of a practicum component means that even teachers with education degrees are ill-equipped for the challenges and reality of the classroom. Unfortunately, many of the teachers hired in the United Arab Emirates and in the rest of the Gulf do not possess an education degree but are instead subject specialists. This can be seen clearly in Figure 4.4, which shows that 70% of English language teachers in RAK in the United Arab Emirates hold a bachelor of arts degree in a field other than education or English. These recruits have no pedagogical training at all, and some of those in the RAK study stated that they were promised pedagogical training when they were recruited, but it never materialized (Ridge, 2010).

The hiring of teachers without any pedagogical training points to larger issues relating to hiring within Ministries of Education. In the United Arab Emirates under the 2008 hiring system, Emirati principals traveled to Egypt, Jordan, and Syria to recruit teachers by placing ads in

Figure 4.4. Academic Background of English Language Teachers in RAK

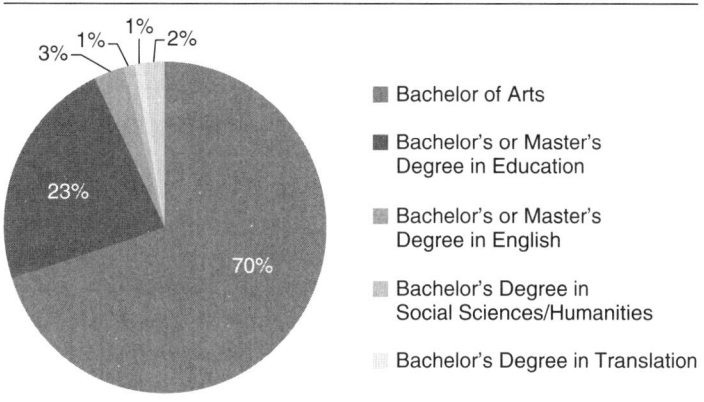

Source: MOE, UAE (2012).

the local newspaper. The principals then returned to the UAE and shortlisted applicants. Suitable candidates were interviewed and selected, which sounds simple enough. However, one principal who took part in the recruitment process stated that he believed the most important qualification for teachers was a content-related degree (he holds bachelor's and master's degrees in geography) because pedagogy was the easy part and could be learned on the job (Ridge, 2009). Also in the United Arab Emirates the committee approach to hiring can mean that English teachers, for example, are recruited by those who may not possess a good command of English themselves. There is no requirement on the part of the MOE that candidates produce an internationally recognized proof of English competency, such as IELTS or TOEFL results.[4] The result of this was seen in a study on English teachers in the United Arab Emirates in which some expatriate teachers were found to have paper-based TOEFL scores of under 350 (Dave & Ridge, 2013). With this approach toward recruitment, coupled with the poor regard for the importance of pedagogy, the result has been to reinforce the poor quality of teachers in boys' schools in the United Arab Emirates, rather than to raise the levels over time. The lack of attention to who is recruited, and from where, also means that boys, in particular, are often served by teachers who are unable to give national students the type of education the United Arab Emirates needs and wants. While there is less information about other GCC countries, it is reasonable to hypothesize that similar issues abound. In short, there are large differences between the training and skills of male, expatriate teachers and female, national teachers, which may be important to understanding at least some of the gender differences between girls and boys in the Gulf.

Working Conditions

Another important factor having an impact on teacher commitment, and therefore quality, is working conditions, which include compensation and treatment of expatriate teachers. In the United Arab Emirates, expatriate teachers in 2008 were paid almost half that of the salary of Emirati teachers. Expatriate Arab teachers make up 80% of the male teaching workforce but only 15% of the female teaching workforce, which creates a situation in which teachers in boys' schools are, in general, paid a lot less than teachers in girls' schools (Ridge, 2009). The case is similar for Bahrain, Kuwait, and Qatar, where expatriate Arab male teachers' salaries were 20% lower than those in neighboring GCC countries, excluding Saudi Arabia, where expatriate teachers are paid even lower than expatriates working in Qatar (Brewer et al., 2007). It is also noted that expatriate teachers in Qatar also relied largely on supplemental income from private tutoring (Brewer et al., 2007).

In addition to the lower wages, working conditions are also very different for expatriate teachers. The highly stratified nature of Gulf society is also relevant to the existence of a gendered teaching–learning gap. Expatriate teachers can be perceived by their national students and parents as inferior because they come from poorer Arab nations. Observations made during the research phase indicates that the respect for teachers that Ridge (2009) was told used to exist in schools in the United Arab Emirates may have eroded over time as the country became more prosperous. Heavy reliance on and need for cheap foreign labor in the United Arab Emirates has led some Emirati citizens to resent those they need ("Sending Home the Foreigners," 2013). Although they have no desire to do the jobs expatriates do, with Emiratis representing only 20% of the population in the United Arab Emirates, they can feel threatened by the large numbers of expatriates living in the country. Expatriate teachers working in public schools were observed being mocked by students for their accents and were spoken to rudely and dismissively (Ridge, 2009). Expatriate teachers are also aware of the precarious position they occupy: they are all on 1-year renewable contracts, and they learn from the newspaper whether they have lost or retained their jobs for the following academic year (Ridge, 2009). This unfortunate practice applies to most, if not all, GCC countries and genders equally, and does little to instill a sense of security or good feeling toward the various Ministries of Education. In 2013, for example, a Nepalese chemistry teacher at one of Qatar's most prominent private schools, Qatar Academy, was fired from his school, arrested for "insulting" Islam, and deported back to his country (Kaphle, 2013). The accusation was made with little evidence other than a student's description of the events. In 2010, in Saudi Arabia, several expatriate female teachers were also fired from their jobs without any notice and with no apparent reason (Anbar, 2010). One teacher reports, "They have not renewed my contract despite my 19-years' experience in the field of female adult education and the fact that my work performance is excellent" (Anbar, 2010).

Expatriate teachers from poor countries have everything to lose if they upset students or their families. It was reported that expatriate teachers feel powerless if they are in a showdown with a student and his family. In the United Arab Emirates, for example, rather than supporting the school or its teachers, staff reported that Emirati parents show unwavering support for their children regardless of the circumstance (Ridge, 2009). It appears that expatriate teachers, males in particular, are incentivized to act in ways that are not necessarily in the interests of the student but will enable them to keep their jobs. This is not uncommon among most expatriates as job security continues to be an impending issue of concern.

Early research on teachers in the United Arab Emirates carried out by Gardner (1995) and Clarke (2006) examined teacher education, test scores, and salaries. Gardner believed that the low salaries paid to non-Emirati teachers in comparison to their Emirati counterparts (at the time) and the use of short-term labor contracts for non-Emiratis would negatively impact the future creation of a quality teaching force in the United Arab Emirates. Nearly 15 years later, Ridge (2009), also conducting research on teachers in the United Arab Emirates, found that what Gardner had predicted had indeed occurred; however, while Gardner had forecast this to affect all students in the United Arab Emirates, the large numbers of Emirati women entering the teaching profession in the subsequent years has meant that girls' schools are now almost completely staffed by Emirati teachers. Thus, while there are issues with teacher quality, the issue has taken on a gendered dimension due to the changes that have taken place in the past 10 years, with boys' schools remaining largely staffed by expatriate male teachers.

Impact on Boys' Education

The impact of uncertain working conditions and varying levels of educational qualifications has manifested itself in different ways, all of which negatively impact the education of boys. First, Ridge (2010) found that male expatriate teachers are significantly more likely than their female counterparts to be the sole wage earners, typically supporting not only their immediate but also their extended families. Male expatriate teachers therefore have more expectations placed on them than their female counterparts. The combination of a low wage, high job insecurity, poor promotion possibilities, and heavy demands from their families means that male teachers are often highly incentivized to make as much money as they can in the time they are in the United Arab Emirates. The one easy avenue open to these teachers to make extra money is to offer private tutoring to their students. In her study *Private Tutoring Trends in the UAE*, Farah (2011) found that 52.5% of male expatriate teachers were giving private tutoring to their own students. Other studies find that, in addition to offering private tutoring, some male expatriate teachers undertake other kinds of wage-supplementing employment, such as driving taxis in the evening (Shaheen, 2010). As the current assessment system used by government schools and private Arabic schools is based on memorization, private tuition lessons require no additional skills beyond the ability to drill students. The cumulative effect of many teachers in boys' schools offering private tutoring but relatively few girls' teachers making this choice is no doubt a critical factor in determining the quality (or lack thereof) of boys' education. This could be manifested in teachers not covering all content material, giving unequal assistance to students, and/or being physically exhausted and unable to give full attention to their teaching duties.

Second, Ridge (2010) also found that male teachers (her sample contained only expatriate males) were less student-centered and less pedagogically skilled than their female counterparts. Evidence of the poor quality of male teachers in UAE government schools was found through data from the observations of 32 teachers at four different intervals in the emirate of Ras Al Khaimah (Ridge, 2009). These observations allowed for an examination of teaching quality on a teacher-by-teacher basis at eight schools in RAK, and results were then aggregated to identify overall differences between male and female teachers. The results of the teacher observations supported the finding that female teachers, both Emirati and expatriate, are more competent than their male counterparts. The teacher observations uncovered a significant ($p = .02$) difference in teaching quality between male and female teachers, with female teachers having, on average, higher ratings than male teachers (Ridge, 2009).

In addition to the observation data, student achievement data from the MOE for the students taught by these teachers also revealed differences in achievement between males and females. It can be seen in Figure 4.5 that the largest difference in student achievement is in math, whereas the smallest difference is in biology.

When the achievement data for students of the teachers in the RAK study were compared to the data from the teacher observations[3] using a Mann-Whitney *U* test, there was a significant ($p = .001$) difference overall, with students (girls) taught by women scoring on average 73%, and students (boys) taught by men scoring 67% across the four subjects (Ridge, 2009).

Figure 4.5. Grades 10–12 Student Achievement by Subject and Gender for Eight Schools in RAK

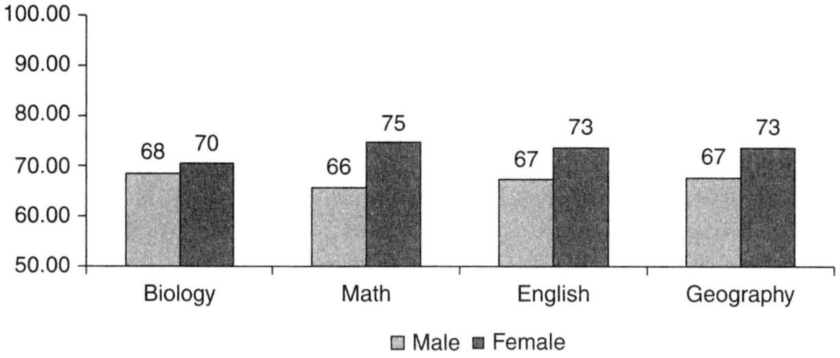

Subject	Male	Female
Biology	68	70
Math	66	75
English	67	73
Geography	67	73

Source: Ridge (2009) as cited in Ridge, 2010.

Third, the precarious situation in which expatriate teachers find themselves not only leads to poor student outcomes but also impacts the school as a whole. Box 4.1, taken from Ridge's (2009) study, describes the environment of boys' schools. Created by poorly motivated, insecure teachers, many prefer to take the path of least resistance, such as allowing cheating rather than holding students to high standards, which may in turn lead to the teacher losing his job. This aversion to taking risks could be seen in field experiments with public school English language teachers in RAK, conducted as part of a study on English language teacher effectiveness, where expatriate teachers were found to be at least four times as risk-averse as their Emirati counterparts (Dave & Ridge, 2013). The rampant grade inflation observed in the difference between boys' scores on internal standardized tests in the United Arab Emirates versus the grades given to students by their class teachers is another example of how disempowered, disengaged teachers actually undermine the future of entire generations.

While the general level of teacher quality in the Gulf is not among the best in the world, stark differences have emerged between male and female teachers. In those countries in the GCC that rely heavily on expatriate teachers, differences in teacher quality have now split across gender and nationality lines due to the rapid expansion of work and teacher education opportunities for national women. This, coupled with an acute shortage of national men in the education profession, has left secondary boys' schools particularly dependent on male expatriate teachers. These teachers have been found to have less training in pedagogical skills and be less effective in the classroom (Gardner, 1995; Ridge, 2010). This should not be surprising, given that it is unlikely that these expatriate teachers served a probationary period or even received pedagogical training or

Box 4.1. Learn or Leave? Boys' Schools in the United Arab Emirates

In complete contrast to girls' secondary schools, the classrooms in the boys' secondary schools were bare other than the graffiti on the walls and the rubbish strewn across the floor. While boys reported that they liked school in general, they were much more negative about the particular school they attended. During observations of classes in boys' schools, the teaching style was found to be 90% lecture format, with perhaps a maximum of 5 to 10 minutes for student engagement. The overall school environment appeared harsher and rougher as compared to girls' schools, more like life in a remand center than life at home. School seemed to be viewed by boys as a poorly resourced social club they had been forced to attend. The impression given was that these boys saw going to school, in many cases, as serving time, as something that had to be done but not as something they necessarily enjoyed.

Corporal punishment was observed by the researchers and reported frequently by the students. When the researcher asked the boys about the use of corporal punishment, one replied, "This is normal, it makes you a man" (field notes, Thursday, January 29, 2009). In front of researchers, boys who misbehaved were typically asked to leave the class, but boys who slept in the back of the classroom, did very little, or failed to complete their work in lessons were unchallenged and left alone. As long as they did not interrupt the lesson, teachers seemed not to care what the boys did or did not do. This lasted until just before exams, when a flurry of memorization took place, and teachers tried to get all the boys to memorize everything. If that failed, according to extensive reports, some teachers sold exam papers, answers, and questions to students who had been too lazy to study.

A standardized English test was introduced in 2003, and the mock exam paper was circulated to teachers four days prior to the exam for a proper trial run. The researcher was told that the teachers told all their students what was in the mock exam so they would not look bad. The results, therefore, looked promising, and the organizing body (an external government institution) seemed happy. Then came the actual exam, in which students all went to a central location to take the exam under the tightest supervision; the results were terrible, as one would predict. Prior to this, one principal lamented to the researcher about how his students should be allowed to take the exam in their school, which he said would be much more "comfortable" for them (field notes, n.d.). The

Box continues on next page

> **Box 4.1. (continued)**
>
> principal meant it would be easier for students to cheat, and the school would not look so bad because grades would not be so low. It is this attitude that real academic success is unimportant, cheating is acceptable, and appearances rather than reality are what really matters, that is contributing to the devaluation of secondary education in the United Arab Emirates, particularly boys' secondary education.
>
> *Source*: Ridge (2009)

practicum sessions in their home country. Coupled with unequal and uncertain working conditions, this has created a cohort of teachers who not only seek out additional employment opportunities outside the classroom, but also do not see themselves as an integral and important part of the education system of the GCC countries, and as such see little point in investing in it themselves.

CONCLUSION

Boys' education in the GCC countries has been stagnant at best, and deteriorating at worst, since the introduction of mass schooling in the Gulf. Although both boys and girls have access to the same funding, facilities, and curriculum, the use of lower-paid, expatriate, male teachers who are far less engaged or appreciated by the system has, at least in part, contributed to a situation in which boys across the Gulf States are disengaged with school. The school environment described by Ridge (2009) in RAK in the United Arab Emirates can be found, anecdotally, to various degrees throughout the Gulf States. In countries such as Oman that do not have the same shortage of national male teachers, the low university requirements for becoming a teacher (MOE, Oman, & World Bank, 2012; Mullis et al., 2012b), coupled with the low status of the profession, may have also resulted in the disengagement of Omani male teachers. Omani male teachers also seem to be completely unaware of the seriousness of the issue, with a recent report, *Education in Oman: The Drive for Quality* (2012), finding that both teachers and students had unrealistic assessments of their performance. The report discussed how student surveys from the 2007 TIMSS found boys saying they were confident about their ability in mathematics and teachers saying they were "very well-prepared" to teach the topics covered in the science and mathematics tests. The results, however, in the words of the report, "suggest a misplaced level of confidence…that may encourage a culture of complacency" (MOE, Oman, & World Bank, 2012, p. 84).

There appears to be a strong reason to hypothesize that female teachers in general are far more enthusiastic about teaching and far more likely to invest more of themselves in their work than many of their male counterparts, particularly because a teaching career is not considered low status for women. As a result, boys across the region receive an education that is far from engaging or motivating. While external factors may certainly contribute to boys' lack of achievement and retention, it is hard to dismiss the role of the school and, in particular, the teacher.

Research on the United Arab Emirates finds that teachers have a statistically significant impact on a student's decision to stay in school and on student achievement, all things being equal (Ridge et al., 2013). It is therefore reasonable to focus on the role that teachers play in both retention and achievement. Despite the failures of the education system with regard to boys, it is not only the education sector that creates disincentives to male achievement and to their continuing education. As the Gulf States have developed, they have increasingly sought to employ nationals at the top levels of all offices. Conferences and speeches on nationalization, and an almost unparalleled belief in a fabricated narrative of competence without experience or education, further undermine national educational aspirations at the macro level and give the wrong signals about the value of education to young people at the micro level. Inasmuch as schools push young men away, labor policies also pull young men away from school with incentives that will, if left unchecked, create societies in which unskilled, inexperienced youth may dominate. The next chapter explores the issue of nationalization more thoroughly and looks at the consequences of nationalization policies on the educational aspirations and achievements of young men in the GCC countries.

5

Placating the Populace

Nationalization, Gender, and the Threat to Education

> Empowerment, education and Emiratization. Those three aspects are our foremost priority as a government. (H. H. Sheikh Mohamed bin Rashid Al Maktoum, 2013)

As examined in previous chapters, a significant gender gap has emerged between males and females in the GCC countries with regard to educational attainment and achievement. Paradoxically, however, despite national males having less and lower-quality education, they are more likely to be employed than females. Women form a minority in national workforces, ranging from around 25% in the United Arab Emirates (McMeans, 2010) to 12% in Saudi Arabia (Dickinson, 2013). While the reasons for this pattern cannot be attributed to one single factor, there is strong evidence that suggests that increasingly aggressive nationalization programs across the GCC countries are exacerbating gender differences favoring males in the workforce while simultaneously creating perverse incentives whereby males perceive little or no advantage from continuing their education beyond secondary school. Interestingly, while theoretically these policies should also have a negative impact on female participation, the impact of nationalization policies on women appears to be mitigated by cultural factors that limit women's mobility and longevity in the labor market.

The push for nationalization across the region in large part stems from the heavy dependence of the GCC countries on foreign labor. Not only are governments concerned with providing citizens with jobs, they are also concerned with maintaining national cultural identities. Labor nationalization has also become the GCC's primary tool for sustainable human resource management (HRM), and the inclusion of national youth in the workforce is a prominent concern, especially in light of the Arab Spring.[1] Expatriates constitute anywhere from 23% (in Saudi Arabia) to 80% (in the United Arab Emirates) of resident populations and account for about one-third of the total population of the GCC countries (Randeree, 2012). Furthermore, in the private-sector workforce expatriates account for between 52% (in Oman) and 99% (in the United Arab Emirates) of total employees (Morada, 2010).

Nationalization policies in the Gulf originate in the rentier bargain through which governments and rulers of resource-rich countries redistribute wealth to their citizens to remain in power (Hertog, 2012). Key to the rentier bargain in the Gulf States is the provision of jobs for nationals (Randeree, 2012). This was traditionally done by providing employment in the public sector, but in all GCC nations the public sector is increasingly unable to absorb new hires (Forstenlechner & Rutledge, 2010), and states are now looking to the private sector to make up the shortfall. This is being achieved through nationalization programs that mandate quotas and preferences for nationals, in much the same style as affirmative action in the West aimed to level the playing field for disadvantaged minorities (Cunningham, 2002; Faundez, 1994; Randeree, 2012).

This chapter examines the impact of current nationalization programs on incentives for education, particularly for males. It first looks more closely at the rentier state in the Gulf and the rise of nationalization policies in the region. Next, it looks at nationalization and implications for the education sector. Then it examines common characteristics in nationalization policies across the GCC countries, followed by a look at existing nationalization programs in each of the states of interest. The chapter concludes with a discussion of the impact of current nationalization policies on males and females, and the urgent need for a more meritocratic approach to employment of nationals to provide the right signals to both males and females about the value of education.

THE RENTIER STATE AND THE RISE OF NATIONALIZATION INITIATIVES

Resource-rich GCC nations are often analyzed through the lens of rentier state theory, which examines the ways in which Gulf governments redistribute oil revenues to nationals in the form of "cradle-to-grave" welfare benefits, such as the provision of health care and housing assistance, free education, and constitutionally guaranteed jobs, typically in the public sector (Al Khazraji, 2009). Arguably, these direct transfers of wealth create a "rentier mentality" that placates citizens and fosters within them a favorable disposition toward the government, thus helping to prevent social unrest of the sort witnessed in the Arab Spring, where unemployment was a key factor in regional uprisings (Levins, 2013). Yet, coupled with nationalization policies that guarantee jobs to under qualified or under experienced nationals, the rentier mentality also delinks educational attainment, gainful employment, and income in the minds of citizens (Minnis, 2006). This combination may have deleterious effects on both student performance (Mazawi, 1999) and persistence in education. It can also result in GCC nationals expecting relatively higher salaries and advanced positions. If these expectations are not met, this can lead nationals to choose voluntary or "luxury" unemployment (Al Qudsi, 2005) and then living off state benefits or family rather than joining the workforce.

In the early days of the GCC, low population rates and the development of new governance structures allowed for the creation of public-sector jobs, which were able to employ all national males who sought to enter the labor market. However, indigenous populations across the region have grown, and the public sector is no longer able to absorb all the new entrants to the labor market. To avoid widespread discontent, governments across the region began introducing nationalization programs to promote employment of nationals in the private sector beginning in the mid-1970s (Randeree, 2012). In the GCC states the private-sector workforce consists of anywhere from 29% of nationals to around 1% to 2% of nationals, as illustrated in Table 5.1 (Forstenlechner & Rutledge, 2010; Qatar Statistics Authority, 2012).

The task of luring nationals to the private sector has been challenging for governments in the region, with resistance coming from both employees and employers. The private sector has been traditionally eschewed by nationals due to a number of factors, including longer working hours, lower salaries, and the perception of less job security (Al Waqafi & Forstenlechner, 2012; Randeree, 2012), although new legislation has made it extremely difficult in many GCC countries to fire nationals (Forstenlechner, Madi, Selim, & Rutledge, 2012). Complicating efforts to promote nationals

Table 5.1. Private-Sector Employment of GCC Citizens

Country	Nationals in Private Sector (%)	Percent of Employed Nationals in the Private Sector	Year of Measurement
Bahrain[a]	29	NA	2011
Kuwait[b]	18	NA	2012
Qatar	<1[c]	2[d]	2012
Saudi Arabia	16[e]	10[f]	2011
United Arab Emirates	0.5[g]–4[h]	NA	2012

Sources: (a) Randeree (2012); (b) "Employment in Private Sector Sees Rise" (n.d.); (c) Qatar Statistics Authority & Diplomatic Institute (2012); (d) Government of Qatar Planning Council (2005); (e) Info-Prod Research Ltd. (1999); (f) "Private sector may not keep pace with Saudi Youth Bulge—IMF" (2013); (g) Al Khan (2013); (h) Forstenlechner & Rutledge (2010).

working in the private sector is the lax enforcement and consistency of working regulations in the public sector. One major issue that governments struggle with is years of poor enforcement of attendance; this is reported by Kuwaiti employers to be nearly three times more common for nationals than for expatriates (Brinkley, Hutton, Schneider, & Ulrichson, 2012). Another issue is that of erratic and often excessive pay rises in the public sector. In 2008, for example, the federal government in the United Arab Emirates raised public-sector salaries by up to 70% in a single increase (Salem, 2012). Similarly, extravagant increases took place again across the GCC countries following the Arab Spring; in 2011, for instance, the United Arab Emirates issued a 100% pay raise for indebted Emiratis in order to "help them get their ambitions in a stable and comfortable life" (Gara, 2011). Similarly, Saudi Arabia and Qatar responded to the social unrest brought about in the Arab Spring by offering generous salary packages/ increases to nationals through investment in a $130 billion stimulus package (Gara, 2011). In the same year Qatar also announced a 50% to 120% pay raise for public-sector employees (Gara, 2011). Together, these three countries, among the most financially stable in the GCC, also offered to provide a stimulus package worth $20 billion for the citizens of Oman and Bahrain, the two countries in the GCC most impacted by unrest resulting from the Arab Spring (Gara, 2011).

Alongside the creation of unrealistic salary expectations in the GCC public sector, there has also been a preoccupation with titles, with public-sector employees often being rapidly promoted to the position of manager. This has created an expectation among nationals that they will achieve the title of manager within a very short span of time (Baxter, 2009). When this is not achieved, it can lead to employee dissatisfaction and even resignations. Despite these difficulties, which are well recognized, governments in the region seem to be unwilling to make fundamental changes to the public-sector working environment that would level the playing field and make private-sector employment at least as attractive as public-sector employment (Forstenlechner & Rutledge, 2010).

For Gulf nationals working in the private sector, the longer working hours, fewer benefits, and lower salaries also lead to dissatisfaction, especially in comparison to their colleagues working in the public sector. Compounding this issue is the preference that private-sector employers often have for more highly skilled, affordable expatriate labor (Al Khazraji, 2009). As a result, neither nationals themselves nor private-sector employers are enthusiastic about nationalization policies in the private sector, and governments have been compelled to offer a number of concessions to both parties to achieve even the most modest advances in the numbers of nationals working in the private sector (Forstenlechner & Rutledge, 2010). Even with these concessions and incentives, voluntary

Table 5.2. Age Structures of National GCC Populations (2011)

COUNTRY	0–14 YEARS (%)	15–24 YEARS (%)	15–64 YEARS (%)
Bahrain	20	15.9	77.3
Kuwait	25.6	15.4	72.2
Oman	30.6	20.2	66.2
Qatar	12.5	13.9	86.7
Saudi Arabia	28.2	19.6	68.7
United Arab Emirates	20.6	13.8	78.4

Source: World Bank (2011).

unemployment rates across, the GCC countries continue to rise, with nationals often preferring no work to working in the private sector (Shediac & Samman, 2010).

Decreasing fertility rates in the Gulf indicate that the coming years will be characterized by "demographic gift," a term that means the working-age population will be much larger than the population of dependents (Klasen & Lamanna, 2009). However, this gift will also increase pressure on governments to provide more employment opportunities to meet demand. In 2008, nationals aged 15–64 accounted for between 64% and 83% of the populations in Gulf countries (Gonzalez, 2010). According to the World Bank (2011), that age group accounted for between 66% to nearly 87% by 2011, as presented in Table 5.2.

In 2009, GCC unemployment rates among national youth aged 15–29 ranged from 8% in Kuwait to an astronomical 28% in Saudi Arabia (Forstenlechner & Rutledge, 2010), while UAE estimates ranged from 6.5% to 30% (Lewis, 2009). A 2010 study by Booz & Company indicated that unemployment for those aged 25–29 ranged from 22% in Qatar to 33% in Bahrain (cited in Braxton, 2011). Overall, unemployment in the 15–29 age range accounts for more than three-quarters of total unemployment in the Gulf States (Al Qudsi, 2005). High youth unemployment is becoming more problematic for governments, not only because it perpetuates economic dependence on foreign labor and decreases consumption (Braxton, 2011), but also because it leads to discontent and carries with it the potential of social unrest. Even when youth are classified more narrowly within the 15–24 age range (which means a greater proportion of young people are still students), unemployment is still an acute problem for both genders, as illustrated in Table 5.3.

In terms of gender, Table 5.3 shows that youth unemployment is higher for females than for males in all countries except Kuwait. This is despite the fact that women are more highly educated than men. However, with double-digit

Table 5.3. Youth Unemployment by Gender Among Gulf Nationals

COUNTRY	UNEMPLOYED FEMALES, 15–24 YEARS (%)	UNEMPLOYED MALES, 15–24 YEARS (%)
Bahrain[a]	32.6	25.7
Kuwait[a]	10	11.8
Oman[b]	~33 overall	
Qatar[a]	8.9	0.4
Saudi Arabia[a]	45.8	23.6
United Arab Emirates[a]	21.81	7.9

Sources: (a) World Bank (2011); (b) International Labour Organization (ILO) (2010).

youth unemployment in all Gulf countries, Qatar aside, governments are faced with increasing pressure to create jobs for both males and females.

Youth unemployment is not only economically and politically problematic, there are also social implications relating to increasing crime and incarceration rates (Carmichael & Ward, 2001). Despite the demographic gift that Gulf States will enjoy, unless increased levels of education can be translated into national workforce participation, the youth bulge will do little to promote long-term economic growth or relieve government welfare burdens. Rather, it could have a far more detrimental and destabilizing effect. With regard to gender, the Arab Spring has demonstrated that it is young men in particular who are angry and frustrated with the lack of economic opportunities that they have. As the burden of provision for the family primarily lies with males in the region (Abudabbeh, 1996), even if they have lower unemployment rates as compared to women, the existence of double-digit unemployment figures for males and females in some GCC countries poses serious challenges for individuals and families.

THE ISSUE OF NATIONALIZATION AND IMPLICATIONS FOR THE EDUCATION SECTOR

Nationalization initiatives are now an integral part of the policy landscape through which GCC governments believe they can ensure stability and prosperity and also achieve economic diversification to become knowledge economies rather than hydrocarbon economies. Strategies such as the UAE's Vision 2021 (UAE Government, 2010), Bahrain's Vision 2030 (Government of Bahrain, 2008), the Kingdom of Saudi Arabia's Vision 2020 (Ministry of Economy and Planning, Saudi Arabia, 2002), and Qatar's National Development Strategy 2011–2016 (GSDP, 2011) have sections highlighting each country's dedication to nationalization efforts. However, it appears that governments have failed to consider the impact of these policies on the education sector. In short, as young people believe they have a right to employment by virtue of their nationality rather than by merit, the incentive for education is greatly diminished. In addition, lower male unemployment rates as compared to those for females signals that gender may be more important than education in terms of obtaining a job, which further serves as a disincentive for males to continue their education.

Key to sustainable nationalization efforts, therefore, is establishing the relevance of education for employment for nationals. This needs to begin with bolstering human capital in the education sector in order to equip future generations of nationals for the workforce. However, as has been discussed, Gulf countries are struggling to attract nationals to both teaching and academia. National male teachers are especially scarce, which is problematic because evidence suggests that students whose teachers are from the same ethnic and geographic backgrounds as their pupils are more engaged (Ridge, 2010). In Qatar, only 30% of teachers are nationals, and male national teachers comprise only 28% of all male teachers (Toumi, 2011). Qataris may therefore be responding to wage disincentives, since salary scales for teachers are the same regardless of nationality, which means that Qataris (who have a far higher reservation wage) are paid the same as expatriates. Extra allowances may be added for special skills and qualifications (Toumi, 2010), but that opportunity excludes the large number of teachers who struggled even to pass licensing exams (Toumi, 2011).

Saudi Arabia also has had trouble incorporating nationals into the field of teaching. Education is considered a "nurturing" field and therefore is regarded as more appropriate for women, according to the dominant Wahhabi theology (Metz, 1992). However, national men are sorely needed in the field since schools are strictly gender segregated. In 2007, 93% of degrees granted to females were in education or the humanities (Al Munajjed, 2009), though the figure fell to 63% in 2011 (Dickinson, 2013). While a minimum wage of 5,600 riyals/month was instituted for Saudi teachers in 2011, many schools struggle to pay these salaries even with the promise of government subsidies. Expatriate teachers' salaries average just 2,000–3,500 riyals (Shaheen, 2011), making them a more attractive alternative when faced with limited budgets. In 2010, around 200 young Saudi men protested in front of the Ministry of Education (MOE), Riyadh, angered by a perceived shortage of teaching jobs for college graduates (Lindsey, 2010).

Bahraini nationals have also expressed similar discontent over their unemployment in the education sector. In 2011, a group of more than 600 nationals criticized the MOE for hiring so many teachers from other Arab countries and staged protests to demand jobs (Torr, 2011). One Bahrain Training Institute (BTI) student had seen what she referred to as injustice second hand through her aunt and reported, "My aunt graduated as a teacher seven years ago and she has never worked, there is no space for us because they bring people from abroad" (Torr, 2011). A Bahraini teacher who also participated in the protests claimed that despite her strong academic and professional background, she and many other national teachers were unable to afford proper housing because of the lack of jobs (Torr, 2011). Interestingly, it has been reported that Bahrainis represent the largest proportion of the Gulf national workforce in both the public and private sectors in Kuwait, with many Bahrainis working as teachers with a salary and benefits package negotiated between the two governments as part of a bilateral agreement ("Kuwaiti Jobs for Bahraini Teachers," 2002).

Oman has been the most successful of the GCC countries with regard to nationalization of the teacher workforce. The percentage of Omani teachers rose rapidly from 8% in 1980 to 89% in 2009 (MOE, Oman, & World Bank, 2012). However, there have been concerns among Omanis around the hiring of expatriates to fill teacher positions while some national teachers remain unemployed. These concerns were voiced in a 2010 protest staged by approximately 250 qualified Omani teachers in front of the MOE in Ruwi. One frustrated protestor blamed the MOE and claimed, "They keep hiring Arabic-speaking expatriates at our cost and that's not fair." A ministry official responded to the teachers' frustration and reported the Omani candidates had failed to pass a written qualifications test required to fill teaching positions in the country (Vaidya, 2010).

Nationalization efforts in the education sector in the United Arab Emirates have also been intensifying in part because of restrictions imposed on the hiring of Arab nationals from countries involved in the Arab Spring. While never publicly stated, unofficial visa restrictions are reported by education authorities as making it difficult to hire new expatriate teachers or replace older ones who need to retire. As a result, the United Arab Emirates has an increasingly urgent need to train national male teachers (Salem, 2013a). However, male enrollment rates at teacher-training colleges continue to fall. In Sharjah, the number of men enrolled in university teaching courses dropped from 45 in 2010 to only 13 in 2011 (Ahmed, 2013), while at the Emirates College of Advanced Education only 6 males graduated in the 2012 academic year. In terms of higher education, the Higher Colleges of Technology have Emirati directors at 5 of the 18 campuses, but only 10% of total employees are Emirati (Salem, 2013b). While Ministries of Education and Higher Education and Scientific Research give preference to nationals, they accounted for just 20% of applicants in 2013 (Ahmed, 2013), and as such, even if every applicant were hired, there would still not be enough to fill existing vacancies. Recruiting national males is also difficult due to social stereotypes and stigmas. In a survey of Emirati teachers, 70% said teaching is "not a respectable job for men," and anecdotally there even appears to be a stigma against marrying male teachers (Ahmed, 2012c).

There are also issues relating to the retention of national male teachers. Emirati teachers of both genders state that there is a need for better mentoring if they are going to stay in the profession (Ahmed, 2012a), but Gulf countries often struggle to find experienced national teachers to act as mentors. In Oman, for example, professors of education often have postgraduate degrees but little practical teaching experience. The United Arab Emirates, like other countries in the GCC, is introducing a short orientation program for new teachers. However, as teachers are allowed to retire after only 15 to 25 years of service, there are a limited number of seasoned nationals in the profession who could act as mentors for new entrants (Ridge, 2010). Retention is also difficult due to the low status accorded to the profession and the fact that it is often seen as a profession of last resort, as discussed in Chapter 4. In Oman, the top two survey responses from males regarding why they had entered the teaching profession were that they had "no other alternatives" in university or no other job offers when seeking employment, although they still intended to look for other jobs in the future (MOE, Oman, & World Bank, 2012). Nationalization efforts need to focus on both attracting high-quality national males to the education workforce and then retaining them, or boys in particular will continue to have few role models who demonstrate the value and importance of education.

In addition to a lack of role models for boys at the school level, the poor quality of public education at both the school and university levels has meant that the actual skills boys come out with are often deficient or ill-suited for labor market demands (Al Munajjed & Sabbagh, 2011; Farah, 2012; MOE, Oman, & World Bank, 2012), especially for the private sector. In Gulf countries, the distribution of university degree attainment in various fields often does not match what is needed in the labor force; there is a perceived over enrollment in the largely theoretical branches of the social studies and humanities and a lack of students pursuing engineering, sciences, and other technical fields (Bahgat, 1999; Baki, 2004; Gonzalez, 2010; MOE, Oman, & World Bank, 2012; Randall, 2011). In the next section we will examine nationalization policies more closely, beginning with a look at the common elements across the GCC countries and then at individual countries.

COMMON CHARACTERISTICS AND CHALLENGES OF GCC NATIONALIZATION POLICIES

Virtually all GCC nations face demographic imbalances characterized by "an overdependence on an expatriate workforce and on the government job-provision mechanism (for citizens)" (Forstenlechner & Rutledge, 2011).

Yet, each country has historically employed different measures in attempts to diversify and encourage nationals to participate in the workforce, as shown in Table 5.4. Strategies range from setting labor quotas and facilitating public-sector job creation to fostering positive national rhetoric toward employment, offering vocational preparation courses, funding entrepreneurship initiatives, and organizing programs that incentivize citizens (especially women) to join the private sector (Randeree, 2012). In some cases, significant discrepancies in labor data between sources make detailed analysis of the labor market in each country difficult (Hertog, 2012), but general trends can be observed.

Common across the GCC countries is that the appeal of the public sector is based on perceptions of greater prestige, higher wages, earlier retirement (often after 15–20 years), shorter hours, and better benefits packages than the private sector offers (Randeree, 2012; Harry, 2007).

In much of the private sector in the region, employers actually have disincentives to hire national workers. Not only do expatriates earn lower wages and often have more skills and experience than nationals (Al Khazraji, 2009), they are easier to hire and let go since there are no quotas or regulations protecting their jobs. Additionally, the regional stereotype of Gulf nationals as lazy and under qualified (Al Waqafi & Forstenlechner, 2012; "Labour Market Problems Threaten Relations," 2007; Nelson, 2004) creates a discourse that

Table 5.4. Early Nationalization Programs in the GCC Countries

Country	Date	Features of Nationalization Program	Source
Bahrain	2008	$25 monthly employer tax on expats	Forstenlechner & Rutledge (2010)
Kuwait	1997	Manpower and Government Restructuring Program (MGRP) for training and private-sector job placement	Markaz Research (2012)
Oman	1995	Quotas, expat visa control, certain jobs reserved for Omanis	Forstenlechner & Rutledge (2010)
Qatar	1997	Goal of 20% Qatari employees in all sectors	Felder & Vuollo (2008)
Saudi Arabia	2003	70% Saudization required by 2007	Looney (2004)
United Arab Emirates	1990s; 2004	Public-sector job provision; resolution to integrate nationals into private sector through quotas, training, etc.	UAE Government (2010)

is often detrimental to their gaining employment in the private sector. Furthermore, nationals in the GCC countries have been anecdotally reported to have a reputation for "job-hopping," that is, leaving one company for another before their training is complete and thus wasting resources spent on training. Expatriates have less mobility since their visas are legally tied to their employers, and thus represent a safer investment of both time and training (Stasz et al., 2007). Reportedly, these reasons also explain why some national employers are just as reluctant as expatriate employers to hire fellow nationals (Forstenlechner & Rutledge, 2010).

While nationalization programs are not gender specific, it is clear that they have a gendered effect due to a number of cultural factors. First, women are far less mobile than men and prefer to work close to their homes and families; thus women have fewer choices with regard to workplaces (World Bank, 2013). Second, despite greater freedoms and changing attitudes toward mixed-gender workplaces, many women still prefer to work in single-sex environments, such as schools (Shehadi, Hoteit, Tarazi, & Lamaa, 2011). This preference has led to a surplus of national female teachers in most countries (e.g., 64% of all teachers in Oman are female and 84.5% of primary schoolteachers in the United Arab Emirates are female) (Trading Economics, 2012) and shortages of national women in other sectors. Finally, structural barriers for working mothers, such as comparatively short maternity leave and a lack of child care facilities in the workplace, mean that women are often unable to continue working when they have young children (Al Mazroui, 2013). Despite these barriers to women's participation, however, there are increasing numbers of Gulf women entering the private sector, as can be seen in Table 5.5.

The emerging trend shown in Table 5.5 is that a greater percentage of national females than national males are employed in the private sector. While there are still strong cultural beliefs in the region that a woman's primary responsibility is to her home and family, and that women bear no responsibility to contribute financially to the household (Goveas & Aslam, 2011; Kirdar, 2010; Ramazani, 1985; Sayed, 2002), with increased education for women, this is beginning to change. National women in the GCC countries are entering the workforce in greater numbers, including the private sector. In the United Arab Emirates, Bahrain, and Kuwait, where there is data to compare female and male nationals working in the private sector, a higher percentage of the females are nationals vis-à-vis males. Private-sector employers have also reported a preference for female nationals over male nationals due to their better education levels, better English levels, and willingness to work for comparatively lower salaries at junior positions (Rutledge et al., 2011). In addition, reduced mobility may also force women to look for work in the private sector as it may be more geographically suitable than available public-sector positions. Saudi Arabia is the exception because of the smaller relative female participation rates in the labor market

Table 5.5. GCC Employment in the Private Sector by Gender

COUNTRY	FEMALES	MALES	YEAR
Bahrain[a]	23% of employed females in the private sector are Bahraini	14.9% of employed males in the private sector are Bahraini	2012
Kuwait[b]	43.4% of Kuwaitis employed in the private sector are female; 15.5% of employed females in the private sector are Kuwaiti	64.6% of Kuwaitis employed in the private sector are male; 1.6% of employed males in the private sector are Kuwaiti	2008
Oman[c]	17.9% female participation in the private sector	NA	2010
Qatar[d]	0.5% of private-sector employees are female (includes Qatari and non-Qatari)	99% of private-sector employees are male (includes Qatari and non-Qatari)	2007
Saudi Arabia[e,f]	0.8% of private-sector employees are Saudi females	19.2% of private-sector employees are Saudi males	2010, 2013
United Arab Emirates[e]	9.3% of employed Emirati females are in the private sector	6.7% of employed Emirati males are in the private sector (which is 87% male overall)	2012

Sources: (*a*) Labour Market Regulatory Authority, Bahrain (2013); (*b*) Central Statistical Bureau, Kuwait (2012); (*c*) ILO (2010); (*d*) Qatar Information Exchange (2007); (*e*) Al Masah Capital Limited (2012); (*f*) "Saudi Women in Private Sector Up by 330%" (2013).

to begin with (Al Masah Capital Limited, 2012). The next section examines specific nationalization policies in each GCC country and how these policies impact gender and education and what this may mean for men.

NATIONALIZATION, EDUCATION, AND GENDER POLICIES AT THE STATE LEVEL

While there are many similarities between the approaches taken by Gulf countries in terms of nationalization policies and who they target, each country has approached the issue in slightly different ways, which are explored in this section.

Qatar

Although 60% of Qataris are of employable age, only about half of adult Qataris are economically active (QSA & DI, 2012). As of 2011, unemployment rates among Qataris were at 4.1% (GSDP, 2011). Of these unemployed Qataris, just over half have attained only a secondary education degree and 72% are women (GSDP, 2011). While employment rates of Qataris in the public sector amount to 70%, in the private sector, Qataris make up only 1% of the employed population (GSDP, 2012). Despite these rates, Qatar, however, has been able to learn from the successes and struggles of neighbor states that have already reached public-sector saturation and appears to be attempting to prevent the same situation from occurring. For example, new policies have been introduced that aim to encourage entrepreneurship, something that has already been attempted in other GCC countries (QSA & DI, 2012). A National Qualification Framework is also planned to provide vocational training and formal mechanisms linking schools with employers (Randeree, 2012), and Qatar's Science and Technology Park is establishing research programs designed to encourage innovation and research involving Qatari students and private companies (GSDP, 2011). Additionally, Qatar's government sponsors an annual national career fair to encourage employment, mobility, and advancement of nationals across the public and private sectors (QSA & DI, 2012). Public-sector salaries are also highly attractive, and with 96% of working Qataris employed in the public or mixed sectors, they are able to earn average salaries that are two to three times those found in the private sector (Randeree, 2012).

As of 2008, Qataris constituted about half of all public-sector employees in the country (Felder & Vuollo, 2008). While only slightly less than half of Qatar University students indicate a preference for the private sector (GSDP, 2011), few graduates (especially males) have the skills and qualifications for private-sector positions. See Box 5.1 for a discussion of some of the challenges associated with reforming higher education. Despite the fact that the private sector has a preference for university-level education, 56% of Qatari men pursuing postsecondary education chose technical colleges (GSDP, 2011) at the university level a lack of demand has forced Qatar University, the country's premier national university, to downsize or discontinue many of its science/technology programs (QSA & DI, 2012). This appears to be the result of distortions to the labor market coming from the public sector. Current statistics show that the unemployment rate for Qatari men with a university education, at 5.9%, is actually higher than for those men with only an intermediate or secondary education with rates of 1.8% and 1.4%, respectively (Karoly, 2010). Therefore, the signals coming from the public sector with regard to qualifications act as a disincentive for Qatari males to pursue further education qualifications, despite these being desired by the private sector (Karoly, 2010).

Box 5.1. Qatar University's Language of Instruction Dilemma: Caught Between Modernity and Tradition

Qatar University, the country's leading national higher education institution, changed direction in early 2012. Following 10 years of English language instruction at the university, the Supreme Education Council, which functions as the Ministry of Education in Qatar, decreed that the language of instruction would revert to Arabic in 2012 (Khatri, 2012a). While this change in policy was not rolled out across the whole university, it will apply to the faculties of law, international affairs, mass communication, and management (Lindsey, 2012). A similar decision was introduced for primary and secondary schools earlier in 2012. Although no official reason was given for the policy change, some have argued that it indicates a clear effort to strengthen the national identity of Qataris, especially with regard to valuing local culture and traditions (Naif, personal communication, September 7, 2013). More importantly, it could also be interpreted as a backlash against a national initiative undertaken by the country's leadership in the early 2000s at the primary, secondary, and tertiary levels designed ostensibly to improve the competitiveness and employability of Qataris.

This effort involved reforming the public education system to establish "Independent Schools" based on the Western charter school model, in which core subject curriculum is taught in English (all subjects had previously been taught in Arabic) (Brewer et al., 2007). In addition to a focus on English in schools, the government has also invested billions in the creation of Education City, which saw the opening of seven branch campuses from the United States that offer high-quality degree programs, also only in English (GSDP, 2011).

Given the low quality of primary and secondary education in the country, especially in English language, almost all Qatari students choosing to attend higher education have needed to spend their first year in a foundations program that provides them with intensive English language training (among other subjects) (Brewer et al., 2007; GSDP, 2011). While arguments in support of the use of Arabic emphasize the importance of Qataris being fully literate in their mother tongue, the policy change at the university could likely result in lower-quality instruction due to the smaller pool of suitable faculty and instructors who are both subject specialists and fluent in Arabic (Lindsey, 2010). Other consequences of this decision remain to be seen, but it could be reasonably argued that Qataris graduating from Qatar University will now be even less employable in the private sector, where English is firmly established as the lingua franca.

Kuwait

Kuwaiti nationals comprise a relatively large proportion of the total population of Kuwait (48%), yet they account for only 22% of the workforce (Randeree, 2012). Kuwaitis accounted for 94.3% of the public-sector workforce in 2004 (Gonzalez, 2010), but only 2.5% of the private sector in 2005 (Hertog, 2012). Since the Manpower and Government Restructuring Program (MGRP) was created in 1997, Kuwait's immigration policies toward foreigners with families have become more lenient, but efforts to include Kuwaitis in both sectors have also expanded. The government directly subsidizes private companies employing Kuwaiti nationals (Forstenlechner & Rutledge, 2011), and companies are instructed to conduct annual reviews identifying open positions for which they might employ nationals (Randeree, 2012). Furthermore, the government set quotas at "60% Kuwaitization for banks, 15% for the real estate sector, and 2 for manufacturing industries," to be reached by 2008 (Randeree, 2012).

As of 2005, Kuwaiti youth unemployment was estimated at 12% for males and 10% for females; these rates are exponentially higher than the 2% unemployment rate in the overall population (UNICEF, 2011). UNICEF (2011) statistics put youth labor force participation at 24% for females and 42% for males in 2010, suggesting that students of both genders need access to employment opportunities. However, a 2006 survey indicated that 69% of unemployed Kuwaitis had not attained more than a secondary degree (Shediac & Samman, 2010), yet 40% of civil servants also did not even have a high school diploma, indicating the low premium placed on educational qualifications in the public sector (Hertog, 2012). While some have argued that vocational training programs are needed for Kuwaitis to be competitive in the private sector, these types of programs are only just beginning to appear (Saadouli, 2010). It is also reported that Kuwaitis often reject vocational training as a viable option unless they are unable to gain admission to other colleges and universities (Al Enezi, 2007); technical college enrollment accounts for only 2% of secondary education enrollment. In terms of gender the vast majority of those enrolled in technical colleges are males (Al Enezi, 2007), echoing the GCC trend of a preference for males in the region to pursue lower levels of postsecondary education than women. Thus, even with rising youth unemployment levels, the low value placed on education by the public sector is acting as a deterrent for many young Kuwaitis to continue their education, thus making them ineligible for private-sector employment as well.

Saudi Arabia

With 60% of the Saudi population under 20 (Torofdar & Yunngar, 2012) and a lower income per capita than other Gulf countries, youth unemployment is a critical problem for Saudi Arabia and has been estimated at up to 75% for males (Hertog, 2012). Most Saudi youth study at government schools that have a heavy religious education component, resulting in fewer hours spent on subjects such as math and science. As a result, less than 10% have any sort of practical skills that may be beneficial in the job market (Bremmer, 2004). While the Shura Council, the Kingdom of Saudi Arabia's advisory body, planned to achieve 70% Saudization by 2007, the government has apparently abandoned that goal and instead adopted a color-coded system to classify companies based on how well they conform to nationalization goals (e.g., 6% Saudization expected for construction, 19% for media, 49% for banking, etc.) (Randeree, 2012). While the Saudi government created 1.2 million jobs in the private sector between 2004 and 2009, only about 23% of these positions were filled by Saudis (Knickmeyer, 2011). In addition to bolstering local workforce participation, Saudization seeks to reinvest some of the income that foreigner workers send abroad as remittances (Looney, 2004). In 1997, remittances were estimated to equal up to 40% of oil revenues (Azzam, 1997), a number that has no doubt significantly grown since then.

The private sector is anecdotally resistant to employing Saudi nationals for a number of reasons. Companies complain about how inconsistent and short-lived nationalization policies have been, citing little incentive to comply when new ones are enacted (Hertog, 2012). Many prefer to hire foreign workers, who expect salaries less than half of what Saudis receive (Hertog, 2012) and often have more experience than Saudi nationals (Laessing & Alsharif, 2011). Foreign workers can be much more easily controlled, as they are typically unable to shift from the positions and jobs for which they initially secure visas (Madhi & Barrientos, 2003). The Human Resources Development Fund (HRDF) agreed to temporarily subsidize Saudi training and salaries, but up to 75% of recipients of these benefits left their jobs once their salaries were no longer subsidized (Torofdar & Yunngar, 2012). Income gaps between high- and low-wage jobs are growing, which is problematic for Saudi workers without advanced qualifications (Hertog, 2012). In 2011, the government introduced welfare benefits packages for its citizens that were worth 30% of the nation's annual GDP (Knickmeyer, 2011). That same year, 30% of Saudi women searching for jobs were unsuccessful, though 78% of them had university degrees (Knickmeyer, 2011).

There are numerous cultural barriers to the employment of women in Saudi Arabia, which if removed would increase the Kingdom's GDP by an estimated 7% (Islam, 2003). Aside from the practical problems of commuting to work in a country where women cannot legally drive, the prevalent Wahhabi teaching that a woman's primary responsibility is maintaining home and family life also provides a moral disincentive to women pursuing careers outside the home (Baki, 2004). Nevertheless, despite the restrictions on Saudi women in the public sphere, they own more than 16,000 businesses and account for 40% of the country's wealth (Al Banawi & Yusuf, 2011).

While there have been efforts to promote women's employment and a number of developments have taken place, there have been both positive and negative outcomes. At the government's insistence, more private companies now provide child care and offer paid maternity leave (Mellahi, 2011); this appears to have improved conditions for women while still accommodating traditional beliefs. On the other hand, some policies aimed at achieving gender equality have effectively created new barriers to the employment of women. In the field of architecture, for example, companies are required to provide separate offices for female employees, and as of 2009, no female architects had been hired by any Saudi company. Without employment options for women, there is then both reduced demand and a reduced number of qualified female professors for the subject. University architecture programs face practical dilemmas related to bringing male professors into a gender-segregated environment to teach a subject most women now consider a waste of time (Mills, 2009).

Gender-segregated fields like education, nursing, and public administration are considered "nurturing" and more appropriate for women, according to a Wahhabi understanding of gender roles, but this perception is changing. While 93% of degrees granted to females in 2007 were in education or the humanities (Al Munajjed, 2009), this figure fell to 63% in 2011 (Dickinson, 2013). More women are also joining the field of academia (Dickinson, 2013), but competition for teaching jobs remains intense despite increases in government expenditure on education and the expansion of universities. Practicing medicine, a theoretically acceptable occupation for women, requires long years of training and hours on the job that are difficult to balance with family life (Baki, 2004). Thus, there are positive signs, but religious and cultural barriers unique to Saudi Arabia still pose great impediments to Saudi women being able to work, despite their educational credentials and desire to do so.

As for Saudi males in the workforce, they have been found to have lower educational qualifications than their female counterparts (Al Munajjed, 2010b). Thus, men are currently faced with increasingly strong competition in the labor market from more qualified expatriates and female nationals and experience the highest overall unemployment rates in the region, 25% as of 2008 (Shediac & Samman, 2010). With the private sector less willing to hire Saudi men and most of the attention in the newspapers and research remaining on women, young Saudi men have found themselves calling for the state's help through protests and social media (Slavin, 2011). Some, like Saudi Arabia's Abdul Latif Jameel Company, have responded to their calls by establishing training programs to improve their employability

(Shediac & Samman, 2010). By equipping Saudi youth, primarily men, with transferable skills, the company has made it a priority to bridge the gap between private businesses, government institutions, and unemployed youth (Shediac & Samman, 2010). However, there is still much to be done to meet the male employment challenges in Saudi Arabia.

Bahrain

While Bahrainis comprise the majority of their country's population (62% in 2001, Randeree, 2012), those who work in the private sector tend to occupy low or unskilled positions, unlike nationals in most Gulf States. Furthermore, only 30% of working Bahrainis are employed in the public sector, the lowest proportion in the GCC (Gonzalez, 2010), with the public sector reportedly having no additional capacity to incorporate more workers. Since the 1980s, government programs have been targeting training and placement in the private sector. Despite this, Bahraini employees still account for 91% of the public sector and only 29% of the private sector (Randeree, 2012). As of 2007, Bahrain's Ministry of Labor had reduced unemployment from 16% in 2002 to 3.6%, but the unemployment rate among youth remained around 25% (Gonzalez, 2010).

In 2005, The National Employment Project began as a follow-up to previous internship and technical training programs that had been initiated by Tamkeen, a government agency working to develop enterprises and improve the worker productivity, and by the MOE (Karolak, 2012). The project aims to provide vocational training and aid in job searches, and 74% of its beneficiaries are female. An unemployment benefits program also started in 2007, but many citizens reportedly applied for benefits without any real intention of seeking a job (Ahmed, 2010). Additionally, Bahrain's MOE has begun to incorporate technology into all levels of public education to better prepare students for the workforce (MOE, Bahrain, 2008), while a microcredit loan system has become popular among entrepreneurs (Al Gharaibeh, 2011). In 2010, Bahrain became the first Gulf State to implement a Decent Work Country Programme in conjunction with the ILO (Goveas & Aslam, 2011). The program announced the establishment of a Labour Market Regulatory Authority to handle employment policy and licensing, a Labour Fund to support training and leadership development for youth, an unemployment insurance policy, educational reforms for vocational training, and suggested legal reforms to further women's empowerment in the workplace (ILO, 2010).

With regard to gender and employment, Bahraini men faced 12.5% unemployment in 2004 (Gonzalez, 2010), and nationalization policies have tended to favor female employees. Tamkeen, for example, is developing training programs that target Bahrainis across a wide variety of industries with roles traditionally occupied by female expatriates, such as airline cabin crew and nursing jobs. In fact, to increase women's employment in the private sector, Bahrain's legal code now allows companies to count Bahraini women as two people when tallying to reach their nationalization quotas (Karolak, 2012). While there has been talk of introducing a monthly tax on private companies who support expatriate visas, national ministers have repeatedly delayed enactment in response to social unrest (Broomhall, 2012). Social unrest in Bahrain seems to be driven by young men, which is unsurprising given that Bahrain has the highest male youth unemployment level in the region, 25% (World Bank, 2013). It is therefore interesting that nationalization programs in Bahrain continue to focus more on women, though this may change in light of ongoing social unrest, which appears to be largely driven by discontented young males (Torr, 2011).

United Arab Emirates

The United Arab Emirates has the greatest proportion of foreign workers in the GCC (88% in 2008) (Mashood, Verhoeven, & Chansarkar, 2009), and therefore has a greater need to integrate citizens into the workforce in the interest of long-term economic and social stability. In 2003, 75% of all local university students in the United Arab Emirates were women, but only between 9% (Thomas, 2000) and 14.7% (Abdulla, 2006) of Emirati women were employed full-time. The overall unemployment rate for locals reportedly fell dramatically from 20.8% in 2012 to 14% in 2013 (Al Makahleh, Badih, & Sabry, 2012; Sabry & Zaman, 2013). The National Human Resources Development and Employment Authority (Tanmia) is responsible for implementing nationalization policies, and tends to focus on equipping Emiratis for the workplace rather than imposing mandatory quotas on companies. The United Arab Emirates has increased public-sector employment opportunities, but labor officials suggested that the market was near saturation in 2009 and that open positions do not match the skills of national job seekers ("Emirati jobs 'are a bigger challenge than downturn,'" 2011). Therefore, future nationalization policies are focusing on bolstering national employment in the private sector, where starting salaries are one-half to one-third of those found in the public sector (Hertog, 2012), and where Emiratis constitute less than 1% of nearly 4 million employees (Issa, 2013b). As in other Gulf nations, surveys find that employee rights, job security, working hours, and salary are still the most important determinants of career decisions for UAE nationals (Al Waqafi & Forstenlechner, 2012; Godwin, 2006; Nelson, 2004; Wilkins, 2001). Hoping to change perceptions, national rhetoric has begun to emphasize greater opportunities for advancement in the private sector

(Simpson, 2013a). Some have even suggested that Emiratis who turn down more than three job offers after receiving vocational training should be denied government unemployment benefits (Issa, 2013a).

In the last decade, private-sector nationalization focused largely on employment in the banking sector, which reached 34.4% Emiratization in 2009 (Randeree, 2012). Human resources and administrative positions are meant to be filled exclusively by locals as per government recommendations in 2007 ("Labour Market Problems Threaten Relations," 2007). Despite nationalization quotas being voluntary, Emirati employment in the trading industry increased from 0.019% to 4% from 2004 to 2007, as employers are reportedly recognizing more of the cultural benefits of having employees with local knowledge (Randeree, 2012). Absher, a cooperative program between the government and private companies, provides job placement services and discounts at local businesses for Emiratis employed in the private sector (Ahmed, 2013). Emirati employment is growing at a rate of nearly 17% for females but only 6% for males, but unemployment rates are still lower for males than for females (2% versus 12%) (Shediac & Samman, 2010). Currently, Emirati females with university degrees are more likely to become entrepreneurs than to join the private sector (which often means banking), where women tend to be less educated (Randeree, 2012).

Oman

In 2008, around 86% of Omanis in the workforce worked in the public sector, with an additional 8.6% in the mixed sector and 4.7% in the private sector (Gonzalez, 2010). Yet Omanization policies target the private sector to a greater extent than the rest of the GCC, setting limits on incoming foreign labor and encouraging entrepreneurship (Mashood et al., 2009). However, with 83% of its population under the age of 35 (OBG, 2010), youth unemployment may have contributed to antigovernment protests in February 2011 (Hamdan, 2011). In response to these protests, the government increased the minimum wage and increased public-sector job creation (Hamdan, 2011). Numerically, more Omanis are employed in the public sector than in the private, but they still constitute a minority in comparison with foreign workers, who account for 54% of the workforce (Mashood et al., 2009). While private-sector Omanization rates remain low, diversification of nationalization across sectors has been greater than in other Gulf countries that have larger reserves of oil. National employment is still concentrated in the banking sector, which achieved over 90% Omanization in the 2000s, but only 25% of Omanis in that sector have a tertiary education as compared to 85% of expatriates (Hertog, 2012).

In 2010, Oman joined Bahrain in developing a Decent Work Country Programme with the ILO, which included plans to further develop vocational training and reform the Oman Labour Law (ILO, 2010). Currently, less than half of Omani male job seekers who have never worked before have received short-term vocational training (MOE, Oman, & World Bank, 2012). Omani women comprised roughly 17% of the workforce in 2000 and 16% in 2006 (MOE, Oman, & World Bank, 2012), but they are still more likely to work in the government sector in traditional fields such as social services, education, and health care. Vocational training and the expansion of professional organizations for Omanis have so far focused largely on women, including the formation of an Omani women's center and multiple training centers to teach women traditional skills so they can make and sell handicrafts for profit (Al Khaduri, 2007). Total female workforce participation in 2011 was 26%, while male participation was 78% (Buckley & Rynhart, 2011), but the concentration of male Omani employment in certain sectors suggests both genders need more training in order to take advantage of employment opportunities in a wider variety of sectors.

UNINTENDED OUTCOMES

Across the GCC countries all states are making pronounced efforts to engage nationals in the workforce. When there is an explicit gender component to nationalization programs, it is typically to promote the involvement of women in the workforce due to women's relatively lower participation rates, as shown in Table 5.6.

However, current nationalization programs in the region are not addressing the issue of low levels and quality of male education. Instead, nationalization programs that compel companies and government agencies to prefer nationals to nonnationals automatically confer a comparative

Table 5.6. GCC Workforce Participation by Gender

COUNTRY	WOMEN (%)	MEN (%)
Bahrain	39	87
Kuwait	43	82
Oman	28	82
Qatar	52	95
Saudi Arabia	18	74
United Arab Emirates	44	92

Source: World Bank (2011).

advantage on national males who can access the workforce more easily than their female counterparts. This signals to young men that by virtue of their nationality alone they are entitled to a job. As such, young men do not perceive that their level of education or the quality of their education could potentially be a barrier to securing a job (Jones, 2013). Young men also do not think that education, or for that matter experience, is a necessity to climb the career ladder. This can result in resentful attitudes and/or disengagement if they do not get the job, position, or salary they feel entitled to (Randeree, 2012). As the public sector in all GCC countries is close to reaching capacity, or at least the capacity that governments are willing to absorb, nationalization policies are now focusing on attracting nationals to the private sector. This approach has been met with resistance from employees who prefer the working conditions of the public sector, and also from employers, who cannot always meet pay expectations and often require more experience and greater education levels.

As a result, it appears that governments across the region are switching strategies to more strategically engage youth. In addition to incentivizing the private sector to employ more nationals, governments are now encouraging young nationals to become entrepreneurs through a host of initiatives at the school level. However, it is far from clear whether these programs will successfully create a generation of entrepreneurs. In Oman, the government is experimenting with incorporating part-time vocational training into existing academic programs and publicizing technical schooling as a viable educational path (MOE, Oman, & World Bank, 2012). In the United Arab Emirates, students are encouraged to become entrepreneurs through a number of initiatives such as the Mohammed bin Rashid Entrepreneur Development Programme called "Tejar Dubai," which includes mentoring programs, training workshops, bringing university students and businesses together through marketing fairs, and social networking initiatives (Wam, 2013). Another program in the United Arab Emirates offered through the Khalifa Fund assigns aspiring entrepreneurs to industrial projects that have been designed by private-sector companies that will benefit if the projects are successful (Malek, 2011). The private sector is also active in promoting entrepreneurship, with corporations such as Shell funding programs for young entrepreneurs in the region (Goveas & Aslam, 2011).

The feeling seems to be that if nationals cannot be lured into the private sector, the solution may be that nationals become business owners themselves. However, recent research conducted in the United Arab Emirates by Jones (2013) found that ostensibly vocational schools (ATHS)[2] designed specifically to foster both vocational education and entrepreneurship, while having the effect of improving student attitudes toward entrepreneurs (students admired entrepreneurs), were not successful in creating students who wanted to be entrepreneurial themselves. In addition, Jones found that these students articulated heightened levels of entitlement with regard to being given a government job and access to welfare. Thus, these government efforts to promote private-sector employment or entrepreneurship actually inadvertently produced greater entitlement attitudes and expectations of public-sector employment. Programs to promote entrepreneurship, therefore, may need much more careful evaluation concerning what their actual outcomes are, as there are indications that, rather than creating future business owners, they are actually promoting a discourse of entitlement that is further undermining the value of education.

At the heart of the difficulties facing nationalization programs is the poor quality of education experienced by the majority of nationals in government schools across the region. Males, as stated earlier, receive a very poor quality of education, which is exacerbated by a lack of national role models within the cadre of teachers in the majority of GCC countries. Nationalization programs enable young men with little and low-quality education to obtain positions above the level of their actual experience or education. This substantiates unrealistic job expectations by other Gulf males and simultaneously devalues education itself. By emphasizing nationality over education and experience in the labor market, the quality of the public sector, private sector, and the education sector are all undermined, resulting in a vicious cycle. The aspiration of most Gulf States—that of becoming a knowledge economy—will remain out of reach if knowledge is not the commodity valued most by the labor market. Male and female nationals who do obtain a good-quality education are so rapidly promoted that they often become victims of their own success; they are placed in senior positions quickly, without the necessary soft skills to manage people beneath them or the experience to make thoughtful decisions.

As women become more educated across the Gulf and governments seek to include them in the workforce for various reasons, there is little doubt that they will eventually hold more senior positions than will men (Rutledge et al., 2011). In fact, in the United Arab Emirates and Qatar many women already do (Rutledge et al., 2011). This situation poses its own set of problems because men and women in the GCC countries have been segregated during their educational paths and socially throughout their lives, and thus find the workplace a difficult place to begin to understand and relate to the opposite sex. Stories from government departments are layered with toxic and bitter gender feuds, with reports of men resenting women as managers and women feeling frustrated and threatened when they get promoted (Shehadi et al., 2011). This will be an additional challenge for both government and private-sector employers and employees in the coming years.

In short, nationalization programs have helped to facilitate the entry of many more Gulf nationals into the workforce. However, they have not signaled the right messages regarding the value of education to males in particular. These programs appear to further undermine the already tenuous state of boys' education and do not provide the right incentives for young men to either study hard or continue their education. Additionally, nationals who do continue their education may experience high levels of dissatisfaction if high-paying, senior jobs are not immediately accessible. The next chapter examines why education remains critical for the development of the Gulf, despite the messages of the labor market and how the current state of boys' education and the neglect of the development of males across the region may lead to potentially explosive social repercussions.

6 The Value of Education Beyond Work

Implications for Gender

Throughout this book we have been examining gendered aspects of education in the GCC countries and how girls are achieving more and persisting longer, while boys are being left behind on both fronts. We have also looked at the labor market and the paradox that, despite their educational successes, women are more likely to be unemployed or, if they are employed, to be working in lower-paid jobs. The function of education in the Gulf is thus often and understandably questioned by outsiders as to its value and purpose, especially if educational achievement is disconnected from labor market rewards. In general, education is typically viewed as a critical part of ensuring the social and economic development of a nation. Governments across the globe therefore spend billions of dollars investing in education based on the belief that education offers benefits or returns to both the individual and society. These returns to education are typically conceived and measured in terms of whether they are private monetary returns, private nonpecuniary (nonmonetary) returns, or social returns.

In the GCC countries little research has been done on the returns to education in general; so when questions arise about the value and purpose of education in these societies, where employment or income appears guaranteed, answers are far from clear. Some research on private returns to education has been done in the United Arab Emirates, Kuwait, and Qatar—all of which finds that there are positive returns to education and that these returns are stronger for males than for females. While there is currently scant empirical research on the private nonpecuniary returns to education or on the social returns to education, the positive findings with regard to private monetary returns lead to the question of why so many males are not choosing to continue their education. For governments the policy of ignoring the poor performance and persistence of males also makes little sense; even if there are currently no empirical studies for the region, the existence of social returns to education is already proven elsewhere.

This chapter explores the potential of education in the GCC countries to benefit both individuals and society. It also examines how ignoring the reverse gender gap in education is exacerbating a new gender divide in both health and crime that will impact not only males but females and society as a whole. The chapter begins with a discussion of the returns to education and what the literature finds in terms of pecuniary, nonpecuniary, and social returns. It then examines the situation in the GCC countries for each of these types of returns. This is followed by a discussion of the social returns to education in the GCC countries as they relate to health and crime rates and subsequent costs to society. The chapter concludes with a discussion of how, in the light of growing gender imbalances in health and crime rates, greater attention to the disadvantages facing boys in education has the potential to have far-reaching benefits for women and society at large.

RETURNS TO EDUCATION

Before examining the case of the GCC in particular, it is important to understand the established literature on returns to education. Adam Smith pioneered the notion of returns to education in *The Wealth of Nations* (1776), where he claimed that an investment in education and training is seen as an investment in human capital and produces similar, if not better, results than an investment in physical capital. This notion was later extended by Theodore Schultz and Howard Becker in the 1960s; they suggested that education can increase productivity of labor and thus eventually contribute to economic returns in the form of real wages. Psacharopoulos (1985) and Barro (2001) also furthered this research through their comparative studies of both developed and developing countries; they found that education generates higher economic growth by attracting technology and adjusting the levels of physical capital upward to suit improvements in education. However, with rising student debt and other costs of education, economists became more concerned with the narrowing gap between the monetary costs and rewards of getting an education, particularly a college education (Oreopoulos & Uros, 2013). The departure away from a focus on private monetary returns to education to a focus on the nonpecuniary and social benefits was initiated by Haveman and Wolfe (1984). These authors found education to be linked to improvements in personal health, consumer efficiency, savings, and marital relations. A number of social returns were also noted, including improved family health and fertility, reduced rates of crime, and social cohesion. Lochner and Moretti (2004) found that the social benefit from reduced criminal behavior that comes as a result of higher educational attainment is the equivalent of 14% to 26% of the financial reward. A calculation of monetary benefits alone is misleading, and consideration of social benefits, in this case, increases the gap between costs and benefits of education. Similarly, Gorssman (2005) and

Oreopoulos (2007) suggest that an additional year of schooling increases the chances of avoiding health-damaging behavior like smoking, thus increasing the life expectancy of the population as a whole. Finally, education has also been found to be linked positively with job satisfaction and lower unemployment in the United States (Oreopoulos & Salvanes, 2011). We will now look at each of the three main categories of returns to education—private monetary returns, private nonpecuniary returns, and social returns—in the wider literature before moving on to look at each of these in the context of the Gulf.

Private Monetary Returns

Private monetary returns are by far the most discussed and measured returns to education. These are the financial returns that accrue to an individual as he or she acquires additional years of education. Globally, a plethora of literature confirms the correlation between earnings and education. Psacharopoulos's (1981) investigation of patterns in 32 developing and developed countries presented in 53 different studies reveals that returns are highest at the primary level of education; that private returns exceed social returns, particularly at the tertiary level; and that returns are relatively higher in developing as opposed to developed countries. He also finds that the rate of return to a year of typical schooling is approximately 14% for least developed countries, 10% for intermediately developed countries, and 8% for advanced countries (Psacharopoulos, 1981).

Another comparative study, which focused on three countries in the Middle East—Egypt, Iran, and Turkey—found that returns to education are positive (at 5.3% in Egypt, 7.6% in Iran, and 12.4% in Turkey) and increased for all countries at each level of education from the 1980s through 2006 (Salehi-Isfahani, Tunali, & Assaad, 2009). This study also found that returns to vocational education and training are lower than those observed for general upper secondary in Egypt and Iran, similar to patterns across other developing countries (Salehi-Isfahani et al., 2009). The authors hypothesize that the reason Turkey does not experience this same pattern is because its economy is overall more open to accepting job seekers with a vocational training background. Finally, Salehi-Isfahani and colleagues (2009) suggest that returns to university education have increased between the 1980s and 2006 to align with greater labor market competitiveness in all three countries examined.

Prodromidis and Prodromidis's (2008) study on private returns to education in Greece between 1988 and 1999 confirms the existence of extensive returns to education and also draws the primary empirical conclusions around that phenomenon. First, rates of return for female high school and university graduates exceed those of male graduates. Second, rates of return for high school graduates increase for the first few years, reach a maximum, and then decrease, following an inverted U-shape throughout the span of 11 years. Finally, university graduates experience a constant increase in their returns from education over time.

In Kenya, Kimenyi, Mwabu, and Damiano (2006) conducted a nationwide study of private returns based on data from 1994 and found that rates of return grew at every educational level. That is, they increased from 7.7% at the primary level to 23.4% at the secondary level and finally to 25.1% at the university level. However, statistically significant differences were found between geographical regions; urban locations were associated with higher returns to education than rural regions, which encouraged those who work in Kenya's major cities to pursue more education. Similarly, in rural areas, university graduates were found to earn lower wages than high school graduates, which discouraged the pursuit of higher education for those working in rural areas.

Country-specific case studies from the United States are the most widely available and are also consistent with human capital theory. In the United States, Card (1999) estimated the private returns to education to be around 10% (table 5, pp. 1843–1844). Using evidence from studies done with identical twins, Card found the returns to education to be in the range of 10%–15% (p. 1851). In another U.S. study by Hout (2012), he found that salaries rise almost linearly with educational qualifications. Having a bachelor's degree instead of a high school diploma increases prime-age men's occupational standing up to 69 points from a base of 45 points and increases prime-age women's occupational standing up to 59 points from a base of 34 points. For both genders this translates to a 20% increase in annual salaries (Hout, 2012, p. 382). It is clear that there are greater returns to education in the United States for men than for women. On the other hand, contrary to the findings from U.S. studies, Lewin-Epstein and Semyonov (1994) studied the ethnic Arab population in Israel and found that for every year of education men's earnings increased by 7% and women's by 8%, with increased occupational status for both men and women (p. 640).

However, it is not only the number of years of study that were found to impact earnings, it is also the type of study that occurred. Literature that looks at specific majors in college in the United States consistently finds that quantitative, technical, and vocational subjects have higher returns than others. Jacobson, LaLonde, and Sullivan (2005) estimated the returns for quantitative majors to be around 10% per year, compared to 3%–5% for humanities and social sciences majors. Jepsen, Troske, and Coomes (2009) found that health degrees gave the highest returns, followed by other vocational degrees, including business degrees, while some humanities disciplines were not statistically related to returns.

There is therefore compelling evidence from across the globe that greater levels of education, particularly having a bachelor's degree versus a high school diploma versus not completing high school, will translate into greater earnings over the course of a lifetime. In addition, the type of degree studied also has an impact on future earnings; scientific and technical degrees yield greater returns to education than humanities degrees. The fact that these findings hold true in countries across the world, regardless of culture, language, or religion, means that there is almost always an individual financial benefit from attaining more education, holding all other things equal. At what point these become marginal or diminishing returns, however, varies from country to country.

Private Nonpecuniary Returns

Investment in education yields more than just monetary returns for the individual and his or her family. McMahon (1998) reviewed the growing body of literature on the nonpecuniary returns to education and listed health effects, lifelong adaptation, and continued learning, among others, as the positive benefits from education (pp. 317–318).

Health is one area in which private nonpecuniary returns are particularly strong. A number of researchers have established a positive correlation between education and health (Grossman & Kaestner, 1997; Sickles & Taubman, 1986; Taubman & Rosen, 1982). Schafer, Wilkinson, and Ferraro (2013) are among the most recent to contribute to the literature on the correlation between the completion of college degrees and better health. Schafer and colleagues begin by citing the existing literature that supports the notion that college-educated adults have better health when compared with those with less education in areas including "mental health, sense of personal control, self-rated health, disability, chronic conditions and mortality" (2013, pp. 1007–1008). They found that other things being equal, those who complete college are expected to experience lower rates of hypertension, heart problems, and mortality, at 26.4%, 22.8%, and 25.6% respectively, than those who do not. Importantly, they also found that "the benefits of college degree completion were highest among those least likely to attain a degree as a consequence of early misfortune" (2013, p. 1024). The implication of this is that students who drop out of school are the ones who would benefit most were they to complete their studies; such students may be missing out on more than just their education; they are also potentially missing out on a healthier life in the future.

Kenkel (1991) used the 1985 data of over 14,000 males and 19,500 females from the National Health Interview Survey in the United States and empirically confirmed that the more years of schooling completed resulted in a statistically significant reduction in the number of cigarettes smoked, a modest reduction in alcohol consumption, and a significant increase in the amount of physical exercise per week. Another researcher (Leigh, 1989) noted that since the 1964 landmark report by the Surgeon General that linked tobacco smoking to lung cancer, the prevalence of smoking among college graduates in the United States had sharply declined, whereas it had only weakly declined among high school dropouts. Leigh (1989) also noted that tobacco smoking was responsible for 400,000 preventable deaths each year in the United States (based on a report in 1993). The latest 2011 data from the Centers of Disease Control and Prevention (2011) estimated that 24% of adults with a high school diploma were smokers and that this figure dropped to 9% for adults with an undergraduate college degree.

Outside of the United States, a similar study in Italy used nationally representative data and found that education contributes to better health and health-related behavior of men and women (Braga & Bratti, 2012). Specifically, each effective year of lower secondary schooling was found to reduce women's body mass index (BMI) by 4.3%, which in total amounts to a reduction of 12.8% across all 3 years of lower secondary schooling. Lower secondary schooling was also found to be associated negatively (–24 percentage point) with the likelihood of women being obese. However, no such effects were observed for men, which is consistent with observations from the United States. While men did not experience direct benefits to their health, higher probabilities of health-improving behaviors were observed for this subsample. That is, every additional year of lower secondary schooling was associated with higher chances of exercising regularly (at least once a week), higher chances of going for cholesterol and glycemia checks, and lower chances of following a set dietary regime.

International comparisons, highlighted in Cutler and Lleras-Muney (2012), tell a similar story about the nonpecuniary benefits of education. Integrating literature from both developed and developing countries, Cutler and Lleras-Muney found that across the globe, more education is often associated with better health. However, they noted that the conditions that mark better health differ between most developed and developing countries. For instance, in developing countries those who are more educated have higher BMIs and are thus less likely to be undernourished and/or anemic, but are more likely to be obese or overweight. In contrast, in developed countries those who are better educated have lower BMIs than their noneducated counterparts, and are thus less likely to be overweight or obese. In other words, education is found to be "protective for the outcomes that are known to be bad for health" (Cutler & Lleras-Muney, 2012, p. 8).

People with more formal education during their early years are also more likely to learn more in their later years. Not only does learning apply to learning in school, it also applies to learning new skills on the job and adapting to new technologies (McMahon, 1998; Mincer, 1981). According to Mincer (1981), "Schooling improves the efficiency with which people can absorb learning on the job" (p. 198). That is, investing in human capital not only accumulates additional knowledge, it also helps produce new knowledge that can be used to develop innovative and more technically advanced ways of performing the same job. Eventually, higher efficiency on the job as a result of learning allows wage earners to invest more in the labor market.

In addition to health and learning, there are also psychological benefits from greater levels of education. Oreopoulos and Salvanes (2011) worked with the data from the U.S. General Social Surveys in the period 1972–2000 and reported that high school graduates were 8 percentage points happier (self-reported) than high school dropouts, and college graduates were 5 percentage points happier than high school graduates (self-reported). Even after controlling for income, high school graduates still were 4 percentage points and college graduates 2 percentage points happier than the group beneath. In discussing the results, they attributed the amount of happiness to success in the labor market, better health, happier marriages, and a decrease in risky behaviors, including criminal activity (Oreopoulos & Salvanes, 2011, pp. 179–180).

Finally, there are intergenerational benefits of education that accrue to the families of those who are better educated. Research has shown a negative correlation between parents who are well-educated and the likelihood that their children would drop out of school (Duncan, Brooks-Gunn, & Klebanov, 1994; Haveman & Wolfe, 1995). Davis-Kean (2005) added another layer to the existing literature by separating the racial groups and found that while there was a significant difference between African Americans and European Americans, there was still a positive correlation between parents' years of schooling and their children's academic achievement.

Private nonpecuniary returns are therefore significant, especially in terms of health and well-being. They are also intergenerational, in that they accrue to the families of individuals as these individuals go on to have children of their own. When people are more educated, they not only earn more income, they are also more likely to be happier, healthier, and live longer. These returns, again, are stronger for those at greater risk—those from lower socioeconomic groups. In terms of gender, there are also findings that show that benefits to health differ between males and females, with each benefitting in different ways from having greater levels of education.

Social Returns

In addition to the private returns to education, which accrue to individuals, there are also important social returns to education that benefit society as a whole (Topel, 1999). The theory argues that when members of society gain more education, the whole society gains both economically and socially. If the rate of return is high, the obvious policy implication is that "a reallocation of resources from other uses to the education sector may be in order," as few other public investments would have comparably high returns (Wolfe & Haveman, 2002, p. 119). Studies on social returns, however, are fewer in number, and while the private monetary returns can be measured with reasonable accuracy, it is more difficult to measure the returns of education to society in general (Hout, 2012; Morreti, 2004; Riddell, 2004).

The first and most discussed social return to education comes in the form of economic growth. Education builds human capital, a critical component of economic growth (Barro & Lee, 2011; Hanushek & Kimko, 2000; Riddell, 2004). An educated society translates to better-skilled workers and higher labor productivity, thus increasing the output of goods and services. Having well-educated members also aids in the transfer of knowledge and technology from more developed countries (Barro & Lee, 2011). For developing countries and countries that want to shift to knowledge-based economies, greater educational attainment is often seen as the key to economic prosperity in the future.

Hanushek and Kimko (2000) and Barro (2001) performed cross-country regressions and found that test scores were positively related to the growth rates of real GDP per capita. Hanushek and Kimko included 150 countries in their regressions and concluded that "labor-force quality has a consistent, stable, and strong relationship with economic growth" (2001, p. 1203). Barro used data from OECD countries and samples of rich and poor countries and came to the same conclusion. Although he did not find economic growth to be significantly related to male schooling at the primary level, he did find that growth is significantly related to secondary and higher levels of education for males. In contrast, he found no statistically significant relationship between growth and education at the secondary and higher levels for women suggesting that women were not as highly utilized in the labor market as men in 100 countries between 1965 and 1990.

In contrast, he found no statistically significant relationship between growth and education at the secondary and higher levels for women

Social returns, in the form of greater public welfare savings for governments, are also accrued through greater levels of education. Studies find that education improves health, reduces the crime rate, and decreases incarceration costs and welfare spending, all of which lead to less government spending today and also benefit generations far into the future. Citing a study done in Texas and California by Murdock et al. (2003), Hout (2012) noted that for every $1.00 invested in state universities in Texas, the state received a return of $4.00. This amount came from the money saved from lower use of public assistance, lower crime and incarceration, and higher payback in the form of sales, property, and state income taxes. In California, the net return was $3.65 based on a similar study done in 2005 (Hout, 2012, p. 392).

Criminal activity in a community is negatively related to the average level of educational attainment of its members. Lochner and Moretti (2004) found strong negative correlations between education and crime. High school completion reduces the chance that an individual will commit a crime, after controlling for factors such as location, year, type of crime, and age level. Lochner and Moretti also found that dropping out of high school had a larger effect on reducing violent crimes (e.g., murder, assault) than property crimes (p. 23). Thus, society has a real incentive to prevent high school dropouts, as not only does dropping out of school take away future positive externalities such as increased future productivity and wages and increased federal government savings estimated at $1.4 billion annually, but—more importantly—it can create serious negative externalities for society in the form of higher crime rates.

In addition, greater levels of education indirectly benefit society through human capital spillover. Moretti (2004) investigated whether having educated workers would make other workers more productive, thus creating positive human capital externalities. He found that manufacturing plants located in cities where the number of college graduates grew at a faster rate had larger increases in productivity than manufacturing plants in cities where the number of college graduates grew more slowly. Moretti reached this conclusion after controlling for each individual plant's level of human capital.

More education for individuals may lead to social cohesion and may enable society to better adapt to technological and social changes (Wolfe & Haveman, 2002). An educated person is also more likely to participate in civic life. This includes making informed choices when voting and more engagement with one's community (Hauser, 2000). Schooling is also positively related to improving trust of others and to increased involvement in organizations and community projects (Helliwell & Putnam, 1999), and to reducing the chance of violence during protests (Hall, Rodeghier, & Useem, 1986).

Trent and Medsker (1968) followed the paths of 10,000 high school graduates in the period 1959–1963 and found that those who pursued further education were "less stereotyped and prejudiced in their judgments, more critical in their thinking, and more tolerant, flexible, and autonomous in attitude" (pp. 129–130). This significant gain occurred regardless of the type of higher institution attended, suggesting that more education leads to more tolerance and less prejudice. Trent and Medsker linked the increase in social maturity to "openness to ideas, tolerance of different points of view, and self-direction" (p. 197). Other researchers after Trent and Medsker have reinforced this positive correlation (Astin, 1977, 1993; Bowen, 1977; Pascarella & Terenzini, 1991). Bowen (1977) concluded that college education "increases moderately their psychological well-being as well as their understanding, human sympathy, and tolerance toward ethnic and national groups and toward people who hold differing opinions" (p. 433). Astin (1977) used over 2 decades of data from the Cooperative Institutional Research Program, which had surveyed some 200,000 students from 300 postsecondary institutions in the United States. His conclusion echoed the other researchers', in that he found increases in "commitment to participate in programs to clean up the environment, to promote racial understanding, and to develop a meaningful philosophy of life" (Astin, 1977, p. 397). Pascarella and Terenzini, in their book *How College Affects Students* (1991), review over 2,600 empirical studies and suggest that "college is linked with statistically significant increases in the use of principled reasoning to judge moral issues," which in the long term is consistently linked to "a range of principled behaviors, including resisting cheating, social activism, keeping contractual promises, and helping those in need" (pp. 366–367).

There is also evidence that the more schooling one has, the more time and money one invests in charitable causes, even after controlling for income level (Dye, 1980; Freeman, 1997; Hodgkinson & Weitzman, 1988). Hodgkinson and Weitzman (1988), for instance, found that college graduates volunteered twice the amount of hours and donated 50% more of their income than high school graduates.

Cyclical Benefits

Significant benefits from education can be seen for males, females, and society at large, which should make investing in education a priority for governments the world over. While we can understand returns to education in terms of private and societal, in reality all of the positive effects for the individual do flow back to their society and create a constructive cycle that feeds back to the family unit. For instance, when young people stay in school and obtain jobs as opposed to the alternative of dropping out of school, they contribute to a safer, more prosperous, and healthier neighborhood that, in turn, provides a healthy environment for children to live and learn.

Hout (2012) claims that the biggest surprise in recent literature regarding the benefits of education concerns those who miss out on education—the dropouts. Evidence from the United States shows that the students who benefit most from education are not the most talented, who do tend to complete high school and college degrees, but those in the middle and/or lower range. Brand and Xie (2010) found that students who were unlikely to go to college because of their economic and noneconomic background would benefit more from completing high school and attending universities than typical college students. Thus, making sure students who are at risk of dropping out stay and complete their education would reap even greater rate of returns to the individual, the society, and the nation as a whole. With this in mind, we now turn to the GCC countries to examine the existing studies on returns to education and how the lack of focus on boys' education is leading to growing inequalities in health and behavior that are having increasingly adverse effects—not only on individuals, but also on families and societies.

RETURNS TO EDUCATION IN THE GCC

Empirical studies on returns to education in the GCC countries are comparatively few, and most consider private monetary returns. However, overall findings are consistent with the international literature, highlighting the significance of education in contributing to wages for both males and females, and contributing progressively to national economic growth. Studies in which gender was considered are also relatively consistent regionally and find that returns to education are stronger for men than for women and higher in the private sector than in the public sector. We will look at each category of return in kind before discussing the implications of this for education and gender.

Monetary Returns

In one of the earliest studies conducted in the region in 1989, entitled "Returns to Education, Sectoral Pay Differentials and Determinants in Kuwait," Al Qudsi used the human capital model to estimate the private monetary returns to education of three groups of workers (composed of nationals and nonnationals) in the private and public sectors of the economy in Kuwait, based on data from the 1983 National Labor Survey. He found that returns to education were greater in the private sector in Kuwait than in the public sector, while overall wages were higher for public-sector employees than for those in the private sector. Holding everything else constant, returns to education across both sectors was found to be higher for nationals than for nonnationals, regardless of educational attainment. Al Qudsi's findings guide his policy recommendation to evaluate the current wage dynamics in the public sector to ensure it is aligned with productivity and labor market requirements.

In Qatar, a 2011 study from the Department of Social Development General Secretariat for Development Planning (GSDP) on the monetary returns to schooling found that "the monetary gain for males completing a university degree is more than twice that for females and yet the male progression to higher education is substantially lower than female progression" (p. 8). Monetary returns were found to be stronger for younger generations than for older, and in the 18–39 age group, returns from 1 year of university were 8.7% for females compared to 11.4% for males. Overall, the report found that for men the return to postsecondary education is around 11%–14%, while for women it is slightly lower, around 8%–11%.

In the United Arab Emirates, a study by Fatma Al Marri and Mike Helal (2011) found that there are positive returns to education for male and female nationals in Dubai. According to their research, male Emiratis experience higher returns than do females, overall. For males, "the average annual income for early school leavers appears to be around AED 100,000 while it approaches AED 200,000 for those who have successfully completed secondary school" (Al Marri & Helal, 2011, p. 115). Al Marri and Helal also found that males who attain a tertiary qualification earn around AED 300,000, if not more, annually; thus, at the secondary level, male Emiratis are expected to earn, on average, twice the wages of a dropout, and at the tertiary level, at least three times the wages of a dropout. While these results were not based on a representative sample of the United Arab Emirates, the findings suggest the existence of increasing returns to higher levels of education in the Emirates.

More recently in the United Arab Emirates, Squalli (2012) conducted a larger, empirical study on a wider sample of 30,043 unemployed Emiratis and 376 employed Emiratis from across all Emirates to estimate the expected returns to education and work experience. He found that expected wages for both males and females dropped initially, with each additional year of schooling resulting in an 11.8% drop in expected wages for males attaining 0 to 8.7 years of schooling and a 7.8% drop in expected wages for females attaining 0 to 6.4 years of schooling. The tide turns, however, beyond the 8.7-year mark for men and the 6.4-year mark for women. According to Squalli (2012), "Beyond these years, the expected return for an additional year of schooling is 0.6% higher for males and females alike" (p. 12). The first part of the relationship between wages and education suggests a possible mismatch between productivity brought about by a combination of an Emirati entitlement mentality (Jones, 2013) and compensation based on seniority and/or *wasta* (social connections) (Squalli, 2012). The second part is in line with previous literature from across the globe on positive returns to secondary and college education (Psacharopoulos, 1981).

Similar patterns have been observed in Saudi Arabia, where, with only a few exceptions, according to Karoly (2010), "Wages increase monotonically as the level of education increases" (p. 28). However, Karoly found that not only were returns to education between the secondary and tertiary levels higher for males than for females but they were also higher for nonnationals than for nationals. For example, the wage premium between secondary and tertiary school was found to be 242% for expatriate males and a much lower 176% for Saudi males; in contrast, expatriate women experienced a 145% wage premium and Saudi women a 131% premium (Karoly, 2010). According to Karoly (2010), gender and nationality differentials can be explained by occupational and sectoral differences across the groups, whereby male and female nationals working in high-status occupations in the public sector are more likely to experience higher wages in comparison to their counterparts in lower-status occupations in the private sector.

It is therefore clear that there are at least private monetary returns to education in the GCC countries, thus disputing the belief that education is irrelevant for nationals and in particular for males. However, there appears to be little awareness of the potential returns to education by either governments or individuals. The lack of awareness on the part of governments is evidenced in statements made in the UAE Yearbook, for example, stating that males are satisfied with a secondary education as that provides them with access to a good job, the implicit belief being that males do not require more education to do well at work (National Media Council, 2010). For individuals, the lack of awareness of the returns to education for males in particular is evidenced by them dropping out of school in far greater numbers to typically pursue employment opportunities (Al Munajjed & Sabbagh, 2011; Ridge et al., 2013), when their earnings would be far greater if they completed school. However, beyond private monetary returns to education, there is also evidence of nonpecuniary and social returns, which we will examine next.

Potential Nonpecuniary and Social Returns

Governments across the GCC countries are becoming increasingly concerned about a number of issues involving youth, especially in light of the "youth bulge" and the Arab Spring. In particular, issues of youth dropouts, unemployment, health, and crime are coming to the forefront, with crime less publically discussed than other issues. While education and problems with the quality of education are frequently discussed in relation to addressing unemployment, there has been little discussion of how education could also be a key factor hindering or helping issues related to health and crime. In addition, there is also little public acknowledgment that in both health and crime, young men in the region are at far greater risk than women—making addressing issues in boys' education important for reasons other than employment. This section will look briefly at the nonpecuniary benefits of education in relation to school dropouts and unemployment, and then address the less-studied issues of health and crime in the region and how education may be the missing link.

Early school leaving and the labor market. In a study examining the relationship between early school leaving and unemployment in Dubai, Al Marri and Helal (2011) studied working-age Emirati male and female populations in Dubai and found that, particularly for males, leaving school early was consistently linked to lower labor market outcomes. According to the authors, 16% of uneducated Emirati males are unemployed and, similarly, 10% of those who dropped out of school before completing their secondary education are out of a job. For secondary school completers the unemployment rate is much lower (at 2%), and the unemployment rate is below 1% for those with a postsecondary qualification. For females, the study found very little correlation between attrition and labor force outcomes, suggesting that—for females—leaving school early is often unrelated to seeking employment.

In another study conducted by Ridge and colleagues (2013) examining the whole United Arab Emirates, staying in school was found to be statistically and significantly related to other individual nonpecuniary benefits in school and at home. The study used a mixed-methods comparative approach to examine the patterns and perceptions of dropping out of school for a nationally representative sample of male Emiratis, and found that with every one-level increase (i.e., moving from primary to secondary school) in a mother's education, the chances of the male Emirati child dropping out of high school were 22% lower. This confirms previous international literature on the intergenerational effects of education on children (see Haveman & Wolfe, 1995). Quantitative and qualitative analyses also indicated that staying in school was also correlated with having smaller, more cohesive families, stronger relationships with peers and teachers at school, and greater parental support for education (Ridge et al., 2013).

Finally, a recent comparative study by Wilkins (2011) on foreign universities that operate campuses in the Gulf countries reveals "that higher education in the Gulf States is helping to transform Gulf societies, by increasing labour market nationalisation, reducing youth unemployment, reducing the emigration of highly skilled labour, reducing currency outflows caused by nationals studying overseas, and by contributing to the creation of more highly diversified, knowledge-based economies" (p. 81). According to Wilkins (2011), one of the primary benefits of international campuses has been the introduction of part-time study, which allows GCC nationals to continue working while they undertake their higher education studies. With these options available, branch campuses have contributed substantially to the increased higher education participation rates across the GCC countries. The study also suggests that young nationals studying at these international campuses have been able to acquire the knowledge and skills necessary for employment in the highly competitive private sectors.

Health. In the media across the GCC countries, discussions of health, and particularly lifestyle diseases such as obesity and diabetes, are becoming commonplace (Al-Adawi, 2006; Barker, 2013; Booz Allen Hamilton, 2012; Slackman, 2010; Stott, 2012). Slackman (2010) singled out Qatar in a *New York Times* article discussing high obesity rates, particularly among males. With nearly 37% of boys between the ages of 12 and 17 found to be obese in Qatar in 2003–2004, and rates steadily growing over time, there is a rising concern about the health prospects for Qatari children. Qatar has one of the highest childhood obesity rates among boys in the region, according to the International Association for the Study of Obesity ([IASO], 2013). An unnamed member of the Al Thani Qatari ruling family is quoted in the *New York Times* article as saying, "The typical Qatari student skipped breakfast, then ate a snack and lunch at school. When students return home they are given another lunch, generally a heavy meal of rice and lamb. Later, they snack on cake and tea. And then at night they eat dinner, often fast food that is delivered" (as cited in Slackman, 2010). Table 6.1 illustrates the childhood obesity rates by gender and country across the GCC countries, for years when data were available. It can be seen that boys in both Qatar and Kuwait are substantially (10 percentage points or more) more obese than girls, while girls in Bahrain are substantially more obese than boys. In the United Arab Emirates and Saudi Arabia there is little difference between the genders.

The United Arab Emirates has been the subject of far more research on health and lifestyle diseases than other countries in the region, and there is a wealth of literature on obesity and diabetes in particular. In their article "Dietary habits associated with obesity among adolescents in Dubai, United Arab Emirates," bin Zaal, Musaiger, and D'Souza (2009) state,

Table 6.1 Childhood Obesity Rates in the GCC Countries by Gender

Country	Prevalence of Childhood Obesity (%)		
	Male	Female	Year(s)
United Arab Emirates	33.0	34.8	2011
Kuwait	60.4	41.4	2010–2011
Saudi Arabia	16.1	18.3	1994–1998
Bahrain	29.9	42.4	2000
Oman	—	—	—
Qatar	36.3	24.8	2003–2004

Source: IASO (2013).

"Recent research in the U.A.E. suggests that the prevalence of childhood obesity is increasing dramatically, surpassing the high levels of obesity found amongst children and adolescents in the U.S. and Europe" (p. 437). Stott (2012), in a study on childhood obesity in the United Arab Emirates, citing a study conducted by Al-Haddad, Al-Numaimi, Little, and Thabitamerican (2000), reported finding a two to three times greater frequency of obesity in the United Arab Emirates than the recently published international standards. Al-Hourani and colleagues (2003) looked at the prevalence of overweight females aged 11–16 years in the United Arab Emirates; their study showed that (at 33%) the subjects aged 11 and 12 years had the highest prevalence of being overweight and were at greatest risk for being overweight.

Also in the United Arab Emirates in 2005, the World Health Organization (WHO), in cooperation with the Centers for Disease Control and Prevention (CDC) and the Ministry of Education (MOE), conducted a UAE-wide Global School-Based Student Health Survey of 7th- to 10th-grade students across governmental and private schools (Fikry & Al-Matroushi, 2005). Survey results revealed that over a third of the students between the ages of 13 and 15 were either overweight or at risk of becoming overweight (Fikry & Al-Matroushi, 2005). The survey also found that only 19.5% of students had any form of exercise or physical activity on a daily basis for at least 1 hour a day, including physical education hours, if offered at school (Fikry & Al-Matroushi, 2005). On the contrary, 38.8% of students spent at least 3 hours a day doing sedentary activities like using the computer or watching TV (Fikry & Al-Matroushi, 2005).

Stott (2012) cites data from a 2006 United Arab Emirates Ministry of Health Annual Report that "showed that of the 304 persons with diabetes mellitus among school-age children 4–19 years old in 2005, 229 (75.3%) were Emiratis and 24.7% Expatriates" (Statistical News, 2006, p. 1). Significantly, the report stated that one of the main contributing factors to diminished exercise tolerance in overweight children with type II diabetes is the lack of physical activity in schools (Statistical News, 2006). In 2012, secondary schools across the United Arab Emirates replaced physical education (PE) classes for Emirati boys with two 45-minute military training classes each week (Al Kadri, personal communication, 2013). For girls in secondary school, while some classes are still allocated to physical education, they are typically not considered important and are often replaced with other classes or activities. In addition, in 2012, it was reported that half of all physical education teachers in government schools in the United Arab Emirates were themselves overweight, and of those 36% of men and 20% of women teachers were in the obese range (Ahmed, 2012b). Linked to this, Stott (2012) discussed a study on the United Arab Emirates by Henry, Lightowler, and Al-Hourani (2004) that looked at energy expenditure in female adolescents. She states that Henry and colleagues found less TV watching on school days (less than 2 hours a day) compared to weekends (3 hours), but no significant difference in any energy expenditure parameters (physical activity level or activity-related energy) between school days and weekends, indicating a lack of physical education in schools (Henry et al., 2004 as cited in Stott, 2012). It should be noted though that in 2013 ADEC announced changes to the PE curriculum that would incorporate health studies in addition to revamping healthy eating policies ("Abu Dhabi Education Council introduces new changes for forthcoming academic year," 2013; "Abu Dhabi Education Council issues healthy eating guides," 2013).

Similar to the United Arab Emirates and Qatar, Kuwait also has high rates of lifestyle disease in both males and females. According to the International Diabetes Federation ([IDF], 2012) and the Food and Agriculture Organization ([FAO], 2013), Kuwait ranks first in prevalence of diabetes and obesity in the Middle East and North Africa (MENA) region and among the top 10 for both in the world. Increasingly, children are becoming victims of diabetes, with type II diabetes patients in Kuwait being the youngest in the world (Dasman Diabetes Institute, 2013). According to the FAO's Nutrition Profile on Kuwait (Al-Hamad, 2006), at least 70% of Kuwaitis' daily food intake consists of fatty products such as heavily fried food, oil, and full cream, much higher than the daily requirement of only 30%. A study conducted by Aljamal and Bagnied (2012) also found that in recent years, Kuwaitis have replaced their traditional diets with very high-fat foods, as a result of rising incomes. Around 80% of respondents interviewed in the study indicated that they either ate out or ordered in fast-food meals three times a week (Aljamal & Bagnied, 2012), which is suggestive of the high diabetes and obesity rates in the country.

Overall, as can be seen in Table 6.2, four out of the six Gulf countries are in the top 10 countries in the world for prevalence of diabetes, and five are in the top 20 for obesity (with this being likely to increase rapidly given current rates of childhood obesity). The lack of PE classes in schools, combined with the poor physical fitness of PE teachers themselves, is unlikely to help this situation. The fact that some governments, such as the United Arab Emirates, have even decreased the number of PE hours to zero for boys points to a serious misunderstanding of the ways in which health and education are linked. In addition to the low number of hours for PE, there are also no classes dedicated to health lessons in order to at least inform students about healthy lifestyles and eating. A 2010 list of approved healthy foods published by the UAE MOE contained items such as chocolate and cheese croissants, showing that officials themselves had very little knowledge about healthy lifestyles (Stott, 2012).

Thus, while there are no economic studies looking at the returns to education in terms of health outcomes in the region, it is clear that there are

Table 6.2. Prevalence of Noncommunicable Lifestyle Diseases in the GCC Countries and the World

Country	Prevalence of Diabetes (%)[a]	Global Ranking[a]	Prevalence of Obesity (%)[b]	Global Ranking[b]
	2012		2008	
United Arab Emirates	18.87	11	33.7	15
Kuwait	23.86	6	42.8	8
Saudi Arabia	23.38	7	35.2	11
Bahrain	22.40	9	32.6	19
Oman	10.16	57	22.1	68
Qatar	23.33	8	33.1	17
Nauru	30.07	2	71.1	1
World	8.5	—	11.7	—

Sources: (*a*) IDF (2012); (*b*) FAO (2013).

currently some very real trends in lifestyle diseases, in particular that are linked to education. There is a great need for more research in this area as there is strong evidence from elsewhere that suggests that if people are more educated, then they are less likely to suffer from these diseases. This again makes the argument that in the case of males in the GCC countries, encouraging them to stay in school would not only increase their potential earnings but also improve their health.

Crime. Health is not the only area where the potential for positive returns to education is yet to be fully considered in the GCC countries. Crime rates across the GCC countries are also on the increase, and youth crime, in particular committed by males, is reaching new levels (International Centre for Prison Studies [ICPS], 2011). While underreported, statistics that are available indicate that there are growing problems with criminal behavior such as theft, assault, and even murder among national populations ("2 Emirati men sentenced in youth's rape case," 2007; Agence France Press [AFP], 2013a,b; Al Amir, 2013a–c; Al Khoori, 2013b; AP, 2013; Toumi, 2013c,d; Tutton, 2010; Vaidya, 2013). While the overall rates of homicide (at least those publically reported) are low in comparison to the rest of the world, prisoner rates vary significantly. The United Arab Emirates and Saudi Arabia both have significantly more prisoners per 100,000 of the population than the world average, while Kuwait and Bahrain are not far behind. Only Qatar and Oman have very low rates, although the most recent data for Qatar is over 10 years old (Table 6.3).

Table 6.3. Crime Rates in the GCC Countries and the World

Country	Homicide Rate per 100,000 Population[a]	Year	Annual Prevalence of Opiate Drug Use as a (%) of the Population Aged 15–64[b]	Year	Prisoner Rate per 100,000 Population[c]	Year
Kuwait	2.2	2009	0.17	2004	137	2010
Bahrain	0.5	2011	—	—	136	2010
Oman	0.7	2008	—	—	61	2002
Qatar	0.9	2008	—	—	41	2008
Saudi Arabia	1.0	2007	0.06	2006	178	2009
United Arab Emirates	0.8	2006	0.02	2004	238	2006
World	7.6	2003–2008	0.3–0.5	2008–2009	146	2010

Sources: (a) UNODC (2013); (b) UNODC (2011); (c) ICPS (2011).

While there are currently no studies examining returns to education in relation to crime or incarceration trends, in a study on school dropouts in the United Arab Emirates researchers studied men in a central prison in the at country (Ridge et al., 2013). They found that in total, 246 men, both Emirati and non-Emirati, were serving time in prison as of September 2013. Twenty-one percent of them were Emirati, and were serving time for crimes such as consuming or dealing drugs (49%), check fraud (19.6%), and theft (13.7%). Of these 51 Emiratis, approximately 73% had dropped out of school before completing their education (Ridge et al., 2013). While these figures do not prove any causality between dropping out of school and imprisonment, they are definitely suggestive that Emirati males who leave school may be at a higher risk of getting incarcerated (Ridge et al., 2013). This is also the case for non-Emirati male inmates, whereby an alarming 95% have dropped out of school.

As suggested by the 49% of Emirati prisoners serving time for drug-related crimes in the United Arab Emirates prisons, drug use is emerging as a particularly large problem across the GCC countries. In 2006, Saudi Arabia accounted for nearly a quarter of all amphetamine seizures worldwide (Constantine & Meenaghan, 2008). Seizures continued to rise and amounted to 12.8 metric tons in 2008, out of a total of 15.3 metric tons for the Near and Middle East/Southwest Asia region as a whole (UNODC, 2010). According to UNODC's World Drug Report 2010, "Lebanon, Turkey, the United Arab Emirates and Yemen identified Saudi Arabia as a major destination for amphetamine (or specifically Captagon) trafficked on their territory in 2008, while Gulf States generally were destinations mentioned by the Syrian Arab Republic and Jordan" (p. 208). The United Arab Emirates and nearby GCC states have also been reported to be popular stations in the drug trade route that travels out of the region to Asia and then to Europe (Constantine & Meenaghen, 2008). Figure 6.1 shows that despite the small size of the Gulf States, they are still a significant destination for heroin.

While there is a lack of statistics relating to crime, figures from national newspaper reports claim that there has been an increase in youth crime in many of the countries in the GCC (Al-Hussain, 2009; Al Musalmy, 2010; "Juvenile delinquency on the rise in UAE," 2011; Toumi, 2013c,d). In the United Arab Emirates, "Statistics released by the UAE Ministry of Social Affairs and the Family and Juveniles Prosecution in Dubai show that the number of juveniles who committed robbery and assault in the country, and those who have been housed in the UAE's five juvenile care centers reached 848 in 2009, increasing 32 percent compared to 2008," Al-Awadi said in a study published by the Abu Dhabi-based Emirates Centre for Strategic Studies and Research ("Juvenile delinquency on the rise in UAE," 2011). Figures also revealed that 258 of the juveniles registered by the ministry in 2009, or 38% of the total number, were born to

Figure 6.1. Destinations of Heroin Consignments Seized in Pakistan, by Region (2002–2010)

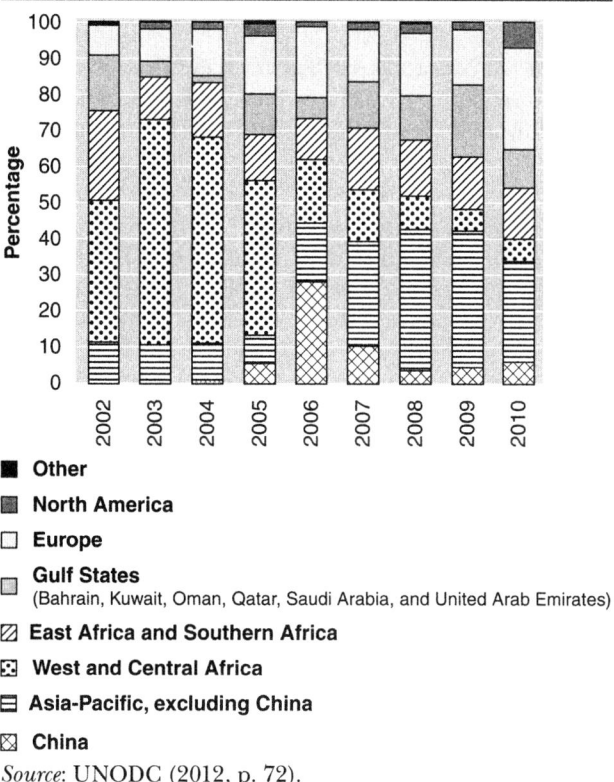

Source: UNODC (2012, p. 72).

national parents, while juveniles with a UAE national father and a foreign mother amounted to 425, a ratio of 62% of the total housed in care centers (Kilpatrick, 2011).

In Saudi Arabia, seven young national men were executed for armed robbery committed when they were 15 ("Saudi Arabia executes 7 for juvenile crime," 2013). According to a report released by The Saudi Arabian Monetary Agency (SAMA) at the end of 2003, as cited in Al-Hussain (2009), crime rates among jobless youth grew by 320% from 1990 to 1996. By 2005 the crime rate is expected to grow by 136% (SAMA, 2003, as cited in Al-Hussain, 2009). This figure is particularly significant since until just a few years ago Saudi Arabia had a low crime rate, so much so that the country could boast being practically crime-free ("Downward spiral of unemployment and juvenile delinquency," 2004). Even in Qatar, reports of murder committed by youths are now appearing in local papers, the most recent involving the story of four young males who murdered a security guard in order to steal an expensive car for a joy ride ("Two youth sentenced to death for murder," 2013).

Similarly, in Oman, a rise in youth crime has also been reported over the past few years (Al Musalmy, 2010), and recent reports state that males are again disproportionately involved. Batool bint Hasan al Lawati, director of the Department of Juvenile Affairs, told the *Muscat Daily* that male juvenile offenders outnumber their female counterparts by a wide margin: "Ninety-six per cent of juvenile offences in 2010 were committed by males while those by females were as low as four per cent of the total. Offences by females are mostly resolved in a friendly manner" (Al Musalmy, 2011). Kuwaiti officials are also concerned with youth crime and a lack of reliable statistics on which to base policies ("Parents indifference, net cause of 'juvenile crime,'" 2013).

While there is little available in terms of official statistics, from the data that are available it is evident that young men, in particular, appear to be more likely to commit a crime, consistent with global research on crime and gender (Hagan & Nagel, 1983; Steffensmeier & Allan, 1996). There are therefore potentially significant social returns to education for these young men, their families, and society, in addition to the potential private monetary and nonpecuniary returns. Keeping students in school has been shown to have a negative impact on crime rates, and the fact that very few females across the GCC countries commit crimes again points to the need for targeted education policies to engage boys.

THE VALUE OF EDUCATION BEYOND THE LABOR MARKET AND THE IMPLICATIONS FOR GENDER

For governments in the GCC, education most certainly has symbolic value in terms of signifying modernity and giving the appearance of the redistribution of wealth through upholding the social contract. It is also recognized as key to providing skilled national employees who will be able to contribute to economic growth and diversification. Finally, education provides governments in the region a platform through which they can inculcate particular values, such as nationalism, trust in the government (Jones, 2013), and religious beliefs (Center for Religious Freedom of the Hudson Institute, 2008). However, education holds much more potential in the GCC countries than merely signaling modernity and creating competent employees or compliant citizens. The little literature that is available on returns to education in the region, coupled with statistics on health and crime, demonstrates that there are also real social and economic values to education that, if taken advantage of, would benefit both individuals and governments.

When considering private and social returns to education in the GCC countries, it is important to note that there are some clear gender patterns emerging from the data that are contradictory to current policies and behavior. The first pattern is that private monetary returns are greater for males than for females. However, trends in boys' education across the GCC countries demonstrate that boys are unaware of the benefits of continuing their education, both financially and in terms of their health and well-being. Governments also seem to be unaware of the cumulatively negative impact that the current gender-blind education policies are having on boys and men. Compared to females, young males in the GCC countries are more at risk of dropping out (Ridge et al., 2013), committing a crime (ICPS, 2011), being incarcerated (ICPS, 2011), being overweight (Stott, 2012), and dying younger, often as a result of traffic accidents (Saudi Aramco, n.d.). This not only disadvantages the individual, but will also disadvantage any children they have, and the health and incarceration costs will burden governments financially. It is important to also note that young men from lower socioeconomic backgrounds are far more at risk than those from wealthier families, and thus any interventions would need to be targeted for this group (Ridge, Farah, & Shami, 2013).

As women become better educated and live longer, the gap between men and women in the GCC countries will continue to widen and will not be confined just to education. It is not impossible to imagine that GCC women in the future may face challenges similar to those currently facing women in the West. For example in the African American community, 72% of women are currently single (unmarried, widowed, divorced) (Washington, 2010) and U.S. African American males are more likely to go to prison than to university (Stephenson, 2013). This has resulted in a lack of Black male role models, which is now having devastating intergenerational effects that then perpetuate a cycle of low educational attainment, poverty, crime, and family breakdown (Simmons, 2010). Similarly, a 2013 report, *Fractured Families: Why Stability Matters*, by the Centre for Social Justice (CSJ) found that a million children in the United Kingdom are currently growing up without a father, and the report finds similar linkages between educational attainment and a host of negative life choices that impact men and women, as well as society at large. The West has failed to address issues with boys and men that are now having widespread social and economic impacts; the countries of the GCC are on track to see the same problems unless these issues are addressed early. Key to addressing these problems is the education sector. The final chapter of this book considers the future of education and gender in the GCC countries.

7 The Future of Gender, Education, and Development in the Gulf

> Approximately 70% of the graduates are women, 65% of them are government employees and around 30% have assumed leadership positions. I have noticed that women generally work harder and are more keen to learn, hence they have a bright future ahead of them. In my office alone, for instance, 85% of the employees are women. Thus, we have high expectations from them and excellent future plans are ahead. *But to the men, I say: Beware they may as well take over your leadership positions.* (H. H. Sheikh Mohamed bin Rashid Al Maktoum, 2013)

In many ways, what is occurring with regard to gender in the resource-rich countries of the GCC is consistent with trends found in other high-income countries around the world. Globally, as discussed in previous chapters, women are becoming more educated and, as a result, are also gaining important ground in the workforce. Despite a few lingering cultural or social barriers, women are becoming more visible in senior positions and there is a steady narrowing of the wage gap between men and women (Autor & Wasserman, 2013; Rendall, 2013). Autor and Wasserman (2013) write that men's real wages in the United States have actually been stagnating while women's have been rising. Some argue that part of the reason for this trend is a profound global shift in labor demand as a result of new technologies, which have, as Rendall (2013) writes, resulted in a shift from "brawn" to "brain." As manufacturing and industrial sectors have become highly mechanized, the need for men's physical attributes has dramatically declined (Autor & Wasserman, 2013; Rendall, 2013). What was uniquely men's work is no longer so, there are fewer and fewer factories, and while some sectors in the developing world still rely on men, manual work there is in decline too, particularly for routine production tasks, in favor of cheaper and more efficient machines (Autor, 2010; Rendall, 2012). In the 2009 recession, Autor and Wasserman (2013) found that men were more likely to lose their jobs than women, with women's careers seemingly more recession-proof at every educational level, with the exception of the most highly educated category. Alongside these changes in the type of labor demanded, women have also been steadily gaining the upper hand through acquiring more education of the type that firms now desire. In today's workforce, soft skills are far more the order of the day. Women, because of their better education (Autor & Wasserman, 2013), seem inherently better suited to the workplace of the future. Thus, we may well be entering what some writing on the GCC countries are calling a time when "only women will work" (Foley, 2010).

What does this mean for men though, and what does it mean for society at large? Is the fight for gender equality over if women are now better educated and on their way to becoming more employable and, at a minimum, equally paid? Or are we reaching a crossroads in terms of creating a more inclusive definition of gender that refers to both men and women, which will mean that we address inequalities for males with the same intensity that we have addressed inequalities for females?

To date, issues relating to boys and men across all sectors have received scant attention from policymakers or academia. Current global trends hint at a crisis facing males that is changing the social fabric with potentially irreversible consequences (Centre for Social Justice [CSJ], 2013). In 2012 in the United Kingdom, 95% of all prison inmates were males (Poole, 2012; Ministry of Justice, UK, 2013), and of those inmates, 90% had been excluded from school (Poole, 2012). Men in the United Kingdom, as compared to women, are also more likely to be the victims of violent crimes (Berman & Dar, 2013), three times more likely to commit suicide (Powell, 2013), and two and a half times more likely to die before the age of 25 (Poole, 2012). They are also more likely to have learning difficulties (Wellcome Trust Sanger Institute, 2009), and if they manage to graduate from university, they are still 50% more likely to be unemployed than their female counterparts (Asthana, 2010; Poole, 2012). As mentioned in the previous chapter, the report *Fractured Families: Why Stability Matters* (CSJ, 2013) highlights that in 2012 in the United Kingdom, over 1 million children were growing up without a father, and around 15% of these children will never know or see their father. In addition, these children also tended to live in areas where there was also an acute shortage of positive male role models, including schoolteachers. The report coined the term *man deserts* to describe these areas (CSJ, 2013).

The ongoing neglect of the challenges facing boys in the education sector, despite some sporadic attention here and there, is something that should be troubling parents, educators, and policymakers alike (CSJ, 2013), yet it barely receives a mention in comparison to issues relating to girls. Stoet and Geary (2013, p. 2), in a paper on sex differences in mathematics and reading, write that "in contrast to the sex differences in mathematics, the difference in reading, favoring girls receives relatively little attention, despite the fact that the average sex difference in reading was three times larger than the sex difference in mathematics." Recent statistics on education, health, unemployment, and incarceration rates, coupled with the findings of studies that reveal strong effects for fathers or father figures on their son's education and life trajectory, show that there is a strong argument to be made for far greater attention to issues relating to boys and men. Some countries/regions, such as Australia (see Box 7.1), the United Kingdom (see Box 7.2), and the Caribbean (see Box 7.3) have been making efforts to address issues relating to males, but there is still little sign of substantive change in terms of achievement, in particular. In the United States there has been practically no attention given to males in general; however, Black males have recently garnered far more attention.

Historically, governments have found it convenient to place the blame on families for the poor performance and behavior of their children (Coleman, 1966; Lightfoot, 2009). They have blamed mothers or fathers or the absence of them (Garner, 2012; Lightfoot, 2009), but new evidence from a growing number of countries, including our research in the United Arab Emirates, finds strong school and teacher effects that hold even when controlling for family characteristics (Boonen, Van Damme, & Onghena, 2013; Lietz, 2010; Ridge et al., 2013). Teacher effects in particular are now

---

Box 7.1. Boys' Education in Australia: Lighthouse Schools (BELS), 2003–2005

In 2003, the Australian Government founded the Boys' Education Lighthouse Schools (BELS), which worked closely with 350 schools in 50 different clusters to devise projects to improve boys' learning outcomes in Australian schools. The initiative was divided into two stages, Project Stage One followed by BELS Stage Two. Clusters were required to follow a step-by-step approach to improving boys' learning outcomes, which involved identifying the issues perceived to negatively affect boys' learning outcomes, developing effective strategies to address the barriers to boys' learning, and implementing these strategies after consultation with community members. The majority of the strategies that were developed targeted literacy rates; others concerned teacher pedagogy, student engagement, relationship building, and the existence of role models. At least 63% of these projects were found to have a "high" or "very high" positive impact on boys' learning outcomes. Teacher perception reports also indicated that 100% of teachers perceived the projects to be helpful in addressing boys' learning needs. Overall, while the initiative as a whole was found to be a great success, it was unfortunately discontinued in 2005. However, many of the initiative's projects have been integrated as models for other schools to use across Australia.

Source: Cuttance et al. (2006)

well documented, and the impact of a single teacher on the school life of a child can amount to up to a year's worth of learning. Following on from this can be the difference between staying in or leaving school early (Hanushek, Lavy, & Hitomi, 2008; Rumberger, 2011). Leaving school early leads to a host of other problems in the future, including economic and social disadvantages (Rumberger, 2011); thus keeping boys in school and keeping them engaged while they are there is critical to addressing some of the wider societal problems that are often beyond the control of governments and policymakers. This chapter reviews what has gone before and highlights both the challenges and opportunities for education to address the issue of gender and disadvantage in the GCC countries if governments will allow it. The chapter will first summarize what we now know about the gender gap in the GCC countries and then explore the main reasons why governments in the GCC countries may not be incentivized to address issues relating to males, that is, the barriers to change. Finally, it will examine opportunities for the education sector across the region to begin making a meaningful contribution to improving the life chances of both boys and girls in the region.

THE GENDER GAP IN THE GCC

As discussed in the preceding chapters, in the GCC countries females now do better than males across major educational, health, and social indicators, as summarized in Table 7.1. With regard to education at all levels, with the exception of Oman and Qatar at the primary level, there are more girls enrolled than boys. Boys in all countries are more likely to drop out of school. Girls outperform boys from participating GCC countries across reading, math, and science in both PISA and TIMSS. If we look at the numbers of national teachers in all countries, there are more female national teachers than males. At the tertiary level, not only are females more likely to attend than males, but there are also more girls graduating than males even in the scientific fields.

In terms of health, males are more at risk than females. There are more countries where males are obese in the region; in addition, men from the region are also more prone to have diabetes (National Health Service [NHS], 2011) and have a shorter life expectancy than women (Desjardins, 2004). While data are scarce on suicide rates, in the two countries where there are available data (Bahrain and Kuwait), males are more likely to commit suicide than females, consistent with global trends. Males are also more likely to be in prison than females in all countries in the GCC. Data from the United Arab Emirates also showed that in one emirate there were no female nationals in the central prison, versus national males accounting for 21% of the male prison population. There appears to be reluctance by governments in the region to imprison national women, whereas there is little

Table 7.1. Measures of the Gender Gap in the GCC Countries and Country Placements

Measure	Countries with Higher Rate for Girls Than Boys	Countries with Higher Rate for Boys Than Girls	Countries in Which Boys and Girls Are Equal
Primary Net Enrollment Ratio[a]	Bahrain, Kuwait, United Arab Emirates	Oman, Qatar	Saudi Arabia
Secondary Net Enrollment Ratio[a]	Bahrain, Kuwait, Oman, Qatar, Saudi Arabia, United Arab Emirates		
Tertiary Gross Enrollment Ratio[b]	Bahrain, Kuwait, Oman, Qatar, Saudi Arabia, United Arab Emirates		
Secondary school drop-out rates[b]		Bahrain, Oman, Qatar, Saudi Arabia, United Arab Emirates	Kuwait
PISA Reading[c, d, e]	Qatar, United Arab Emirates		
PISA Math[c, e]	Qatar		
PISA Science[e]	Qatar, United Arab Emirates		
TIMSS Grade 8 Math[f]	Bahrain, Oman, Qatar, United Arab Emirates		
TIMSS Grade 8 Science[f]	Bahrain, Oman, Qatar, Saudi Arabia, United Arab Emirates		
Tertiary science graduates[a]	Bahrain, Oman, Qatar, Saudi Arabia, United Arab Emirates		
National teachers[g]	Bahrain, Kuwait, Oman, Qatar, Saudi Arabia, United Arab Emirates		
Youth obesity[h]	Kuwait, Qatar	Bahrain, Saudi Arabia, United Arab Emirates	
Diabetes mellitus[i]		Bahrain, Kuwait, Oman, Qatar, Saudi Arabia, United Arab Emirates	

Table 7.1. (continued)

Measure	Countries with Higher Rate for Girls Than Boys	Countries with Higher Rate for Boys Than Girls	Countries in Which Boys and Girls Are Equal
Life expectancy[j]	Bahrain, Kuwait, Oman, Saudi Arabia, United Arab Emirates	Qatar	
Suicides[k]		Bahrain, Kuwait	
Unemployment rates[l]	Kuwait	Bahrain, Oman, Qatar, Saudi Arabia, United Arab Emirates	
Wages[m]		Bahrain, Oman, Qatar, Saudi Arabia, United Arab Emirates	
Prison population[n]		Bahrain, Kuwait, Oman, Qatar, Saudi Arabia, United Arab Emirates	

Sources and notes: All data are taken from the most recent year available as of 2013. If a country is not mentioned for a measure, there are no data available for that country for the corresponding measure(s); (*a*) UIS (2013); (*b*) Ridge et al. (2013); UIS (2012); UNICEF (2008); (*c*) Dubai represented the United Arab Emirates in the 2009 PISA; (*d*) The only GCC countries to participate in the 2009 PISA were Qatar and the United Arab Emirates; (*e*) Walker (2011); (*f*) Mullis et al. (2012a); Martin et al. (2012); (*g*) Nagy (2013); "Girl Power" (2013); Ministry of Education, Oman, & World Bank (2012); GSDP (2012); Hamdan (2005); Ridge (2010); (*h*) IASO (2013); (*i*) Sicree, Shaw, & Baker (2011); (*j*) World Bank (2013d); (*k*) WHO (2011); (*l*) World Bank (2013e); (*m*) ILO (2013); Arnold (2013); (*n*) ICPS (2011).

hesitation when it comes to men (Al Khoori, 2013a). An example of this can be found in the 2013 sedition trial in the United Arab Emirates in which 94 people were charged: all 69 of the men were found guilty, but all 25 of the women were acquitted (Al Khoori, 2013a). The only category in which women are not faring as well as men is the labor market, where women are more likely to be unemployed and to have lower incomes.

It is important to note at this point that males who are economically disadvantaged are far more at risk than those from higher socioeconomic groups (Autor & Wasserman, 2013; Ridge et al., 2013). This is consistent with the literature from Organisation for Economic Co-operation and Development (OECD) countries which shows that the biggest determinant of a person's life trajectory is not gender or race, but class (as defined in economic terms). The growing number of private schools in the region has meant that wealthy families are able to send their children to higher-quality co-educational international schools typically staffed by higher-paid, better-qualified teachers from the West (KHDA, 2013). While girls still outperform boys in most of these private schools, the difference between genders is smaller than that found in public schools (KHDA, 2012a).

Compounding the issue for less well-off males is that, due to cultural norms and expectations in the Gulf, it is males who are expected to take care of their mothers and female siblings, both emotionally and financially (Ridge et al., 2013). When families break down or polygamy occurs (polygamy accounts for nearly 25% of families in RAK, United Arab Emirates, according to Ridge, 2009), an additional burden is placed on those boys already most at risk of leaving school early. As the divorce rate climbs to around 20% (2008) in Saudi Arabia, 24% (2007) in Bahrain, 25.62% (2008) in the United Arab Emirates, 34.76% (2009) in Qatar, and 37.13% (2007) in Kuwait (Al Munajjed, 2010a), this burden will continue to be an issue solely facing males, but the issue is currently unacknowledged by either the community or policymakers. The reasons behind the reluctance of governments to acknowledge and address these issues are explored next.

Box 7.2. Boys' Reading Commission in the United Kingdom, 2012

The Boys' Reading Commission was a joint venture between the All-Party Parliamentary Literacy Group and the National Literacy Trust established in January of 2012 to investigate the scale of the gender gap in reading, explore reasons why boys in the United Kingdom were falling behind, and provide recommendations for addressing the challenge in schools, at home, and in the community. One of the primary findings of this initiative was that 76% of UK schools saw boys underperforming in reading, in comparison to girls. This gender gap increases from 7 percentage points at age 7, to 8 percentage points at age 11, to 12 percentage points at age 13, and finally to 14 percentage points by secondary school. After finding no biological connection to this gender gap, thus demonstrating that its existence is not inevitable, investigators sought out other potential factors contributing to the gender gap. They found that the gap begins at home with parental support provided biasedly in favor of girls, continues at school where teachers are given few resources to direct at boys, and is finally perpetuated in society where boys are faced with male gender identities that do not value reading. With reference to these findings, the Commission established a set of recommendations for moving forward; these included encouraging schools to promote reading for pleasure, involving fathers in their sons' reading strategies, ensuring that teachers have a library of books that target disengaged boys, and establishing a nation wide approach to boys' literacy.

Source: National Literacy Trust (2012)

BARRIERS TO CHANGE

It would be wrong to say that governments across the GCC are unaware of the statistics highlighted in this book on boys and men, and it would be equally wrong to say that governments are completely uncaring about these imbalances. Governments in the region are, however, strongly incentivized both internally and externally to continue to focus on women and girls, despite realities on the ground. Four key barriers to change are explored below.

Adherence to International Treaties and Agreements That Focus on Women and Girls

All GCC states are signatories to the Millennium Development Goals, Education for All, the Convention on the Elimination of All Forms of Discrimination against Women, and the Convention on the Rights of the Child (Georgetown University, n.d.). These four international treaties and agreements require that signatory countries maintain a focus on women and girls (UNICEF, 2013; Verveer, 2010) until—at least—gender equality (as defined by the agreement) is reached. It is therefore in the best interest of GCC states to continue to refer to and discuss issues relating to women and girls, as discussed in Chapters 2 and 3. However, as boys or men are not featured in these agreements, or in any others for that matter, there is simply no need to discuss or even mention them in the reports that are produced to comply with reporting regulations. As a result, not only are references to boys and men missing in international reports, national reports often drawn from these reports also then fail to mention males.

A Desire to Signal Modernity for Trade and Influence

As discussed in Chapter 3, countries in the GCC do not merely only talk about women and girls because they have signed on to international agreements, they also choose to focus on them to demonstrate to the West that they are modern nation states. Governments in the region have not been slow to learn that one thing that pleases the Western press, and therefore elected Western governments, is to talk about women's empowerment. The GCC wishes to attract trade and tourists to its shores, and it knows that this will be a far easier job to do if they are viewed as countries that support women. As mentioned before, an example of how the woman card is played can be found in the campaign to attract the World Expo 2020 to Dubai, in which Princess Haya reportedly "charmed and impressed the large audience in Paris and delivered an eloquent case for Dubai's plans" (Simpson, 2013b). Elected Western government officials have no desire to be seen supporting countries that are portrayed as oppressors of women, as this directly threatens votes and thus their staying in power. The GCC is fully aware of this; just as they have learned to temper their language on Israel to ensure the support of the United States (Janofsky, 2013), they also strategically emphasize the achievements of women for the same reason.

Political Expediency

While rulers of the GCC countries are unelected, they still have to maintain popularity to ensure that their citizens are content for the status quo to continue. One easy political win is to promote the rights of women and to talk of the value of women to the nation. While Saudi Arabia remains an outlier in this case, the other GCC countries have gone to great lengths to demonstrate to their people their commitment to women and girls. Everyone has a mother; so talking about and promoting education and work opportunities for women is to please both men and women. In the national imaginings, there is often talk of not only the father but also the "mother of the nation" (Sheikha Fatima bint Mubarak Al Ketbi of the UAE). Behind the scenes, the role of women in both family and politics in the region should not be underestimated. As such, it is not only to external stakeholders but also to internal ones that governments in the region speak about the importance of women. Discussing men and boys, however, is potentially a higher-risk endeavor, especially in terms of assisting them. Local media and policymakers continually make derogatory comments about boys and men, implying that their biggest problem is that they are lazy (Young, 2013). There is no recognition that they face real barriers to improving themselves that girls do not. If the same language was used about girls, there would be an uproar, but about men and boys there is scarcely a whimper.

Increasing Availability of High-Quality Private Education

The final reason why governments and those in power in the GCC have little incentive to address issues related to poor quality of education, in particular that of boys, is that their children—particularly their boys—no longer attend public schools. As the GCC has employed greater numbers of expatriates in senior positions, and as businesses, embassies, and consulates have opened up across the region, schools were needed to educate the children of these highly paid Westerners—otherwise attracting them to the region would be almost impossible. The schools that were built to cater to expatriate children, however, are now also the schools of choice for local elites. In Dubai, over 56% of Emiratis send their children to private schools (KHDA, 2013), and while these are of varying quality, the children of the wealthiest are to be found in the best British and American schools. The pattern is the same throughout the Gulf. While local families are typically happy to send their girls to international primary schools, they are less likely to keep them in co-educational environments past puberty; some choose to send their daughters to public secondary school, but not their sons. Of the Emirati children in private schools, 57% are males (KHDA, 2013). The result is that the imperative to reform public schools becomes far less urgent or compelling if those in authority do not have any real connection to the schools themselves. As boys from wealthy families are less likely to be in public schools, there is even less attention given to boys' schools.

It is clear that there are very real gains for governments in the region to address and speak to issues relating to women and girls. However, there are very few gains to be made from speaking about or introducing policies focusing on men and boys. In fact, to do so could potentially only further reinforce the existing Western view of the Gulf as a patriarchal, misogynistic region that only cares about men (AbuKhalil, 2005). Governments in the region, elected or otherwise, have absolutely no intention to do this. In addition, the growing disconnect between ruling elites and the public education system reduces the urgency and personal motivation to take action. Nonetheless, there is the potential for change to happen, quietly, equally, and in ways that would be objectionable to no one—through the education sector. It would, however, have no immediate benefit or publicity. It is not a quick win like announcements of Emirati women envoys to the UN (Salama, 2013), but it would be a long-term gain to boys, their families, their future families, and society at large.

THE POTENTIAL OF GULF EDUCATION SYSTEMS TO ENSURE OPPORTUNITY FOR ALL STUDENTS

No one can argue that access to education has been transformative for the women of the GCC countries. While there have certainly been benefits for men, it could be argued that these have been less and more spillover effects, in a sense. However, there are several simple ways, based on research, by which, boys' education could be improved that would benefit both males and females.

Improve the Quality of Teaching in Preparatory and Secondary Boys' Schools

Of greatest importance, as emphasized throughout this book, is to improve the quality of teaching in government preparatory and secondary boys' schools, which are solely staffed by males. In terms of national males this means ensuring that they are challenged and rewarded appropriately and in comparison to other public-sector jobs. There needs to be public recognition of the service that they provide to their country as educators. Also, greater attention must be paid to teacher-training programs for all nationals to ensure that they are high quality and include a significant practicum component for teachers of both genders. Entry to teacher-training programs needs to be carefully monitored to ensure that those admitted have adequate skills. In the United Arab Emirates, TOEFL testing of 269 English language teachers in 2013 revealed that 71% of Emirati teachers scored below 500, which is the minimum score for undergraduate university entrance (Dave & Ridge, 2013). These teachers were all graduates of local teacher-training courses, and their poor performance raises serious questions relating to content knowledge. Quality assurance of local teacher-training programs would assist in ensuring that well-qualified teachers (both men and women) enter the classroom.

For expatriate male teachers, there needs to be a thorough means of selection in order to ensure that the best teachers are hired, with an emphasis on teachers having some prior experience as well as good content knowledge. There also needs to be a change in the type of contracts offered to these teachers so that they feel more secure and invested in the Gulf education sector. Upon arrival in the Gulf, they should be given a proper induction to the system and regular professional development opportunities. Expatriate teachers should be offered the same opportunities for career advancement in order to create a competitive environment by which the best teachers are rewarded, as measured across a range of indicators. There could also be the possibility that teachers who stay for at least a certain number of years have the opportunity to apply for citizenship, which encourages greater loyalty to the host country.

Introduce Practical Curricular Subjects

Despite attempts to reform curricula in the GCC countries, most notably in Qatar (Brewer et al., 2007) and Abu Dhabi (Olarte, 2010), there has been little change in terms of what is taught for the past 20 years. Curricula remain centered on traditional subjects, with more creative, practical, or physical ones excluded or marginalized. For boys, particularly those at risk of dropping out, the inclusion of subjects such as design and technology, media, fine art, and physical education has the potential to keep them engaged and in school. The biggest challenge to introducing these subjects is the lack of qualified teachers to teach them, as currently very few schools of education offer specializations in these areas. While the College of Education at Sultan Qaboos University in Oman provides art and physical education programs, other GCC education colleges tend to offer only the basics such as Arabic, Science, Math, English, and Islamic studies. For example, in the United Arab Emirates currently there are no universities offering a Bachelor of Education with a focus on health or physical education (Olarte-Ulherr, 2013), although the Abu Dhabi Education Council (ADEC) and Higher Colleges of Technology have announced plans to deliver these and other select specializations in the future (Ahmed, 2012b; Zaman, 2013b). As such, there is a need to develop not only school curricula but also university curricula, and that they match. Ideally, these would be developed together in order to ensure consistency.

Establish Comprehensive Career Programs

There are currently a number of initiatives in the United Arab Emirates, Qatar, and Oman to introduce career guidance in schools (Supreme Education Council, 2011; "Waljat College Invites All Students to Career Guidance Session," 2013; Zaman, 2013a). However, guidance counselors need to be properly trained and informed to be effective. Part of this program should be a work experience component, wherein students spend time in workplaces, trying out possible careers to get a real sense of what that type of work is like. While some private schools offer internship programs, there are no documented work experience programs in GCC government school curricula. National boys who typically imagine entering the military or police have little idea about what that actually looks like or what other careers they might enjoy. Through work experience programs youth get the chance to try out new things or test existing aspirations. These programs would benefit girls equally, but again would support those boys most at risk of leaving early and encourage them to stay in school to pursue other options. Finally, career programs need to explain clearly to boys, most importantly those at risk, the economic value of staying in school so these young people fully understand and develop a long-term perspective about why staying in school will help them earn more.

Hold Schools Accountable for Identifying and Engaging At-Risk Students

Two of the biggest predictors of dropping out are repeated and frequent absences and poor grades (Ridge et al., 2013). However, in the GCC countries, schools are not held accountable for following up on at-risk students to find out why they are not coming to school, what is happening at home, or how the school might be of assistance. In particular for boys it appears that teachers and schools have little interest or responsibility for investigating when students either do not come to school on a regular basis or have poor grades often and across many subjects (Ridge, 2009). Schools need to be accountable for their students and they need to be connected to the students' families as well. A comparative study of systems in Cuba, Chile, and Brazil by Carnoy (2007) found that one of the secrets to the high performance of Cuban students was that teachers and schools in Cuba were grounded and connected to the communities they were in. By rewarding those schools that help and retain students and requiring all schools to be active in this area, there is great potential to help at-risk youth to stay in school.

Introduce a Service Component to Curricula

Finally, in order to reduce the entitlement mentality that is currently being fostered throughout the GCC countries and to help Gulf nationals see the benefit of giving back to their societies, introducing a practical service component to school curricula would prove valuable. This could take the form of some type of community service, such as volunteering at care facilities for the elderly, tutoring younger students, or helping out at a charity. Being involved in service work has been found to be statistically correlated with increases in academic learning outcomes of high school and college students alike, through an improvement in critical thinking and problem-solving skills (Cohen & Kinsey, 1994; Hedin, 1989). Other studies have found that community service also contributes to a student's personal development and character by generating personal values, building motivation, and improving communication skills (Astin & Sax, 1998; Eyler, Giles, Lynch, & Gray, 1997). Thus, community service would benefit both the community and the students involved. It can be undertaken at the school, class, or individual level, but would be organized through the school to ensure that all students participate. Such programs particularly assist boys at risk, as it shows them that there are others who are also in need and that they themselves can help (Kerr, 2013). Often these students have never had the chance to help someone else, which builds self-confidence and a feeling that they have something to contribute to society.

While the above suggestions are by no means exhaustive, each of them benefits boys as well as girls, whether directly or indirectly. However, as boys are more at risk of not doing well or dropping out before completing school, the potential gains from such programs would be greater for boys. If such reforms were well planned and implemented properly, there would be a good possibility of retaining and engaging those students most at risk. Education systems in the Gulf are relatively small and centralized; so—at least theoretically—it would be far easier to implement these changes than in a larger country like the United States.

Box 7.3. Regional Caribbean Initiative on Keeping Boys Out of Risk in Latin America and the Caribbean, 2009

The Regional Caribbean Initiative on Keeping Boys Out of Risk was formed jointly by the World Bank and the Commonwealth Secretariat in 2009 to address the issue of boys who are at risk of dropping out of school, perpetrating crime and violence, and being unemployed or in poverty in Latin America and the Caribbean. The initiative was five-fold and included a contest for best educational initiatives targeting boys, a conference to share experiences in meeting the needs of underachieving boys, a fair to identify best-practices to be used across the Latin American and Caribbean regions, the establishment of a common action plan for countries in the region, and the development of a library of materials and resources for dissemination. Upon investigation of the problem at hand, the initiative found that boys are not only faring worse than girls in terms of literacy, but that boys are also less represented in secondary education than girls, despite being initially more highly represented at the primarily level. This became an indication of males dropping out at the secondary level and eventually doing worse in the labor market and in life. With this finding in mind, the initiative sent out a call for proposals on best practices that target at-risk boys. The call received submissions from 11 countries within Latin America and the Caribbean, and enabled the sharing of innovative projects that have had positive on-the-ground results. After the call, a conference was held that identified a common action plan for participating countries that included undertaking activities such as developing early intervention programs offering remediation to at-risk students in grade 4, introducing students to productive activities employed during idle time, and designing a comprehensive approach to the delivery of technical and vocational education programs for boys.

Source: World Bank & Commonwealth Secretariat (2009a, b)

REIMAGINING GENDER AND EDUCATION IN THE GULF STATES

There is indeed a paradox in the Gulf States; countries that are most well known as being oppressive of women are actually seeing the rise of women in ways that their Western counterparts find simultaneously surprising and enviable. A senior female Emirati from the Ministry of Education, who traveled to Harvard to take part in a Women In Leadership program at the School of Education, commented that she was surprised to hear the kinds of discrimination and barriers faced by women working in educational leadership in the United States. She, in contrast, felt that she had never experienced such things in the United Arab Emirates (S. Farah, personal communication, 2013). Figures released in 2013 estimated that the annual revenue of businesses in the GCC countries run by women was at US$5 billion, making women serious economic players in the region (Soman, 2013). In the Arab world, women in the GCC countries stand out as better educated, more employed, and increasingly holding more positions of leadership. However, lingering stereotypes based largely on Saudi Arabia and on the black covering (the abaya) that women in the region wear keep the image of the oppressed Gulf woman alive. The notion of the oppressed woman cannot exist, though, without an oppressor, and it is in that role that men of the region have been cast. Following September 11, 2001, men were cast in the additional and complementary role of potential terrorists (Ewing, 2008). In a 2004 briefing paper for The Corner House, Hendrixson captures this dichotomous view of men and women in the region in her title, "Angry Young Men, Veiled Young Women Constructing a New Population Threat." It should therefore be no surprise that when countries in the region wish to signal that this is not the way things are, they choose to focus on the successes of women. As women and girls from the region have been excelling in their education for some time, it has been easiest to speak of these successes to Western audiences.

Internally, governments of the region have also needed rallying points to highlight social and economic developments. Again, the educational achievements of women and girls have been an easy and popular story to tell. Contrary to what many outsiders may believe, both the men and women of the GCC countries are happy and proud of the successes of their daughters, mothers, aunts, and sisters. It is one of the rare parts of the world where on a Saturday afternoon you will see many men taking their children (boys and girls) out alone to the local mall. This is not to say that there are still no challenges facing women in the region, especially challenges embedded in the legal framework, that threaten a woman's independence on different levels, as discussed in Chapter 3. However, while the successes of women and girls in the region are heralded internally and externally, the poor achievement and retention of boys goes unmentioned, except perhaps to serve as a comparison point for girls.

The blame for this one-sided approach to gender cannot be laid solely at the feet of the governments of the Gulf. They merely echo a global discourse constructed by Western governments and academia. The common view of gender relations in the West appears to be that it is a zero-sum game (Linder, 2008), whereby if one sex benefits the other loses, but that is not the way it has to be. Rather, we need to see gains to one group as gains to both, and losses to one group as losses to both. Studies from a range of disciplines and organizations are warning of profound social shifts arising from disadvantaged males (CSJ, 2013; European Commission, 2009; Harding, 2009; Husseini, 2009). Had these reports been about women and girls, there is little doubt that there would be both international and national attention given to the issue and programs rolled out across countries. However, the lack of a cohesive voice for men has meant that these reports receive a few days of local press and then disappear. Meanwhile, across the world, young males continue to languish in school and to be more likely to commit crimes, among a host of other social issues. Between 1982 and 2012, 67 mass shootings took place in the United States, killing and injuring around 1,000 people (Follman, Aronson, & Pan, 2013). All except one were committed by males and close to half took place in schools or workplaces. Yet, the debates that swirl around in the aftermath of such tragedies focus on gun regulation (Follman et al., 2013) instead of what is going so wrong that boys are almost always the sole perpetrators of such crimes.

There has been little attention given to schools and the role they play in helping young men become meaningful, fulfilled members of society. In the Gulf, while mass shootings are not the order of the day, increasing reports of male violence, typically toward other males (Aghaddir, 2013; Al Khoori, 2013c; Duffy, 2013; "Lebanese killed in sword attack at Kuwait mall," 2012), have not promoted any examination of the education systems in which these boys have been socialized. Current research demonstrates that schools and teachers can impact students; so now, more than ever, education systems in the region need to be scrutinized and issues related to gender addressed. Unless governments in the Gulf start to address the growing inequalities for boys and see gender as something pertaining to both males and females, there will be a cost for families and societies in the region.

For governments in the GCC, openly addressing issues related to boys is likely to generate fierce criticism. This is due to the fact that they will have to contend with taking a policy stance that is unpopular in the West and they will have to do it in the context of already being stereotyped as societies that are patriarchal and male dominated. In charting a new path, countries in the region will have to find new advisors who will not simply echo dominant global discourses on education and gender. They will need to start trusting their own experts, experiences, and statistics in order to effectively address their own particular challenges relating to gender. In a sense, governments across the GCC stand at a crossroads. For a sustainable and stable future of their own making, they will need to decide what they care more about—their people or their image. Some may argue that they have already chosen, but I prefer to wait and see.

Notes

Introduction

1. In this book, the term *West* will refer to Australia, New Zealand, the United States, Canada, and Western European countries. The term *Global South* will refer to all remaining countries.

Chapter 1

1. The Cooperation Council for the Arab States of the Gulf (CCASG), also known as the Gulf Cooperation Council (GCC), established in 1981, is a political and economic union of the Arab states bordering the Persian Gulf and located on or near the Arabian Peninsula, namely, Bahrain, Kuwait, Oman, Qatar, Saudi Arabia, and United Arab Emirates.

2. The New School Model was developed by ADEC in 2009 as an innovative tool for learning. It combines a student-centered approach with modern teaching methods, a standardized schooling environment across Abu Dhabi, and biliterate education to improve students' learning outcomes (ADEC, n.d.). To date, its success has been limited.

3. Name adapted from MOE, Oman, and the World Bank report (2012).

4. This figure was taken from a report by Al-Belushi, Al-Adawi, and Al-Ketani in 1999. The statistical book published by the MOE, Oman, in 2002, on the other hand, gives the number 373 (Rassekh, 2004).

Chapter 2

1. For the purpose of this chapter, "school life expectancy" reflects the number of years a person spends within the primary to tertiary stages of education.

Chapter 3

1. Samuel Huntington famously described the "Davos Men" in 2004 as a global elite who "have little need for national loyalty, view national boundaries as obstacles that thankfully are vanishing, and see national governments as residues from the past whose only useful function is to facilitate the elite's global operations."

Notes

2. The GCC consulting market was estimated at close to US$2 billion in 2011–2012, according to Source Information Services (2013). Business in Saudi Arabia accounts for $791 million alone. The greatest growth is in the public-sector market.

Chapter 4

1. Boys' Education Lighthouse Schools Programme (Holland, 2003) and the Hands on Learning Program (Kerr, 2013) are two programs that were developed in Australia with the purpose of re-engaging and motivating students who are at risk of leaving or underperforming at school. In the United Kingdom, Mayor's Mentoring Programme "delivers 12-month mentoring relationships to 1,000 Black boys aged 10–16 who are at risk of offending, or of being not in education, employment or training (NEET)" ("Mayor's Mentoring Programme," 2013).

2. These were based on an instrument modified from an earlier one by Shacter and Thum (2004), and used 12 teaching performance standards: content, lesson objectives, presentation, structure and pacing, activities, questions, feedback, grouping, thinking, motivating, environment, and teacher knowledge of students. Each teacher received a score from 1 to 6 for each of these categories, with 1 being highly ineffective and 6 being exemplary.

3. The 2007 TIMSS, in which Dubai participated for the first time as a benchmarking state, released a report, in December 2008, which stated that teachers in Dubai had been required to take one of these tests, either IELTS or TOEFL. This is not the case, though, in schools located in emirates outside of Dubai.

Chapter 5

1. The Arab Spring refers to a series of antigovernment protests that started in late 2010 in Tunisia and spread across the Middle East and North Africa (Doucet, 2013).

2. Applied Technology High Schools accept students aged 15–18 at four campuses in Abu Dhabi, Dubai, Ras Al Khaimah, and Fujairah. These schools provide professional training for jobs in the energy and industrial sectors, requiring community service and promoting civic responsibility through programs provided in cooperation with the military. The ATHS program aims to absorb one-third of Emirati students from other schools; yet, only the Abu Dhabi campus is open to women; so the schools primarily target the private-sector employability of men (Institute of Applied Technology, www.iat.ac.ae/).

References

2 Emirati men sentenced in youth's rape case. (2007, November 12). *The New York Times*. Available at www.nytimes.com/2007/12/12/world/africa/12iht-dubai.1.8707334.html?_r=0

Abdulla, F. (2005). Emirati women: Conceptions of education and employment (Doctoral dissertation). Available at www.arizona.openrepository.com/arizona/bitstream/10150/195825/1/azu_etd_1048_sip1_m.pdf

Abdulla, F. (2006). *Education and employment among women in the UAE*. Boston, MA: Center for International Higher Education.

Abdulla, F., & Ridge, N. (2011). Where are all the men? Gender, participation and higher education in the United Arab Emirates (Working Paper No. 11-03). *Dubai School of Government*. Available at www.dsg.fohmics.net/en/Publication/Pdf_Ar/WP11-03.pdf

Abdullah, M. T. (2012). Webometrics of top Arab world universities, 2012. Available at www.academia.edu/1726819/Top_10_Middle_East_Universities_2012

Absal, R. (2011, May 20). Public school pupils lag behind in language skills. *Gulf News*. Available at www.gulfnews.com/news/gulf/uae/education/public-school-pupils-lag-behind-in-language-skills-1.810305

Abu Dhabi Education Council (ADEC). (n.d.). Comprehensive new school model. Available at www1.adec.ac.ae/ADEC%20Shared%20Documents/attachments/Comprehensive%20New%20School%20Model_Website%20Version.pdf

Abu Dhabi Education Council (ADEC). (2013). Private schools. Available at www.adec.ac.ae/en/Students/PrvtS/Pages/default.aspx

Abu Dhabi Education Council introduces new changes for forthcoming academic year. (2013, August 26). *Gulf News*. Available at gulfnews.com/news/gulf/uae/education/abu-dhabi-education-council-introduces-new-changes-for-forthcoming-academic-year-1.1224318

Abu Dhabi Education Council issues healthy eating guides. (2013, March 20). *Gulf News*. Available at gulfnews.com/news/gulf/uae/health/abu-dhabi-education-council-issues-healthy-eating-guides-1.1160834

Abu Dhabi National Oil Company (ADNOC). (2013). Energy & UAE. Available at www.adnoc.ae/content.aspx?newid=306&mid=306

Abudabbeh, N. (1996). Arab families. *Ethnicity and Family Therapy, 2*, 333–346. Available at www.isites.harvard.edu/fs/docs/icb.topic545407.files/Abudabbeh.pdf

AbuKhalil, A. (2005, October 11). Women in the Middle East. *Foreign Policy in Focus*. Available at www.fpif.org/women_in_the_middle_east/

Abu-Lughod, L. (Ed.). (1998). *Remaking women: Feminism and modernity in the Middle East*. Princeton, NJ: Princeton University Press.

Abu-Lughod, L. (2002). Do Muslim women really need saving? Anthropological reflections on cultural relativism and its others. *American Anthropologist, 104*(3), 783–790.

Adely, F. J. (2009). Educating women for development: The Arab human development report 2005 and the problem with women's choices. *International

Journal of Middle East Studies, 41(1), 105–122. doi: www.dx.doi.org/10.1017/S0020743808090144

Afkhami, M. (n.d.). Gender apartheid, cultural relativism and women's human rights in Muslim societies. Available at www.mahnazafkhami.net/wp-content/uploads/gender-apartheid-cultural-relativism-and-womens-human-rights-in-muslim-societies_mahnaz-afkhami.pdf

Agence France Press (AFP). (2013a, September 11). Saudi beheaded for murder. *Gulf News*. Available at gulfnews.com/news/gulf/saudi-arabia/saudi-beheaded-for-murder-1.1229852

Agence France Press (AFP). (2013b, September 19). Bahrain jails 5 for attack on government offices. *Gulf News*. Available at gulfnews.com/news/gulf/bahrain/bahrain-jails-5-for-attack-on-government-offices-1.1233033

Aghaddir, A. (2013, September 18). Decomposed body found in Sharjah villa. *Gulf News*. Available at gulfnews.com/news/gulf/uae/crime/decomposed-body-found-in-sharjah-villa-1.1232601

Ahmed, A. (2012a, July 30). Mentoring needed to retain new Emirati teachers. *The National*. Available at www.thenational.ae/news/uae-news/mentoring-needed-to-retain-new-emirati-teachers

Ahmed, A. (2012b, August 6). Shape up or lose your job, overweight PE teachers told. *The National*. Available at www.thenational.ae/news/uae-news/education/shape-up-or-lose-your-job-overweight-pe-teachers-told

Ahmed, A. (2012c, December 10). Lack of local teachers sparks concern about UAE identity. *The National*. Available at www.thenational.ae/news/uae-news/education/lack-of-local-teachers-sparks-concerns-about-uae-identity

Ahmed, A. (2013, April 1). Government schools aim to hire more Emiratis. *The National*. Available at www.thenational.ae/news/uae-news/education/government-schools-aim-to-hire-more-emiratis

Ahmed, D. A. (2010). Bahrain. In S. Kelly & J. Breslin (Eds.), *Women's rights in the Middle East and North Africa: Progress amid resistance* (pp. 1–28). Available at www.freedomhouse.org/sites/default/files/inline_images/Bahrain.pdf

Akeel, M. (2005). Dar Al-Hanan to reopen in new location. *Arab News*. Available at www.arabnews.com/node/276692

Al Amir, S. (2013a, February 13). UAE torture dad sentenced to death, girlfriend jailed for life. *The National*. Available at www.thenational.ae/news/uae-news/courts/uae-torture-dad-sentenced-to-death-girlfriend-jailed-for-life

Al Amir, S. (2013b, September 17). Drug accused was 'helping friend to quit', Dubai court told. *The National*. Available at www.thenational.ae/uae/courts/drug-accused-was-helping-friend-to-quit-dubai-court-told

Al Amir, S. (2013c, September 17). Dubai police beat man until his teeth fell out, hears court. *The National*. Available at www.thenational.ae/uae/courts/dubai-police-beat-man-until-his-teeth-fell-out-hears-court

Al Banawi, N., & Yusuf, N. (2011). Impact of the demand of women higher education: A new dimension case: Saudi Arabia. *Global Science Technology Forum (GSTF) Business Review Journal*, 1(1).

Al Enezi, A. K. (2007). Kuwait's employment policy: Its formulation, implications, and challenges. *International Journal of Public Administration*, 25(7), 885–900.

Al Fahim, M. (2011). *From rags to riches*. Abu Dhabi, UAE: Makarem.

Al Gharaibeh, F. (2011). Women's empowerment in Bahrain. *Journal of International Women's Studies*, 12(3), 96–113. Available at vc.bridgew.edu/jiws/vol12/iss3/7/

Al Khaduri, R. (2007). *Omani women: Past, present and future*. Muscat, Oman: Department of Information and Research.

Al Khan, M. N. (2013, February 19). Two-day weekend for UAE private sector but longer working day, says minister. *The National*. Available at www.thenational.ae/news/uae-news/two-day-weekend-for-uae-private-sector-but-longer-working-day-says-minister

Al Khateeb, H. M. (2001). Gender differences in mathematics achievement among high school students in the United Arab Emirates, 1991–2000. *School Science and Mathematics, 101*(1), 5–9. Available from Amazon.com, e-documents.

Al Khazraji, K. (2009). *Challenges facing workforce nationalization in the Gulf*. Abu Dhabi, UAE: Emirates Centre for Strategic Studies and Research.

Al Khoori, A. (2013a, July 2). UAE sedition trial: 69 guilty, 25 cleared as all accused women walk free from court. *The National*. Available at www.thenational.ae/news/uae-news/courts/uae-sedition-trial-69-guilty-25-cleared-as-all-accused-women-walk-free-from-court

Al Khoori, A. (2013b, September 17). Abu Dhabi couple accused of torturing daughter, 4, to death. *The National*. Available at www.thenational.ae/uae/abu-dhabi-couple-accused-of-torturing-daughter-4-to-death

Al Khoori, A. (2013c, September 18). Men assaulted each other in Ramadan tent, hears Abu Dhabi court. *The National*. Available at www.thenational.ae/uae/courts/men-assaulted-each-other-in-ramadan-tent-hears-abu-dhabi-court#ixzz2ffoid17W

Al Makahleh, S., Badih, S., & Sabry, S. (2012, November 29). UAE unemployment issue to be tackled. *Gulf News*. Available at gulfnews.com/news/gulf/uae/government/uae-unemployment-issue-to-be-tackled-1.1112132

Al Maktoum. (2013, February 11). Mohammed bin Rashid's discussion with Emiratis and Arab citizens at government summit. Available at www.sheikhmohammed.com/vgn-ext-templating/v/index.jsp?vgnextoid=4e6f275128b7d310VgnVCM1000003f64a8c0RCRD&vgnextchannel=679b7eaff07cf210VgnVCM1000004d64a8c0RCRD&vgnextfmt=interview

Al Marri, F., & Helal, M. (2011). *Addressing the early school leaving challenge. Education in the UAE: Current status and future developments*. Abu Dhabi, UAE: The Emirates Center for Strategic Studies and Research.

Al Masah Capital Limited. (2012). GCC women: Challenging the status quo. Available at almasahcapital.com/uploads/report/pdf/report_19.pdf

Al Mazroui, A. (2013, May 6). Working women need support, not an early retirement. *The National*. Available at www.thenational.ae/thenationalconversation/comment/working-women-need-support-not-an-early-retirement

Al Mohsen, M. (2000). An exploratory study on the views of modernization of educated Saudi women (Doctoral thesis, University of Pittsburgh, United States).

Al Munajjed, M. (2009). Women's education in Saudi Arabia: The way forward. *Booz & Company*. Available at www.ideationcenter.com/media/file/Womens_Education_in_SaudiArabia_Advance_Look_FINALv9.pdf

Al Munajjed, M. (2010a). Divorce in Gulf Cooperation Council countries: Risks and implications. *Booz & Company*. Available at: www.booz.com/media/file/Divorce_in_Gulf_Cooperation_Council_Countries.pdf

Al Munajjed, M. (2010b). Women's employment in Saudi Arabia: A major challenge. *Booz & Company*. Available at www.booz.com/media/uploads/Womens_Employment_in_Saudi_Arabia.pdf

Al Munajjed, M., & Sabbagh, K. (2011). Youth in GCC countries: Meeting the challenge. *Booz & Company*. Available at www.booz.com/media/file/BoozCo-GCC-Youth-Challenge.pdf

Al Musalmy, S. (2010, October 5). Juvenile crime on the rise in Oman. *My Week*. Available at www.theweek.co.om/disCon.aspx?Cval=4078

Al Musalmy, S. (2011, February 9). Al Batinah region tops in juvenile delinquency. *Muscat Daily*. Available at www.muscatdaily.com/Archive/Stories-Files/Al-Batinah-region-tops-in-juvenile-delinquency

Al Nabhani, M. (2007). Developing the education system in the Sultanate of Oman through implementing total quality management—The Ministry of Education Central headquarters—A case study (PhD thesis, University of Glasgow).

Al Qasimi, L. (2007, December). How women are empowered through business and entrepreneurship. Speech presented at the Arab International Women's Forum. Dubai, UAE.

Al Qudsi, S. (2005). Unemployment evolution in the GCC economies: Its nature and relationship to output gaps (Labor Market Study No. 22). Abu Dhabi, UAE: Center for Market Research & Information. Available at squdsi.com/downloads/Unemployment%20in%20the%20GCC.pdf

Al Shmeli, S. B. H. (2009). Higher Education in the Sultanate of Oman: Planning in the context of globalization. *International Institute for Education Planning Policy Forum*.

Al Waqafi, M., & Forstenlechner, I. (2012). Of private sector fear and prejudice: The case of young citizens in an oil-rich Arabian Gulf economy. *Personnel Review, 41*(5), 609–629.

Al-Abdulkareem, S. (n.d.). Education development in Saudi Arabia. *King Saud University: Faculty researches and studies*. Available at faculty.ksu.edu.sa/25384/Researches%20and%20Studies%20in%20English/Summary%20of%20Education%20Development%20in%20Saudi%20Arabia-Historical%20Project.doc

Al-Asiri, S. (2001, November 18). Non-Saudi teachers banned. *Arab News*. Available at www.arabnews.com/node/216297

Al-Adawi, S. (2006). Emergence of diseases of affluence in Oman: Where do they feature in the health research agenda? *Sultan Qaboos University Medical Journal, 6*(2), 3–9. Available at www.ncbi.nlm.nih.gov/pmc/articles/PMC3074922/

Al-Awadi, A. R. (1957). Education in Kuwait: The vocational aspect of education. *Journal of Vocational Education and Training, 9*(19), 101–106. doi: 10.1080/03057875780000131

Al-Diwan Al-Amiri. (n.d.). The initials in Kuwait history. Available at www.da.gov.kw/eng/picsandevents/first_time_in_kuwaits_history.php

Al-Faruqi, L. (1987). *Women, Muslim society, and Islam*. Indianapolis, IN: American Trust Publications.

Al-Haddad, F., Al-Nuaimi, Y., Little, B. B., & Thabit, M. (2000). Prevalence of obesity among school children in the United Arab Emirates. *American Journal of Human Biology, 12*(4), 498–502.

Al-Hamad, N. (2006). Nutrition country profile: State of Kuwait. *Food and Agriculture Organization of the United Nations (FAO)*. Available at ftp://ftp.fao.org/ag/agn/nutrition/ncp/kwt.pdf

Al-Hourani, H. M., Henry, C. J. K., & Lightowler, H. J. (2003). Prevalence of overweight among adolescent females in the United Arab Emirates. *American Journal of Human Biology, 15*(16), 758–764.

Al-Hussain, A. A. (2009). Poverty in modern Saudi society causes, consequences, and government policies (Doctoral thesis, Durham University, UK). Available at etheses.dur.ac.uk/2148/1/2148_156.pdf

Al-Rasheed, M. (2003). *A history of Saudi Arabia*. Cambridge, UK: Cambridge University Press.

Al-Sharaf, A. (2006). New perspectives on teacher education in Kuwait. *Journal of Education for Teaching: International Research and Pedagogy, 32*(1), 105–109. doi: 10.1080/0260747050051110

Al-Shehab, A. J. (2010). The impact of private sector competition on public schooling in Kuwait: Some socio-educational implications. *Education, 131*(1), 181–195. Available at eric.ed.gov/?id=EJ917182

Al-Zuhayyan, A. (2012, September 29). Bahraini women's achievements. *Arab News*. Available at www.arabnews.com/bahraini-women%E2%80%99s-achievements

Alamri, M. (2011). Higher education in Saudi Arabia. *Journal of Higher Education Theory and Practice, 11*(4), 88–91.

Aldosari, A. (2007). *Middle East, Western Asia, and Northern Africa*. New York, NY: Marshall Cavendish [Google Books version]. Available at books.google.ae/books?id=j894miuOqc4C&pg=PA246&lpg=PA246&dq=first+public+school+in+Kuwait+1911&source=bl&ots=WMiwvjEgrw&sig=TJBcRIDMWBZ8NDe7PgjQaPDUTPY&hl=en&sa=X&ei=maI2UsudPMeMtQbTjYCYCA&ved=0CEEQ6AEwBTgK#v=onepage&q=UAE&f=false

Ali, K. A. (2002). *Planning the family in Egypt: New bodies, new selves*. Austin, TX: University of Texas Press.

Ali, Y. (1998). Muslim women and the politics of ethnicity and culture in Northern England. In G. Sahgal & N. Yuval Davis (Eds.), *Refusing holy orders: Women and fundamentalism in Britain* (pp. 106–130). London: Women Living Under Muslim Laws (MLUML).

Aljamal, A., & Bagnied, M. (2012). Food consumption and waste in Kuwait: The prospects for demand-side approach to food security. *International Review of Business Research Papers, 8*(6), 15–26. Available at www.bizresearchpapers.com/2.%20Ali%20Aljamal.pdf

Alkhazim, M. A. (2003). Higher education in Saudi Arabia: Challenges, solutions, and opportunities missed. *Higher Education Policies, 16*, 479–486.

Alpen Capital. (2010). GCC education industry. Available at www.alpencapital.com/includes/GCC-Education-Industry-Report-September-2010.pdf

Alphonso, C. (2010, October 21). Failing boys: What other countries are doing. *The Globe and Mail*. Available at www.theglobeandmail.com/news/national/time-to-lead/failing-boys-what-other-countries-are-doing/article1370543/

Alromi, N. (2000). *Vocational education in Saudi Arabia*. State College, PA: Pennsylvania State University.

Anbar, Z. (2010). Several female teachers fired in Saudi Arabia. *Edarabia*. Available at www.edarabia.com/4634/several-female-teachers-fired-in-saudi-arabia/

Arnold, T. (2013, May 24). Gender pay gap in Middle East between 20–40%. *The National*. Available at www.thenational.ae/business/industry-insights/economics/gender-pay-gap-in-middle-east-between-20-40

Associated Press (AP). (2013, September 21). Trafficking case against Saudi princess dismissed. *Gulf News*. Available at gulfnews.com/news/gulf/saudi-arabia/trafficking-case-against-saudi-princess-dismissed-1.1233542

Asthana, A. (2010, July 4). Unemployment fears grow for "hopeless" UK male graduates. *The Observer*. Available at www.theguardian.com/education/2010/jul/04/unemployment-male-graduates

Astin, A. W. (1977). *Four critical years: Effects of college on beliefs, attitudes, and knowledge*. San Francisco, CA: Jossey-Bass

Astin, A. W. (1993). *What matters in college? Four critical years revisited*. San Francisco, CA: Jossey-Bass.

Astin, A. W., & Sax, L. J. (1998). How undergraduates are affected by service participation. *Journal of College Student Development, 39*(3), 251–263. Available at www.coastal.edu/media/academics/servicelearning/documents/How%20 Undergraduates%20are%20Affected%20by%20Service%20Participation.pdf

Australian Council for Educational Research (ACER). (2013). Beginning teacher standards in Saudi Arabia. *ACER eNews.* Available at www.acer.edu.au/ enews/2011/09/beginning-teacher-standards-in-saudi-arabia

Autor, D. (2010). The polarization of job opportunities in the U.S. labor market: Implications for employment and earnings (Paper jointly released by The Center for American Progress and The Hamilton Project). *MIT website.* Available at economics.mit.edu/files/5554

Autor, D., & Wasserman, M. (2013). Wayward sons: The emerging gender gap in labor markets and education. *Third Way.* Available at economics.mit.edu/ files/8754

Avancena, J. (2011, March 14). Number of Saudis studying abroad increases. *Saudi Gazette.* Available at www.saudigazette.com.sa/index.cfm?method=home. regcon&contentid=2011031495826

Ayntrazi, T. (2012, October 14). Educating the Arab world. *Al Arabiya News.* Available at english.alarabiya.net/views/2012/10/14/243699.html

Azzam, H. (1997). Preparing for a global future. *The Banker, 47,* 72–76.

Bahgat, G. (1999). Education in the Gulf monarchies: Retrospect and prospect. *International Review of Education, 45*(2), 127–136.

Bahrain News Agency (BNA). (2011, December 22). Education in Bahrain throughout history. *Bahrain News Agency.* Available at www.bna.bh/portal/en/news/ 486027

Baker, D., & LeTendre, G. (2005). *National differences, global similarities: Current and future world institutional trends in schooling.* Stanford, CA: Stanford University Press.

Baki, R. (2004). Gender-segregated education in Saudi Arabia: Its impact on social norms and the Saudi labor market. *Education Policy Analysis Archives, 12*(28), 1–12.

Ball, S. J. (2007). *Education plc: Understanding private sector participation in public sector education.* New York, NY: Routledge.

Bannon, I., & Correia, M. C. (2006). The other half of gender: Men's issues in development. *The World Bank.* Available at www-wds.worldbank.org/external/ default/WDSContentServer/WDSP/IB/2006/06/20/000090341_200606201 41950/Rendered/PDF/365000Other0ha101OFFICIAL0USE0ONLY1.pdf

Barback, J. (2011). The "decline" of women's studies. *Education Review* series. Available at www.educationreview.co.nz/postgrad-education/may-2011/the-decline-of-womens-studies/#.Uw9CcnmD4Ts

Barber, M., Mourshed, M., & Whelan, F. (2007). Improving education in the Gulf. *The McKinsey Quarterly, 39–47.* Available at relooney.info/SI_ME-Crisis/ 0-Important_89.pdf

Barker, F. (2013, July 24). Obesity: Gulf states world 'heavyweight' contenders. *Al Arabiya.* Available at english.alarabiya.net/en/life-style/2013/07/24/Obesity-Gulf-states-world-heavyweight-contenders-.html

Barro, R. J. (2001). Human capital and growth. *The American Economic Review, 91*(2), 12–17. Available from www.aeaweb.org/atypon.php?return_to=/doi/ pdfplus/10.1257/aer.91.2.12

Barro, R. J., & Lee. J. W. (2011). Barro-Lee dataset. Available at www.barrolee.com/ data/yrsch_old.htm

Baxter, E. (2009, December 21). Emiratis employed by federal government to get 70% pay rise. *Arabian Business Publishing Ltd.* Available at www.arabianbusiness.com/ emiratis-employed-by-federal-gov-t-get-70-pay-rise-9888.html#.Ufi_fvFfocA

Benard, C. (2006). Fixing what's wrong—And building on what's right—With Middle East education. *RAND Corporation*. Available at www.rand.org/content/dam/rand/pubs/reprints/2007/RAND_RP1292.pdf

Berger, M. C., & Leigh, J. P. (1989). Schooling, self-selection, and health. *Journal of Human Resources, 24*(3), 433–445.

Berman, G., & Dar, A. (2013). Prison population statistics. *Ministry of Justice, UK*. Available at www.gov.uk/government/publications/offender-management-statistics-quarterly—2

Bieber, T., & Martens, K. (2011). The OECD PISA study as a soft power in education? Lessons from Switzerland and the US. *European Journal of Education, 46*(1), 101–116.

bin Zaal, A. A., Musaiger, A. O., & D'Souza, R. (2009). Dietary habits associated with obesity among adolescents in Dubai, United Arab Emirates. *Nutrición Hospitalaria*. Available at scielo.isciii.es/scielo.php?pid=s0212-16112009000400007&script=sci_arttext

Bollag, B. (1994). There is no glass ceiling: A female president, the Arab world's first, guides the restoration of Kuwait U. *The Chronicle of Higher Education, 45*.

Boonen, T., Van Damme, J., & Onghena, P. (2013). Teacher effects on student achievement in first grade: Which aspects matter most? *School Effectiveness and School Improvement: An International Journal of Research, Policy and Practice*. doi: 10.1080/09243453.2013.778297

Booz Allen Hamilton. (2012). Exploring the growing challenge of diabetes across the GCC and within the United Arab Emirates. Available at www.boozallen.com/media/file/Diabetes-Report-AR.pdf

Bowen, H. (1977). *Investment in learning: The individual and social value of American higher education*. San Francisco, CA: Jossey-Bass.

Bradley, M. (2010, April 18). Schools fail a whole generation in Egypt. *The National*. Available at www.thenational.ae/apps/pbcs.dll/article?AID=/20100419/FOREIGN/704189820/1002/SPORT

Braga, M., & Bratti, M. (2012). The causal effect of education on health and health-related behavior: Evidence from a compulsory schooling reform. Available at cemapre.iseg.utl.pt/educonf/2e3/files/submissions_to_web/Bratti%20Massimiliano_Braga%20Michela.pdf

Brand, J. E., & Xie, Y. (2010). Who benefits the most from college? Evidence for negative selection in the heterogeneous economic returns to higher education. *American Sociological Review*. Available at personal.psc.isr.umich.edu/yuxie-web/files/working-papers/Brand-Xie-edu.pdf

Braxton, R. J. (2011). Managing the unemployment Tsunami: Education and workforce development. *The Journal of Human Resource and Adult Learning, 7*(2). Available at www.hraljournal.com/Page/7%20Richard%20J.%20Braxton.pdf

Bremmer, I. (2004). The Saudi paradox. *World Policy Journal, 21*(3), 23–30.

Brewer, D. J., Augustine, C. H., Zellman, G. L., Ryan, G. W., Goldman, C. A., Stasz, C., & Constant, L. (2007). *Education for a new era: Design and implementation of K–12 education reform in Qatar*. Santa Monica, CA: RAND Corporation.

Brewer, D. J., Goldman, C. A., Augustine, C. H., Zellman, G. L., Ryan, G., Stasz, C., & Constant, L. (2006). An introduction to Qatar's primary and secondary education reform (Working Paper WR-399-SEC). *RAND Corporation*. Available at www.rand.org/pubs/working_papers/WR399

Brinkley, I., Hutton, W., Schneider, P., & Ulrichsen, K. C. (2013). Kuwait and the knowledge economy. Available at ww.theworkfoundation.com/Reports/309/Kuwait-and-the-Knowledge-Economy

British Broadcasting Corporation (BBC). (2012, December 5). Kuwait profile. *BBC News*. Available at www.bbc.co.uk/news/world-middle-east-14647211

British Broadcasting Corporation (BBC). (2013). Saudi Arabia profile. Available at www.bbc.co.uk/news/world-middle-east-14703523

Broomhall, E. (2012, March 7). Bahrain delays "expat tax" by two years. *Arabian Business*. Available at www.arabianbusiness.com/bahrain-delays-expat-tax-by-two-years-448855.html

Brown, R., Copeland, W., Costello, J. E., Erkanli, A., & Worthman, C. M. (2009). Family and community influences on educational outcomes among Appalachian youth. *Journal of Community Psychology, 37*(7), 795–808. doi:10.1002/jcop.2033

Buckley, G., & Rynhart, G. (2011). The sultanate of Oman: The enabling environment for sustainable enterprises: An "ESSE" Assessment. International Labour Office Employment Report No. 14.

Bullock, K. (2002). *Rethinking Muslim women and the veil: Challenging historical and modern stereotypes*. Surrey, UK: The International Institute of Islamic Thought.

Calderwood, J. (2011, August 19). Kuwait University short of space, segregating sexes blamed. *The National*. Available at www.thenational.ae/news/world/kuwait-university-short-of-space-segregating-sexes-blamed

Callister, P., Newell, J., Perry, M., & Scott, D. (2006). The gendered tertiary education transition: When did it take place and what are some of the possible policy implications. *IPS Policy Quarterly, 2*(3), 4–13.

Cappon, P. (2011). Exploring the 'boy crisis' in education. *Canadian Council on Learning*. Available at www.ccl-cca.ca/pdfs/OtherReports/Gendereport20110113.pdf

Card, D. (1999). The causal effect of education on earnings. *Handbook of labor economics* (Vol. 3, pp. 1801–1863). doi: dx.doi.org/10.1016/S1573-4463(99)03011-4

Carmichael, F., & Ward, R. (2001). Male unemployment and crime in England and Wales. *Economic Letters, 73*, 111–115. Available at files.soc.aegean.gr/sociology/Kitrinou/arthra-se-diafores-thematikes-enotites/i-egklimatikotita-ton-neon/sdarticle35.pdf

Carnoy, M. (2007). *Cuba's academic advantage: Why students in Cuba do better in school*. Stanford, CA: Stanford University Press.

Center for Higher Education Data and Statistics (CHEDS). (2012). *Indicators of the UAE Higher Education Sector*, Volume 1: Abridged.

Center for Religious Freedom of the Hudson Institute. (2008). 2008 update: Saudi Arabia's curriculum of intolerance. Available at www.hudson.org/files/pdf_upload/saudi_textbooks_final.pdf

Centers for Disease Control and Prevention. (2012). Current cigarette smoking among adults, United States, 2011. Available at www.cdc.gov/mmwr/preview/mmwrhtml/mm6144a2.htm?s_cid=%20mm6144a2.htm_w

Central Intelligence Agency (CIA). (2011). Saudi Arabia. In *The world factbook*. Available at www.cia.gov/library/publications/the-world-factbook/geos/sa.html

Central Statistical Bureau, Kuwait. (2012). Annual statistical review. Available at www.csb.gov.kw/Socan_Statistic_EN.aspx?ID=23

Centre for Social Justice (CSJ). (2013). Fractured families: Why stability matters. Available at www.centreforsocialjustice.org.uk/UserStorage/pdf/Pdf%20reports/CSJ_Fractured_Families_Report_WEB_13.06.13.pdf

Chabbott, C. (2003). *Constructing education for development: International organizations and education for all*. New York, NY: Routledge.

Chatriwala, O. (2013). New Emir appoints female cabinet member in Qatar government shake-up. *Doha News*. Available at dohanews.co/post/53940108554/new-emir-appoints-female-cabinet-member-in-qatar

Clarke, M. (2006). Beyond antagonism? The discursive construction of "new" teachers in the United Arab Emirates. *Teaching Education, 17*, 225–237.

Cohen, J., & Kinsey, D. F. (1994). "Doing good" and scholarship: A service-learning study. *The Journalism Educator, 48*(4), 4–14. Available at www.questia.com/library/1P3-5855752/doing-good-and-scholarship-a-service-learning-study

Coleman, J. S. (with Campbell, E. Q., Hobson, C. J., McPartland, J., Mood, A. M., Weinfeld, F. D., & York, R. L.). (1966). *Equality of educational opportunity*. Washington, DC: U.S. Government Printing Office.

Constantine, Z., & Meenaghan, G. (2008, September 9). Gulf region sees rise in drug use. *The National*. Available at www.thenational.ae/news/world/middle-east/gulf-region-sees-rise-in-drug-use

Courington, K., & Zuabi, V. (2011). Calls for reform: Challenges to Saudi Arabia's Education System. *Georgetown Journal of International Affairs, 12*(2).

Crystal, J. (1990). *Oil and politics in the Gulf: Rulers and merchants in Kuwait and Qatar*. Cambridge, UK: Cambridge University Press.

Cunningham, C. D. (2002). Affirmative action: Comparative policies and controversies. In N. J. Smelser, J. Wright, & P. B. Baltes (Eds.), *International encyclopedia of the social and behavioral sciences* (pp. 210–214). Oxford, UK: Elsevier.

Cutler, D. M., & Lleras-Muney, A. (2012). Education and health: Insights from international comparisons (NBER Working Paper No. w17738). Available at ssrn.com/abstract=1981146

Cuttance, P., Imms, W., Godhino, S., Hartnell-Young, E., Thompson, J., McGuinness, K., & Neal, G. (2006). Boy's education lighthouse schools: Stage two final report 2006. *Australian Government*. Available at pandora.nla.gov.au/pan/76883/20070925-1136/www.dest.gov.au/sectors/school_education/publications_resources/profiles/BELS2FinalReport1.pdf

Dasman Diabetes Institute. (2013). Kuwait has the highest rate of diabetes prevalence in MENA region. Available at kuwaitiful.com/information/kuwait-has-the-highest-rate-of-diabetes-prevalence-in-mena-region/

Dave, C., & Ridge, N. (2013). Teacher effectiveness in English language instruction. Manuscript in preparation.

Davidson, C. M. (2008a). From traditional to formal education in the lower Arabian Gulf, 1870–1971. *Journal of History of Education Society, 37*(5), 633–643. doi: dx.doi.org/10.1080/00467600701430020

Davidson, C. M. (2008b). *Dubai: The vulnerability of success*. New York, NY: Columbia University Press.

Davis-Kean, P. E. (2005). The influence of parent education and family income on child achievement: The indirect role of parental expectations and the home environment. *Journal of Family Psychology, 19*(2), 294–304. doi: 10.1037/0893-3200.19.2.294

Department of Education, Employment and Workplace Relations (DEEWR). (2013). Selected higher education statistics. Available at www.deewr.gov.au/HigherEducation/Publications/HEStatistics/Publications/Pages/HomeAspx

De Laat, J., & Vegas, E. (2003). Do differences in teacher contracts affect student performance? Evidence from Togo. *The World Bank*. Available at www-wds.worldbank.org/external/default/WDSContentServer/WDSP/IB/2003/10/24/000160016_20031024103517/Rendered/PDF/269550Vegas0Teacher1contracts.pdf

Del Castillo, D. (2003). Kuwaiti universities return to separating men and women. *The Chronicle of Higher Education, 49*(17), A44–A46. Available at ezproxy.aus.edu/login?url=search.proquest.com/docview/214690518?accountid=16946

Dennis, M. (2008). A new approach to foreign aid: A case study of the millennium challenge account. *Institute for International Law and Justice.* Available at www.iilj.org/publications/documents/dennis.esp12-08.pdf

Desjardins, B. (2004, August 30). Why is life expectancy longer for women than it is for men? *Scientific American.* Available at www.scientificamerican.com/article.cfm?id=why-is-life-expectancy-lo

Dhal, S. (2013, March 13). Admission impossible in Dubai schools? *GulfNews.com.* Available at gulfnews.com/news/gulf/uae/general/admission-impossible-in-dubai-schools-1.1158113

Dickinson, E. (2013, March 11). Finding a job is hard work for Saudi women. *The National.* Available at www.thenational.ae/news/world/middle-east/finding-a-job-is-hard-work-for-saudi-women

Dickson, M., & Le Roux, J. (2012). Why do Emirati males become teachers and how do cultural factors influence this decision? *Learning and Teaching in Higher Education: Gulf Perspectives, 9*(2). Available from lthe.zu.ac.ae/index.php/lthehome/search/authors/view?firstName=Martina&middleName=&lastName=Dickson&affiliation=Emirates%20College%20of%20Advanced%20Education&country=AE

DiPrete, T. A., & Buchmann, C. (2006). Gender-specific trends in the value of education and the emerging gender gap in college completion. *Demography, 43*(1), 1–24.

DiPrete, T. A., & Buchmann, C. (2013). *The rise of women: The growing gender gap in education and what it means for American schools.* Ithaca, NY: Cornell University Press.

Dixon, M., & Le Roux, J. (2012). Why do Emirati males become teachers and how do cultural factors influence this decision? *Learning and Teaching in Higher Education: Gulf Perspectives, 9*(2). Available at lthe.zu.ac.ae

Doha rolls out private school vouchers. (2012, October 1). *The Financial Times.* Available from search.ft.com/search?queryText=doha+rolls+out

Doucet, L. (2013, December 13). Hard winter for the Arab spring. *BBC News.* Available at www.bbc.co.uk/news/world-middle-east-25370833

Doumato, E., & Posusney, M. (Eds.). (2003). *Women and globalization in the Arab Middle East: Gender, economy and society.* Boulder, CO: Lynne Rienner.

Downward spiral of unemployment and juvenile delinquency. (2004, April 17). *Asia News.* Available at www.asianews.it/news-en/Downward-spiral-of-unemployment-and-juvenile-delinquency-637.html

Dubai FAQs. (2010a). Umm Al Quwain private and international schools. Available at www.dubaifaqs.com/schools-uaq.php

Dubai FAQs. (2010b). Fujairah private and international schools. Available at www.dubaifaqs.com/schools-fujairah.php

Duffy, M. J. (2013, July 24). Video of UAE official beating Indian driver sparks debate. *Al Monitor.* Available at www.al-monitor.com/pulse/originals/2013/07/emirati-assault-video-defamation.html#ixzz2ffmNqzdp

Duncan, G. J., Brooks-Gunn, J., & Klebanov, P. K. (1994). Economic deprivation and early childhood development. *Child Development, 65*(2), 296–318.

Dye, R. F. (1980). Contributions to volunteer time: Some evidence on income tax effect. *National Tax Journal, 33,* 89–93.

Economist Intelligence Unit. (2012). Accelerating growth: Women in science and technology in the Arab Middle East. Available at www.managementthinking.

eiu.com/sites/default/files/downloads/Women%20in%20science%20 and%20technology%20WEB.pdf

Egbert, A. (2012). A clearer picture: National and international testing in the UAE. *International Developments, 2*(2). Available at research.acer.edu.au/cgi/viewcontent.cgi?article=1007&context=intdev

Else-Quest, N. M., Hyde, J. S., & Linn, M. C. (2010). Cross-national patterns of gender differences in mathematics: A meta-analysis. *Psychological Bulletin, 136*(1), 103–127. doi: 10.1037/a0018053.

Emirati jobs 'are a bigger challenge than downturn.' (2011, September 27). *The National*. Available at www.thenational.ae/news/uae-news/emirati-jobs-are-a-bigger-challenge-than-downturn

Emiratis throng Abu Dhabi job fair. (2013). *Tawdheef*. Available at www.tawdheef.ae/en/HomePage/MediaCentre/Press-Releases/Emiratis-throng-Abu-Dhabi-job-fair/

Employment in private sector sees rise—Employment growth improves among Kuwaitis, expats. (n.d.). *Kuwait Times*. Available at news.kuwaittimes.net/kuwait-employment-in-private-sector-sees-rise-employment-growth-improves-among-kuwaitis-expats/

Engman, M. (2009). Half a century of exporting educational services: Assessing Egypt's role in education the Arab world. Available at www.ecipe.org/media/publication_pdfs/Engman_HalfCenturyofExportingeducational_services_Egypt102009.pdf

Epstein, D., Elwood, J., Hey, V., & Maw, J. (Eds.). (1998). *Failing boys: Issues in gender and achievement.* Buckingham, UK: Open University Press.

Escobar, A. (1994). *Encountering development.* Princeton, NJ: Princeton University Press.

European Commission. (2009). *Gender differences in educational outcomes: Study on the measures taken and the current situation in Europe.* doi: 10.2797/3598.

Ewing, K. P. (2008). *Stolen honor: Stigmatizing Muslim men in Berlin.* Stanford, CA: Stanford University Press.

Eyler, J., Giles, D. E., Lynch, C., & Gray, C. (1997). Service-learning and the development of reflective judgment. Paper presented at the annual conference of the American Educational Research Association, Annual Conference, Chicago, IL.

Fakkar, G. (2011, July 31). Students decry Egypt's refusal to recognize GCC secondary school certificates. *Arab News*. Available at www.arabnews.com/node/386108

Farah, S. (2011). Private tutoring trends in the UAE. *Dubai School of Government* (Policy Brief No. 26). Available at www.dsg.ae/en/Publication/Pdf_Ar/DSG_Policy_Brief_26_Arabic.pdf

Farah, S. (2012). Education quality and competitiveness in the UAE. *Al Qasimi Foundation* (Policy Brief No. 2). Available at www.alqasimifoundation.com/Files/Pub3-paper(Samar.Farah).pdf

Farah, S., & Ridge, N. (2009). Challenges to curriculum development in the UAE. *Dubai School of Government* (Policy Brief No. 16). Available at www.dsg.ae/en/Publication/Pdf_En/DSG%20Policy%20Brief%2016%20English.pdf

Faundez, J. (1994). *Affirmative action: International perspectives.* Geneva, Switzerland: International Labour Office.

Felder, D., & Vuollo, M. (2008). Qatari women in the workforce. *RAND Corporation* (Working Paper WR-612-QATAR). Available at www.rand.org/content/dam/rand/pubs/working_papers/2008/RAND_WR612.pdf

Fenton, J. (2012, July 9). Qatar cuts down on lessons in English. *Financial Times.* Available at www.ft.com/cms/s/0/c7a87610-c9ac-11e1-bf00-00144feabdc0. html#axzz2eyFD4OPJ

Fikry, M., & Al-Matroushi, M. A. (2005). United Arab Emirates global school-based student health survey 2005. *World Health Organization.* Available at www.who. int/chp/gshs/2005_United_Arab_Emirates_GSHS_Country_Report.pdf

Financial Trend Forecaster. (2008). Historical crude oil prices (Table). Available at inflationdata.com/inflation/Inflation_Rate/Historical_Oil_Prices_Table.asp.

Foley, S. (2010). *The Arab Gulf States: Beyond oil and Islam.* Boulder, CO: Lynne Rienner Publisher.

Follman, M., Aronson, G., & Pan, D. (2013, February 27). A guide to mass shootings in America. *Mother Jones.* Available at www.motherjones.com/politics/2012/07/mass-shootings-map?page=2

Food and Agricultural Organization (FAO). (2013). The state of food and agriculture. Available at www.fao.org/docrep/018/i3300e/i3300e.pdf

Forstenlechner, I., Madi, M. T., Selim, H. M., & Rutledge, E. J. (2012). Emiratisation: Determining the factors that influence the recruitment decisions of employers in the UAE. *The International Journal of Human Resource Management, 23*(2), 406–421.

Forstenlechner, I., & Rutledge, E. (2010). Unemployment in the Gulf: Time to update the "social contract." *Middle East Policy, 17*(2), 38–51.

Forstenlechner, I., & Rutledge, E. J. (2011). The GGC's "demographic imbalance": Perceptions, realities and policy options. *Middle East Policy, 18*(4), 25–43.

Francis, S. M. (2013, February 17). UAE school admissions—75 seats...4,500 apply. *Emirates, 24*(7). Available at www.emirates247.com/news/emirates/uae-school-admissions-75-seats-4-500-apply-2013-02-17-1.495209

Freeman, R. B. (1997). Working for nothing: The supply of volunteer labor. *Journal of Labor Economics, 15*(1), S140–S166.

From access to academic success. (2013, November 20). *Times of Oman.* Available at www.timesofoman.com/News/Article-25949.aspx

Fryer, R. G., & Levitt, S. D. (2010). An empirical analysis of the gender gap in mathematics. *American Economics Journal, Applied Economics, 2*(2), 210–240.

Gallagher, K. (2011). Bilingual education in the UAE: Factors, variables, and critical questions. *Education, Business and Society: Contemporary Middle Eastern Issues, 4*(1), 62–79.

Gara, T. (2011, November 30). UAE raises public sector salaries. *The Financial Times.* Available from www.ft.com/intl/cms/s/0/f59357be-1b4e-11e1-85f8-00144feabdc0.html#axzz2fQ6EBmXL

Gardner, A. (2010). *City of strangers: Gulf migration and the Indian community in Bahrain.* Ithaca, NY: Cornell University Press.

Gardner, W. E. (1995). Developing a quality teaching force for the United Arab Emirates: Mission improbable. *Journal of Education and Teaching, 21*(3), 289–301.

Garner, R. (2012, March 24). "I blame the parents," says chief schools inspector. *The Independent.* Available at www.independent.co.uk/news/education/education-news/i-blame-the-parents-says-chief-schools-inspector-7584103.html

General Secretariat for Development Planning (GSDP). (2011). *Qatar National Development Strategy 2011–2016.* Doha, Qatar: Gulf Publishing and Printing Company. Available at www.gsdp.gov.qa/portal/page/portal/gsdp_en/knowledge_center/Tab/Qatar_NDS_reprint_complete_lowres_16May.pdf

General Secretariat for Development Planning (GSDP). (2012). Qatar's third national human development report: Expanding the capacities of Qatari youth, mainstreaming young people in development. United Nations Development

Programme (UNDP). Available at hdr.undp.org/en/reports/national/arab-states/qatar/Qatar_NHDR_EN_2012.pdf

Georgetown University (n.d.). The GCC Human Rights Project. Available at qatar.sfs.georgetown.edu/academics/research/faculty/nprpgrant/gcchumanright/

Ghainaa Publications. (2008). Woman in Saudi Arabia: Cross-cultural views. Available at www.ghainaa.net/ar/Portals/0/saudi woman english.pdf

Girl power! 72% of Kuwait's teachers are women. (2013, May 13). *Al Bawaba*. Available at www.albawaba.com/editorchoice/kuwait-female-teachers-491462

Global Campaign for Education. (2011). A ten point plan for transforming aid to education. Available at www.campaignforeducation.org/docs/reports/ftf/Fund%20the%20future_education%20rights%20now.pdf

Godwin, S. (2006). Globalization, education, and Emiratisation: A study of the United Arab Emirates. *The Electronic Journal on Information Systems in Developing Countries, 27*, 1–14.

Gonzalez, G. (2010). Education and employment in the private sector: Addressing the skills mismatch in the GCC. In *Education and the requirements of the GCC labor market* (pp. 91–114). Abu Dhabi, UAE: The Emirates Center for Strategic Studies and Research.

Goulding, N., & O'Sullivan, P. (2013, July 21). Norwegian woman: I was raped in Dubai, now I face prison sentence. *CNN*. Available at edition.cnn.com/2013/07/20/world/meast/uae-norway-rape-controversy

Goveas, S., & Aslam, N. (2011). A role and contributions of women in the sultanate of Oman. *International Journal of Business and Management, 6*(3), 232–239. Available at www.ccsenet.org/journal/index.php/ijbm/article/view/9715/6965

Government of Qatar Planning Council. (2005, December 29). *Labor market strategy for the State of Qatar: Main report, volume I*. Qatar: Government of Qatar.

Graduates honoured. (2013, June 7). *Gulf Daily News*. Available at www.gulf-daily-news.com/NewsDetails.aspx?storyid=354825

Grant, M., & Behrman, J. (2010). Gender gaps in educational attainment in less developed countries. *Population and Development Review, 36*(1), 71–89.

Grasgreen, A. (2013, February 21). "The rise of women." *Inside Higher Ed*. Available at www.insidehighered.com/news/2013/02/21/new-book-explains-why-women-outpace-men-education

Grossman, M., & Kaestner, R. (1997). Effects of education on health. In J. R. Behrman & N. Stacey (Eds.), *The social benefits of education*. Ann Arbor, MI: University of Michigan Press.

Government of Bahrain. (2008). From regional pioneer to global contender: The economic vision 2030 for Bahrain. Available at www.evisa.gov.bh/Vision2030Englishlowresolution.pdf

Haddad, Y. (1984). Islam, women, and revolution in twentieth-century Arab thought. *The Muslim World, 74*(3/4), 137–160.

Hafner-Burton, E., & Pollack, M. A., (2002). Mainstreaming gender in global governance. *European Journal of International Relations 8*(3), 339–373. Available at irps.ucsd.edu/ehafner/pdfs/gm_global.pdf

Hagan, J., & Nagel, I. H. (1983). Gender and crime: Offense patterns and criminal court sanctions. *Crime and Justice, 4*, 91–144. Available at www.jstor.org/stable/1147507

Hall, R. L., Rodeghier, M., & Useem, B. (1986). Effects of education on attitude to protest. *American Sociological Review, 51*(4), 564–576.

Hamdan, A. (2005). Women and education in Saudi Arabia: Challenges and achievements. *International Education Journal, 6*(1), 42–64.

Hamdan, S. (2011, April 6). Oman offers some lessons to a region embroiled in protest. *The New York Times.* Available at www.nytimes.com/2011/04/07/world/middleeast/07iht-m07-oman.html?pagewanted=all&_r=0

Hannum, E., & Park, A. (2002). Children's educational engagement in rural China (Draft). Available at economics.ouls.ox.ac.uk/15132/1/engagement.pdf

Hanushek, E. A. (2005). Why education quality matters. *Finance and development, 42*(2). Available at www.imf.org/external/pubs/ft/fandd/2005/06/hanushek.htm

Hanuskek, E. A., & Kimko, D. D. (2000). Schooling, labor-force quality, and the growth of nations. *The American Economic Review, 90*(5), 1184–1208.

Hanushek, E. A., Lavy, V., & Hitomi, K. (2008). Do students care about school quality? Determinants of dropout behavior in developing countries. *Journal of Human Capital, 2*(1), 29–105. Available at hanushek.stanford.edu/sites/default/files/publications/Hanushek%2BLavy%2BHitomi%202008%20JHumCap%202%281%29.pdf

Hanushek, E. A., & Rivkin, S. G. (2012). The distribution of teacher quality and implications for policy. *Annual Review of Economics, 4*, 131–157.

Harby, M. K. (1966). Qatar: Educational planning. *United Nations Educational, Scientific and Cultural Organization (UNESCO).* Available at unesdoc.unesco.org/images/0000/000080/008030eb.pdf

Harding, D. J. (2009). Violence, older peers, and the socialization of adolescent boys in disadvantaged neighborhoods. *American Sociological Review, 74*(3), 445–464.

Harry, W. (2007). Employment creation and localization: The crucial human resource issue for the GCC. *International Journal of Human Resource Management, 18*(1), 132–146.

Hartmann, S. (2008). The informal market of education in Egypt: Private tutoring and its implications. Institut für Ethnologie und Afrikastudien (Working Paper 88). Mainz, Germany: Johannes Gutenberg Universität.

Hasib, N. I. (2013, May 28). Bangladesh praised at women deliver. *Bdnews24.com.* Available at bdnews24.com/health/2013/05/28/bangladesh-praised-at-women-deliver

Hauser, S. M. (2000). Education, ability, and civic engagement in the contemporary United States. *Social Science Research, 29*(4), 556–582.

Hausmann, R., Tyson, L. D., & Zahidi, S. (2009). The global gender gap report. *World Economic Forum.* Available at www3.weforum.org/docs/WEF_GenderGap_Report_2009.pdf

Hausmann, R., Tyson, L. D., & Zahidi, S. (2012). The global gender gap report. *World Economic Forum.* Available at www3.weforum.org/docs/WEF_GenderGap_Report_2012.pdf

Haveman, R., & Wolfe, B. (1995). The determinants of children's attainments: A review of methods and findings. *Journal of Economic Literature, American Economic Association, 33*(4), 1829–1878.

Heard-Bey, F. (2004). *From trucial states to United Arab Emirates.* Ajman, UAE: Motivate Publishing.

Hedin, D. P. (1989).The power of community service. *Proceedings of the Academy of Political Science, Caring for America's Children, 37*(2), 201–213. Available at www.jstor.org/stable/1173962

Helliwell, J. F., & Putnam, R. D. (1999). *Education and social capital.* Cambridge, MA: National Bureau of Economic Research.

Hendrixson, A. (2004). Angry young men, veiled young women: Constructing a new population threat (The Corner House Briefing 34). *The Corner House.* Available at www.thecornerhouse.org.uk/resource/angry-young-men-veiled-young-women

Henry, J. K., Lightowler, H. L., & Al-Hourani, H. (2004). Physical activity and levels of inactivity in adolescent females ages 11–16 years in the United Arab Emirates. *American Journal of Human Biology, 16,* 346–353.

Hertog, S. (2012). Redesigning the distributional bargain in the GCC (Draft). *British Society for Middle Eastern Studies.* Available at brismes2012.files.wordpress.com/2012/02/steffen-hertog-consequences-of-rent-distribution-in-the-gcc.pdf

Higher Colleges of Technology (HCT). (2012). Overview of the HCT. Available at www.hct.ac.ae/files/HCT-Catalog-1213-Overview.pdf

Higher Education Statistics Agency Limited (HESA). (2012). Qualifications obtained by students on HE courses at HEIs in the UK by gender, subject area and level of qualification obtained 2007/08 to 2011/12. Available at www.hesa.ac.uk/dox/pressOffice/sfr183/6995_SFR183_Student_2011_12_Table_7.xls

Hodgkinson, V., & Weitzman, M. (1988). *Giving and volunteering in the United States: Findings from a national survey.* Washington, DC: Independent Sector.

Holland, G. (2003). Focus: Engaging boys through boy-friendly teaching and learning practices/ strategies. Unpublished manuscript. Available at www.google.ae/url?sa=t&rct=j&q=&esrc=s&source=web&cd=8&cad=rja&ved=0CGEQFjAH&url=http%3A%2F%2Fwww.educationalleaders.govt.nz%2Fcontent%2Fdownload%2F715%2F5937%2F&ei=ijALUv7PCNDSsgafmIGoBQ&usg=AFQjCNGdztlmLhYbYLFDpiT0LfIxIdGK-w&bvm=bv.50723672,d.Yms

Hong Kong and Shanghai Banking Corporation (HSBC). (2012). HSBC expat: Expat explorer survey 2012. Available at www.expatexplorer.hsbc.com/files/pdfs/overall-reports/2012/report.pdf

Hout, M. (2012). Social and economic returns to college education in the United States. *Annual Review of Sociology, 38,* 379–400.

Hoteit, L., Moujaes, C. N., Hiltunen, J., & Sahlberg, P. (2012, May 9). Transformation Leadership in education: Three key imperatives for lasting change. Available at www.booz.com/global/home/what-we-think/reports-white-papers/article-display/transformation-leadership-education-three-imperatives

Hussain, T. (2007). Student achievement in Saudi Arabia: The importance of teacher factors (Master of Public Policy Thesis, Georgetown University). Available at repository.library.georgetown.edu/bitstream/handle/10822/555816/etd_th234.pdf?sequence=1

Husseini, R. (2009, October 2). Two-thirds of honour killings committed by economically disadvantaged males—study. *McClatchy—Tribune Business News.* Available at search.proquest.com.ezproxy.aus.edu/docview/457466325

Info-Prod Research Ltd. (1999). IPR country guide—Saudi Arabia. Available at www.infoprod.co.il/country/saudia.htm

Ingvarson, L., & Rowe, K. (2007, 5 February). Conceptualizing and evaluating teacher quality: Substantive and methodological issues. Paper presented at the Economics of Teacher Quality Conference, Australian National University.

International Association for the Evaluation of Education Achievement (IEA). (2011). TIMSS & PIRLS 2011 achievement. Available at timssandpirls.bc.edu/data-release-2011/pdf/Overview-TIMSS-and-PIRLS-2011-Achievement.pdf

International Association for the Study of Obesity (IASO). (2013). Childhood overweight % by region. Available at www.iaso.org/site_media/library/resource_images/Global_Childhood_Overweight_Aug_2013_.pdf

International Centre for Prison Studies (ICPS). (2011). World prison brief. Available at www.prisonstudies.org/info/worldbrief/?search=mideast&x=Middle%20East

International Diabetes Federation (IDF). (2012). *IDF diabetes atlas* (5th ed.). Available at www.idf.org/sites/default/files/5E_IDFAtlasPoster_2012_EN.pdf

International Labour Organization (ILO). (2010). Decent work country programme: 2010–2013. Available at www.ilo.org/public/english/bureau/program/dwcp/download/bahrain.pdf

International Labour Organization (ILO). (2013). Global wage report 2012/13. Available at www.ilo.org/wcmsp5/groups/public/—dgreports/—dcomm/—publ/documents/publication/wcms_194843.pdf

Islam, F. (2003, October 4). Women's place should be in the workforce. *The Guardian*. Available at www.theguardian.com/business/2003/oct/05/islam.saudiarabia

Issa, W. (2013a, April 21). Call for 'three strikes and out' on UAE benefits for jobless who reject work. *The National*. Available at www.thenational.ae/news/uae-news/call-for-three-strikes-and-out-on-uae-benefits-for-jobless-who-reject-work

Issa, W. (2013b, February 13). Holidays boost to make private sector jobs more appealing to Emiratis. *The National*. Available at www.thenational.ae/news/uae-news/holidays-boost-to-make-private-sector-jobs-more-appealing-to-emiratis

Jacobson, L., LaLonde, R. J., & Sullivan, S. (2005). The impact of community college retraining on older displaced workers: Should we teach old dogs new tricks? *Cornells University ILRReview, 58*(3).

Jamal, A. (2013, March 31). 43 private schools in Sharjah seek hike in tuition fees. *The Gulf Today*. Available at gulftoday.ae/portal/e37bbb1e-65d0-4138-a339-79eb5e52be02.aspx

Jamjoom, Y. (2012). Understanding private higher education in Saudi Arabia: Emergence, development and perceptions (Doctoral thesis, Institution of Education, University of London, UK). Available at www.albany.edu/dept/eaps/prophe/Yussra%20Jamjoom%27s%20DISS-PHE%20in%20Saudi%20Arabia.pdf

Janofsky, M. (2013, January 8). The sheikh and I: Ghostwriting for a crown prince in exile. *Los Angeles Review of Books*. Available at lareviewofbooks.org/essay/the-sheikh-and-i-ghostwriting-for-a-crown-prince-in-exile/

Jansen, J. D. (2005). Targeting education: The politics of performance and the prospects of 'Education For All.' *International Journal of Educational Development, 25*(4), 668–380.

Janssen, N. (2005, February 28). Kuwaiti MP plans campaign against women's rights. *Gulf News*. Available at gulfnews.com/news/gulf/kuwait/kuwaiti-mp-plans-campaign-against-women-146-s-rights-1.278944

Jepsen, C., Troske, K., & Coomes, P. (2009). The labor-market returns to community college degrees, diplomas, and certificates. Available at www.ukcpr.org/Publications/DP2009-08.pdf

Jones, C. W. (2013). Bedouins into bourgeois? Social engineering for a market economy in the United Arab Emirates (Unpublished doctoral dissertation). Yale University, CT.

Jones, T. C. (2010). *Desert kingdom: How oil and water forged modern Saudi Arabia*. Cambridge, MA: Harvard University Press.

Juvenile delinquency on the rise in UAE. (2011, August 7). *Emirates 24|7*. Available at ww.emirates247.com/news/juvenile-delinquency-on-the-rise-in-uae-2011-08-07-1.411604

Kaphle, A. (2013, May 9). Qatar jails a Nepali teacher on charges of insulting Islam. *The Washington Post*. Available at www.washingtonpost.com/blogs/worldviews/wp/2013/05/09/qatar-jails-a-nepali-teacher-on-charges-of-insulting-islam/

Karolak, M. (2012). Bahrain's tertiary education reform: A step towards sustainable economic development. *Revue des mondes musulmans et de la Méditerranée, 131*, 163–181. Available at remmm.revues.org/7665

Karoly, L. A. (2010). The role of education in preparing graduates for the labor market in the GCC countries (Working Paper WR-742). *RAND Corporation.* Available at www.rand.org/content/dam/rand/pubs/working_papers/2010/RAND_WR742.pdf

Kelly, S., & Breslin, J. (2010). *Women's rights in the Middle East and North Africa: Progress amid resistance.* Lanham, MD: Rowman & Littlefield.

Kenkel, D. S. (1991). Health behavior health knowledge and schooling. *Journal of Political Economy, 99,* 387–405.

Kennedy, A. (2007). Examining gender and fourth graders' reading habits. Available at www.iea.nl/fileadmin/user_upload/IRC/IRC_2008/Papers/IRC2008_Kennedy.pdf

Kerr, R. (2013). *Hands on learning.* Speech presented at the Gulf Comparative Education Society Conference. Muscat, Oman.

Khalaf, S., & Alkobaisi, S. (1999). Migrants' strategies of coping and patterns of accommodation in the oil-rich Gulf societies: Evidence from the UAE. *British Journal of Middle Eastern Studies, 26*(2), 271–298. Available at sulaymankhalaf.com/pdf/Khalaf-and-Alkobaisi-1999-migrants-strategies-in-the-Gulf.pdf

Khatri, S. S. (2012a). English vs Arabic: Qatar University decision continues to stir controversy. *Doha News.* Available at dohanews.co/post/16690774138/english-vs-arabic-qatar-university-decision-continues

Khatri, S. S. (2012b). Latest Qatar University criticism highlights community divide. *Doha News.* Available at dohanews.co/post/23724201539/latest-qatar-university-criticism-highlights-community

Khatri, S. S. (2012c). Sparking debate, SEC to offer vouchers to Qataris who wish to attend private schools. *Doha News.* Available at dohanews.co/post/28254917958/sparking-debate-sec-to-offer-vouchers-to-qataris-who#ixzz2c2WIY7eK

Kherfi, S. (2012, December). Unemployment and labor market participation of UAE youth: The social-economic situation of Middle East youth on the eve of the Arab Spring. Paper presented at The Social-Economic Situation of Middle East Youth on the Eve of the Arab Spring workshop. Beirut, Lebanon. Available at www.shababinclusion.org/files/1893_file_kherfiuae.pdf

Kilpatrick, J. (2011, August 8). Juvenile delinquency on the rise in UAE. *Education News.* Available at educationviews.org/juvenile-delinquency-on-the-rise-in-uae/

Kimenyi, M. S., Mwabu, G., & Damiano, K. M. (2006). Human capital externalities and private returns to education in Kenya. *Eastern Economic Journal, 32*(3), 493–513.

Kingdom of Saudi Arabia Ministry of Education. (2008). National report on education development in the Kingdom of Saudi Arabia. *United Nations Educational, Scientific and Cultural Organization (UNESCO).* Available at www.ibe.unesco.org/National_Reports/ICE_2008/saudiarabia_NR08_en.pdf

Kirdar, S. (2010). *Women's rights in the Middle East and North Africa 2010: Special report section, UAE.* Washington, DC: Freedom House.

Kirk, D. (2011). The "knowledge society" in the Middle East: Education and the development of knowledge economies. Second annual GCES symposium conference proceedings: Intersections of the public and private in education in the GCC. Available from gulfcomped.ning.com/page/publications

Klasen, S., & Lamanna, F. (2009). The impact of gender inequality in education and employment on economic growth: New evidence for a panel of countries. *Feminist Economics, 15*(3), 91–132.

Knickmeyer, E. (2011, July 19). Idle kingdom: Saudi Arabia's youth unemployment woes go far deeper than most realize. *Foreign Policy*. Available at www.foreignpolicy.com/articles/2011/07/19/all_play_no_work

Knowledge and Human Development Authority (KHDA). (2012a). Dubai TIMSS and PIRLS 2011 report. Available at www.khda.gov.ae/CMS/WebParts/TextEditor/Documents/TIMSS_2011_Report_EN.pdf

Knowledge and Human Development Authority (KHDA). (2012b). The higher education landscape in Dubai 2012. Available at www.khda.gov.ae/CMS/WebParts/TextEditor/Documents/HELandscape2012_English.pdf

Knowledge and Human Development Authority (KHDA). (2013). Private schools landscape in Dubai 2012–2013. Available at www.khda.gov.ae/CMS/WebParts/TextEditor/Documents/PrivateSchoolsLandscapeReport2012-13En.pdf

Krause, W. (2009). Gender and participation in the Arab Gulf. *London School of Economics*. Available at www2.lse.ac.uk/government/research/resgroups/kuwait/documents/Krause.pdf

Kuwait Cultural Office. (2006). History of education in Kuwait. Available at www.kuwaitculture.com/about%20us/history.htm

Kuwaiti jobs for Bahraini teachers. (2002, February 26). *Gulf News*. Available at m.gulfnews.com/kuwaiti-jobs-for-bahraini-teachers-1.379382

Kuwait to recruit 4751 expatriate teachers and 440 expats for other jobs. (n.d.). Available at www.visit-kuwait.com/jobs/237-Kuwait-to-recruit-4751-expatriate-teachers-and-440-expats-for-other-jobs.htm

Labour market problems threaten relations. (2007). *Middle East Monitor, 12*(9), 4. Available at web.ebscohost.com.ezproxy.aus.edu/ehost/pdfviewer/pdfviewer?sid=4450e094-3b2f-45f3-8e23-7b3f0bf70d33%40sessionmgr115&vid=6&hid=113

Labour Market Regulatory Authority, Bahrain. (2013). Bahrain labour market indicators. Available at www.lmra.bh/blmi

Laessing, U., & Alsharif, A. (2011, February, 10). In Saudi Arabia, a clamor for education. *Reuters*. Available at www.reuters.com/article/2011/02/10/us-saudi-education-idUSTRE7190MJ20110210

Lebanese killed in sword attack at Kuwait mall: Report. (2012, December 23). *The Daily Star*. Available at www.dailystar.com.lb/News/Local-News/2012/Dec-23/199652-lebanese-killed-in-sword-attack-at-kuwait-mall-report.ashx#axzz2fboUy9pi

Leigh, J. P. (1998). The Social benefits of education: a review. *Economics of Education Review, 17*(3), 363–368.

Levin, H. M., Belfield, C., Muennig, P., & Rouse, C. (2007). The public returns to public educational investments in African American males. *Economics of Education Review, 26*(6), 699–708.

Levins, C. (2013). The rentier state and the survival of Arab absolute monarchies. *Rutgers Journal of Law and Religion, 14*, 388–423. Available at lawandreligion.com/sites/lawandreligion.com/files/2013%20Vol.%2014%20Levins.pdf

Lewin-Epstein, N., & Semyonov, M. (1994). Sheltered labor markets, public sector employment, and socioeconomic returns to education of Arabs in Israel. *American Journal of Sociology*, 622–651.

Lewis, K. (2009, November 29). Lesson no 1: Improve education. *The National*. Available at www.thenational.ae/news/uae-news/education/lesson-no-1-improve-education

Lewis, M. A., & Lockheed, M. E. (2007, June). Getting all girls into school. *Finance & Development, 44*(2). Available at www.imf.org/external/pubs/ft/fandd/2007/06/lewis.htm

Lietz, P. (2010). School quality and student achievement in 21 European countries. In D. Hastedt & M. von Davier (Eds.), *Issues and methodologies in large-scale assessments* (pp. 57–84). Available from works.bepress.com/petra_lietz/49

Lightfoot, L. (2009, April 4). 'Parents to blame' for problems in UK schools. *The Observer.* Available at www.theguardian.com/education/2009/apr/05/schools-behaviour-teachers-parents

Linder, C. (2008). A zero-sum game? The popular media and gender gap in higher education. *Journal of Student Affairs, XVII,* 48–56. Available at digitool.library.colostate.edu///exlibris/dtl/d3_1/apache_media/L2V4bGlicmlzL2R0bC9k-M18xL2FwYWNoZV9tZWRpYS8zMTE5Nw==.pdf

Lindsey, U. (2010, October 3). Saudi Arabia's education reforms emphasize training for jobs. *The Chronicle of Higher Education.* Available at chronicle.com/article/Saudi-Arabias-Education/124771/

Lindsey, U. (2012, February 7). Debate arises at Qatar U. Over decision to teach mainly in Arabic. *Chronicle of Higher Education.* Available at chronicle.com/article/Debate-Arises-at-Qatar-U-Over/130695/

Lochner, L., & Moretti, E. (2004). The effect of education on crime: evidence from prison inmates, arrests, and self-reports. *American Economic Review, 94*(1), 155–189. Available at www.jstor.org/discover/10.2307/3592774?uid=3737432&uid=2129&uid=2&uid=70&uid=4&sid=21102680676771

Looney, R. (2004). Saudization and sound economic reforms: Are the two compatible? *Strategic Insights, 3*(2). Available at www.google.ae/url?sa=t&rct=j&q=&esrc=s&source=web&cd=1&cad=rja&ved=0CCoQFjAA&url=http%3A%2F%2Fwww.dtic.mil%2Fcgi-bin%2FGetTRDoc%3FAD%3DADA524846&ei=0-8_UuibKY_z0gWJqYG4AQ&usg=AFQjCNEZf3MRMUO3CQcunuayPViPCHJAeQ&bvm=bv.52434380,d.d2k

Madany, I. M., Ali, S. M., & Akhter, M. S. (1988). Note on the expansion of higher education in Bahrain. *Higher Education, 17*(4), 411–415. Available at www.jstor.org/stable/3446928

Madhi, S., & Barrientos, A. (2003). Saudisation and employment in Saudi Arabia. *Career Development International, 8*(2), 70–77.

Mahmoody, B. (1991). *Not without my daughter.* New York, NY: St Martin's Press.

Malek, C. (2011, February 9). Khalifa Fund seeks 10 brave entrepreneurs. Available at old.thenational.ae/news/uae-news/khalifa-fund-seeks-10-brave-entrepreneurs

Malek, C. (2013, October 5). Girls continue to outperform boys in UAE schools. *The National.* Available at www.thenational.ae/uae/education/girls-continue-to-outperform-boys-in-uae-schools

Markaz Research. (2012). GCC Demographic Shift: Intergeneration risk-transfer at play. *Kuwait Financial Centre "Markaz" Research.* Available at www.markaz.com/desktopmodules/crd/attachments/demographicsresearch-markazresearch-june%202012.pdf

Maroun, N., Samman, H., Moujaes, C. N., & Abouchakra, R. (2008). How to succeed at education reform: The case for Saudi Arabia and the broader GCC region. Available at the Booz Allen Hamilton website: www.boozallen.com/media/file/How_to_Succeed_at_Education_Reform.pdf

Martin, M. O., Mullis, I. V. S., Foy, P., & Stanco, G. M. (2012). *TIMSS 2011 international results in science.* Chestnut Hill, MA: Boston College. Available at timssandpirls.bc.edu/timss2011/downloads/T11_IR_Science_FullBook.pdf

Masdar Institute. (2013). Masdar Institute's Ph.D. program receives accreditation from the UAE Ministry of Higher Education and Scientific Research. Available at www.masdar.ac.ae/component/k2/item/6103-masdar-institute-s-ph-d-program-receives-accreditation-from-the-uae-ministry-of-higher-education-and-scientific-research

Mashood, N., Verhoeven, H., & Chansarkar, B. (2009). Emiratisation, Omanisation, and Saudisation—Common causes: Common solutions? Available at www.researchgate.net/publication/228365080_Emiratisation_Omanisation_and_Saudisation-common_causes_common_solutions

Mayor's mentoring programme. (2013). *Mayor of London.* Available at www.london.gov.uk/priorities/young-people/mentoring

Mazawi, A. E. (1999). The contested terrains of education in the Arab states: An appraisal of major research trends. *Comparative Education Review 43*(3), 332–352.

McMahon, W. (1998). Conceptual framework for the analysis of the social benefits of lifelong learning. *Education Economics,* 6, 309–346.

McMeans, A. (2010, May 24). Emirati women held back from the workforce. *The National.* Available at www.thenational.ae/news/uae-news/emirati-women-held-back-from-the-workforce

Meleis, A. I., El Sanabary, N., & Beeson, D. (1979). Women, modernization, and education in Kuwait. *Comparative Education Review, 23*(1), 115–124. Available from www.jstor.org/stable/1187634

Mellahi, K. (2011). The effect of regulations on HRM: Private sector firms in Saudi Arabia. *The International Journal of Human Resource Management, 18*(1), 85–99.

Mettle-Nunoo, R., & Hilditch, L. (2000). Donor participation in the education sector in Ghana. *Action Aid.* Available at www.actionaid.org.uk/sites/default/files/doc_lib/134_1_donor_ghana.pdf

Metz, H. C. (1992). *Saudi Arabia: A country study.* Washington, DC: GPO for the Library of Congress. Available at countrystudies.us/saudi-arabia/31.htm

Metz, H. C. (1993). *Persian Gulf States: A country study.* Washington, GC: GPO for the Library of Congress. Available at countrystudies.us/persian-gulf-states/

Meyer, J. W., Boli-Bennett, J., & Chase-Dunn, C. (1975). Convergence and divergence in development. *Annual Review of Sociology, 1,* 223–246. Available from www.jstor.org/stable/2946046

Michigan State University (MSU). (2012). Kuwait: History. Available at globaledge.msu.edu/countries/kuwait/history

Middle Eastern women to watch. (2005). *Forbes.* Available at www.forbes.com/2005/07/26/cz_05powom_middleeastern_slide.html

Mills, A. (2009, August 3). Reforms to women's education make slow progress in Saudi Arabia. *The Chronicle of Higher Education.* Available at chronicle.com/article/Saudi-Universities-Reach/47519/

Mincer, J. (1981). Human capital and economic growth (Working Paper No. 803). *National Bureau of Economic Research.* Available at www.nber.org/papers/w0803.pdf?new_window=1

Ministry of Business and Trade. (n.d.). Rise with Qatar. *Ministry of Business and Trade, Investment Promotion Department.* Available at www.mbt.gov.qa/English/ForeignInvestor/Documents/MOBT-Brochure%20englo.pdf

Ministry of Economy and Planning, Saudi Arabia. (2002). Vision of the future of the Saudi [In Arabic]. Available at archive.mep.gov.sa/nadwah2020/nadwah/nadwah.htm

Ministry of Education (MOE), Bahrain. (2008). The development of education: National report of the Kingdom of Bahrain (Inclusive education: The way of the future). *The United Nations Educational, Scientific and Cultural Organization (UNESCO).* Available at www.ibe.unesco.org/National_Reports/ICE_2008/bahrain_NR08.pdf

Ministry of Education (MOE), Bahrain. (2013). History. Available at www.moe.gov.bh/en/history/Index.aspx#.Uja5xT_gwpo

Ministry of Education (MOE), Kuwait. (2012). Levels of education in the State of Kuwait [In Arabic]. Available at www.moe.edu.kw/SitePages/kw_his.aspx

Ministry of Education (MOE), Oman. (2011). A glance at the development of education in the Sultanate of Oman. Available at www.moe.gov.om/portal/sitebuilder/sites/EPS/English/MOE/eduinoman.aspx

Ministry of Education (MOE), Oman, & World Bank. (2012). *Education in Oman: The drive for quality.* Muscat, Oman: Ministry of Education Publication No. 23/2012.

Ministry of Education (MOE), Qatar. (2009). Annual Statistics Report. Available at www.qix.gov.qa/portal/page/portal/QIXPOC/Documents/QIX%20Knowledge%20Base/Publication/Population%20Statistics/Education/Source_QSA/Education_Annual_Statistics_Report_SEC_AE_2008_0.pdf

Ministry of Education (MOE), Saudi Arabia (2005). The executive summary of the ministry of education ten-year plan.

Ministry of Education (MOE), Saudi Arabia. (2011). About. Available at www2.moe.gov.sa/english/Pages/about_moe.htm

Ministry of Education (MOE), UAE. (2012). RAK English Teachers Data (Unpublished government data) (Doctoral dissertation).

Ministry of Education (MOE), UAE. (2013a). The evolution of education in the UAE. Available at www.moe.gov.ae/English/Pages/UAE/UaeEdu.aspx

Ministry of Education (MOE), UAE. (2013b). Education statistics. Available from www.moe.gov.ae/English/Pages/opendata.aspx

Ministry of Higher Education and Scientific Research (MOHESR). (2013). CEPA maths scores for September 2006 applications by gender-school-study stream. Available at ws2.mohesr.ae/CEPAAnalysis/GenderSchoolStudyPreference.aspx?Maths=1&Year=2006

Ministry of Justice, UK. (2013). Safety in custody statistics England and Wales: Update to December 2012. Available at www.gov.uk/government/uploads/system/uploads/attachment_data/file/192431/safety-custody-dec-2012.pdf

Minnis, J. R. (2006). First nationals education and rentier economics: Parallels with the Gulf states. *Canadian Journal of Education, 29*(4), 975–997.

Mittleberg, D., & Lev Ari, L. (1999). Confidence in mathematics and its consequences: Gender differences among Israeli Jewish and Arab youth. *Gender and Education, 11*(1), 75–92.

MOE opens door to non-Kuwaiti teachers for '13/14. (2013). Arab Times. Available at www.arabtimesonline.com/NewsDetails/tabid/96/smid/414/ArticleID/190785/reftab/36/Default.aspx

Moghadam, V. (2003). *Modernizing women: Gender and social change in the Middle East.* Boulder, CO: Lynne Rienner.

Monkman, K., & Hoffman, L. (2013). Girls' education: The power of policy discourse. *Theory and Research in Education March 2013, 11*(1), 63–84.

Morada, H. (2010). The role of expatriate workers in supporting GCC economic development. In *Human resources and development in the Arabian Gulf* (pp. 125–143). Abu Dhabi, UAE: The Emirates Center for Strategic Studies and Research.

Moretti, E. (2004). Estimating the social return to higher education: evidence from longitudinal and repeated cross-sectional data. *Journal of Econometrics, 121,* 175–212. Available at emlab.berkeley.edu/~moretti/socret.pdf

Moujaes, C. N., Hoteit, L., & Hiltunen, J. (2011). A decade of opportunity: The coming expansion of the private-school market in the GCC. *Booz & Company.* Available at www.booz.com/media/file/BoozCo-Private-School-Expansion-GCC.pdf

Mullis, I. V., Martin, M. O., Gonzalez, E. J., & Kennedy, A. M. (2003). PIRLS 2001 International Report. Available at timssandpirls.bc.edu/pirls2001i/PIRLS2001_Pubs.html

Mullis, I. V. S., Martin, M. O., Foy, P., & Drucker, K. T. (2011). PIRLS 2011 international results in reading. *International Association for the Evaluation of Education Achievement (IEA).* Available at timssandpirls.bc.edu/pirls2011/downloads/P11_IR_FullBook.pdf

Mullis, I. V. S., Martin, M. O., Foy, P., & Arora, A. (2012a). *TIMSS 2011 international results in mathematics.* Chestnut Hill, MA: Boston College. Available at timssandpirls.bc.edu/timss2011/downloads/T11_IR_Mathematics_Full Book.pdf

Mullis, I. V. S., Martin, M. O., Minnich, C. A., Stanco, G. M., Arora, A., Centurino, V. A. S., & Castle, C. E. (Eds.). (2012b). *TIMSS 2011 encyclopedia: Education policy and curriculum in mathematics and science,* volumes 1 and 2. Chestnut Hill, MA: TIMSS & PIRLS International Study Center, Boston College. Available at timssandpirls.bc.edu/timss2011/encyclopedia-timss.html

Mullis, I. V. S., Martin, M. O., Olson, J. R., Berger, D. R., Milne, D., & Stanco, G. M. (2008). TIMMS 2007 encyclopedia: A guide to mathematics and science edcation around the world. Available at timss.bc.edu/timss2007/encyclopedia.html

Muralidharan, K., & Sundararaman, V. (2010). Contract teachers: Experimental evidence from India. Department of Economics, University of California (UC), San Diego. Available from www.fas.nus.edu.sg/ecs/events/seminar/seminar-papers/31Aug10.pdf

Murdock, S., White, S., Hoque, N., Pecotte, B., You, X., & Balkan, J. (2003). *The new Texas challenge: Population change and the future of Texas.* College Station, TX: Texas A&M University Press.

Nagy, S. (2013, March 11). Bahraini and non-Bahraini women in Bahrain's workforce. *Arabian Humanities.* Available at cy.revues.org/2144

National Center for Education Statistics (NCES). (2010). Fast facts: Degrees conferred by sex. Available at nces.ed.gov/fastfacts/display.asp?id=72

National Health Service (NHS). (2011, October 5). Men 'develop diabetes more easily'. Available at NHS Choices website: www.nhs.uk/news/2011/10October/Pages/males-more-likely-to-get-diabetes.aspx

National Literacy Trust. (2012). Boys reading commission. Available at www.literacytrust.org.uk/assets/0001/4056/Boys_Commission_Report.pdf

NationMaster. (2013). Education statistics. Available at www.nationmaster.com/graph/edu_fem_enr_sha_pri_lev-female-enrolment-share-primary-level# source

National Media Council. (2010). UAE yearbook. Available at www.uaeyearbook.com/Yearbooks/2010/ENG/

National Qualifications Authority (NQA). (2013). The UAE education system: Overview of performance in education. Available at www.nqa.gov.ae

Nelson, C. (2004). *UAE national women at work in the private sector: Conditions and constraints.* Tanmia, Dubai: Centre for Labour Market Research & Information.

Olarte, O. (2009, June 20). Women engineering society launched in Abu Dhabi. *Khaleej Times.* Available at www.khaleejtimes.com/DisplayArticle08.asp?xfile=data/theuae/2009/June/theuae_June439.xml&section=theuae

Olarte, O. (2010, September 14). Abu Dhabi rolls out key school reform plan. *Khaleej Times*. Available at www.khaleejtimes.com/DisplayArticle09.asp?xfile=data/theuae/2010/September/theuae_September322.xml&section=theuae

Olarte-Ulherr, O. (2013, September 4). Current training of teachers inadequate. *Khaleej Times*. Available at www.khaleejtimes.com/kt-article-display-1.asp?xfile=data/educationnation/2013/September/educationnation_September11.xml&section=educationnation

Oreopoulos, P., & Salvanes, K. G. (2011). Priceless: The nonpecuniary benefits of schooling. *Journal of Economic Perspectives, 25*(1), 159–184.

Oreopoulos, P. & Uros, P. (2013). Making college worth it: A review of research on the returns to higher education (NBER Working Papers 19053). *National Bureau of Economic Research*. Available at www.nber.org/papers/w19053.pdf

Organisation for Economic Co-operation and Development (OECD). (2009). Equally prepared for life? How 15-year-old boys and girls perform in school. Available at www.oecd.org/pisa/pisaproducts/pisa2006/42843625.pdf

Organisation for Economic Co-operation and Development (OECD). (2010). PISA 2009 results: What students know and can do. Retrieved August 20, 2013, www.oecd.org/pisa/pisaproducts/48852548.pdf

Organisation for Economic Co-operation and Development (OECD). (2012a). Gender equality in education, employment and entrepreneurship: Final report to the MCM 2012. Available at www.oecd.org/employment/50423364.pdf

Organization for Economic Co-operation and Development (OECD). (2012b, May 22). Tackle gender gap to boost growth, says OECD. Available at www.oecd.org/employment/tacklegendergaptoboostgrowthsaysoecd.htm

Organisation for Economic Co-operation and Development (OECD). (2013). PISA 2012 results: What students know and can do. Retrieved January 5, 2013, www.keepeek.com/Digital-Asset-Management/oecd/education/pisa-2012-results-what-students-know-and-can-do-volume-i_9789264201118-en#page13

Osell, T. (2008, March 26). Is women's studies dead? *Salon*. Available at www.salon.com/2008/03/26/womens_studies/

Oxford Business Group (OBG). (2010). *The report: Oman 2010*. Oxford, UK: Oxford Business Group.

Oxford Business Group (OBG). (2012). *The report: Kuwait 2012*. Oxford, UK: Oxford Business Group.

Parents indifference, net cause of 'juvenile crime': MP urges family cohesion. (2013, March 9). *Arab Times*. Available at www.arabtimesonline.com/NewsDetails/tabid/96/smid/414/ArticleID/166541/reftab/69/Default.aspx

Parpart, J., Connelly, P., & Barriteau, V. (Eds.). (2000). *Theoretical perspectives on gender and development*. Ottawa, Canada: International Development Research Center.

Pascarella, E. T., & Terenzini, P. T. (1991). *How college affects students*. San Francisco, CA: Jossey-Bass.

Pearson helping UAE to develop their school leaders [Web log post]. (2013, June 21). Available at blog.pearson.com/2013/06/pearson_helping_uae.trackback.html

Peterson, J. E. (1989). The political status of women in the Arab Gulf states. *Middle East Journal, 43*(1), 34–50. Available from www.jstor.org/stable/4327879

Peterson, J. E. (2008, November 23–25). Britain and state formation in the Gulf: The case of Abu Dhabi and Shaikh Zayid bin Khalifah. *New Perspectives on Recording UAE History, 4*, 207–213. Available at www.jepeterson.net/sitebuildercontent/sitebuilderfiles/Peterson_Britain_and_Abu_Dhabi.pdf

Peterson, J. E. (2009). Life after oil: Economic alternatives for the Arab Gulf states. *Mediterranean Quarterly 20*(3), 1–18. doi: 10.1215/10474552-2009-011.

Phillips, D. (2004). Towards a theory of policy attraction in education. In G. Steiner-Khamsi (Ed.), *The global politics of educational borrowing and lending* (pp. 54–67). New York, NY: Teachers College Press.

Poole, G. (2012, March 18). Men and boys' inequality—UK statistics. Available at brightonmanplan.wordpress.com/2012/03/18/men-and-boys-inequality-uk-statistics/

Powell, J. (2013). Suicide is a gender issue that can no longer be ignored. *The Guardian*. Available at www.theguardian.com/commentisfree/2013/jan/23/suicide-rates-men-gender-issue

Private sector may not keep pace with Saudi youth bulge—IMF. (2013, July 24). *Reuters*. Available at www.reuters.com/article/2013/07/24/imf-saudi-idUSL1N0FU1B420130724

Prodromidis, K., & Prodromidis, P. (2008). Returns to education: The Greek experience, 1988–1999. *Applied Economics, 20,* 1023–1030. doi: 10.1080/00036840600771197

Psacharopoulos, G. (1981). Returns to education: An updated international comparison. *Comparative Education, 17*(3), 321–341. Available at alihme.wikispaces.com/file/view/Psacharopoulos-comparative+education-1981.pdf

Psacharopoulos, G. (1985). Returns to education: A further international update and implications. *Journal of Human Resources, 20*(4), 583–604.

Quality Assurance Authority for Education & Training (QAAET) (2011). Annual Report 2011. Available at en.qaa.bh/AnnualReportEn.pdf

Qatar Information Exchange. (2007). Annual bulletin of labour force sample survey. Available at www.qix.gov.qa/portal/page/portal/QIXPOC/Documents/QIX%20Knowledge%20Base/Publication/Labor%20Force%20Researches/labor%20force%20sample%20survey/Source_QSA/Labour_Force_QSA_Bu_AE_2007.pdf

Qatar News Agency. (n.d.). Stages of the development of education in Qatar. Available at www.qnaol.net/QNAEn/Main_Sectors/Education/Pages/StagesofthedevelopmentofeducationinQatar.aspx

Qatar Statistics Authority (QSA) & Diplomatic Institute (DI). (2012). The millennium development goals for the State of Qatar. Available at www.qsa.gov.qa/eng/publication/Social_publications/Goal%20English%202012.pdf

Qatar University. (2013). Our history. Available at www.qu.edu.qa/theuniversity/history.php

Raanan, Y. L. (2009). Expanding their future: The social use of education by adolescent Arab girls in the Israeli Galilee (Doctoral dissertation). Available at ProQuest. (Order No. 3357477, The University of Utah).

RAKFTZ. (2013). Schools and skills in RAK. Available at www.rakftz.com/ar/article/business-in-rak/education-rakftz.html

Ramazani, N. (1985, January 1). Arab women in the Gulf. *The Middle East Journal, 39,* 258–276.

Randall, M. (2011). Global trends and their impact on higher education in the UAE. In *Education in the UAE: Current status and future developments* (pp. 183–205). Abu Dhabi, UAE: The Emirates Center for Strategic Studies and Research.

Randeree, K. (2012). Workforce nationalization in the Gulf Cooperation Council states (Occasional Paper No. 9). Center for International and Regional Studies, Georgetown University School of Foreign Service in Qatar. Available at www12.georgetown.edu/sfs/qatar/cirs/KasimRandereeCIRSOccasionalPaper9.pdf

Rassekh, S. (2004). Education as a motor for development: Recent education reforms in Oman with particular reference to the status of women and girls

(Innodata monographs No. 15). *Educational innovations in action.* *United Nations Educational, Scientific and Cultural Organization (UNESCO).* Available at unesdoc.unesco.org/images/0014/001411/141188eo.pdf

Rendall, M. (2012). Structural change in developing countries: Has it decreased gender inequality? *World Development, 45*, 1–16. Available at www.econ.uzh.ch/ipcdp/Publications/Rendall_2013.pdf

Rendall, M. (2013). The service sector and female market work: Europe vs. the United States (Working Paper No. 312). *University of Zurich.* Available at www.econ.uzh.ch/ipcdp/Papers/ipcdp_wp312.pdf

Reynolds, K. (1991). Developing a socialist—feminist vision on education: Conference report of the women for socialism, women and education day school, held on 7 October 1989. *Gender and Education, 3*(1), 81–85. doi: 10.1080/0954025910030106

Riddell, C. W. (2004). *The social benefits of education: New evidence on an old question.* Paper prepared for the conference "Taking Public Universities Seriously," University of Toronto. Available at www.utoronto.ca/president/04conference/downloads/Riddell.pdf

Ridge, N. (2009). Privileged and penalized: The education of boys in the United Arab Emirates (Doctoral dissertation). Available at Teachers College, Columbia University. (UMI Number: 334836).

Ridge, N. (2010). Teacher quality, gender and nationality in the United Arab Emirates: A crisis for boys (Working Paper No. 10-06). *Dubai School of Government.* Available at www.dsg.ae/en/Publication/Pdf_En/Working%20Paper%2010-06%20English.pdf

Ridge, N., Farah, S., & Shami, S. (2013). Patterns and perceptions in male secondary school dropouts in the United Arab Emirates (Working Paper No. 3). *Sheikh Saud bin Saqr Al Qasimi Foundation for Policy Research.* Available at www.alqasimifoundation.com/en/Publications/Publications/PublicationsDetail.aspx?UrlId=5b7010ff-6e67-48e7-9723-25e0c26e6799

Rousseau, R. (2013, April 8). Politics, elections and the "reality" of women's rights in Kuwait. *Diplomatic Courier.* Available at www.diplomaticourier.com/news/regions/middle-east/355-politics-elections-and-the-reality-of-women-s-rights-in-kuwait

Royston, S. (2011, January 27). Saudi Arabia—Why western consultants fail. *Mideast Posts: The Voices of the Middle East.* Available at mideastposts.com/middle-east-business/middle-east-economics-analysis/saudi-arabia-%E2%80%93-why-western-consultants-fail/

Rumberger, R. W. (2011). *Dropping out: Why students drop out of school and what can be done.* Cambridge, MA: Harvard University Press.

Rutledge, E., Al Shamsi, F., Bassioni, Y., & Al Sheikh, H. (2011). Women, labour market nationalization policies and human resource development in the Arab Gulf states. *Human Resource Development International, 14*(2), 183–198.

Saadouli, N. (2010, July). Mechanisms for seeking and developing young entrepreneurs in Kuwait and the GCC region. *Journal of Asia Entrepreneurship and Sustainability, 6*(1), 67–84. Available at www.academia.edu/1376953/Mechanisms_for_Seeking_and_Developing_Young_Entrepreneurs_in_Kuwait_and_the_GCC_Region

Sabbagh, S. (2003). Arab women: Between defiance and restraint [Google Book version]. Available at books.google.ae/books?hl=en&lr=&id=SC7XZY59n5YC&oi=fnd&pg=PR9&dq=western+media,+arab+women+worse+off&ots=9ZX5NImOkV&sig=Dwt9fjrsP8xQuzRcKS5VCIqKRLk&redir_esc=y#v=onepage&q&f=false

Sabry, S., & Zaman, S. (2013, January 9). Emirati unemployment at 14%. *Gulf News*. Available at gulfnews.com/news/gulf/uae/employment/emirati-unemployment-at-14-1.1139425

Salama, S. (2013, August 2). Lana Nusseibeh sworn in as the first female UAE delegate to UN. *Gulf News*. Available at gulfnews.com/news/gulf/uae/government/lana-nusseibeh-sworn-in-as-the-first-female-uae-delegate-to-un-1.1216112

Salehi-Isfahani, D., Tunali, I., & Assaad, R. (2009). A comparative study of returns to education of urban men in Egypt, Iran, and Turkey. *Middle East Development Journal, 1*(2), 145–187. Available at filebox.vt.edu/users/salehi/medj2009.pdf

Salem, O. (2012, June 20). Emiratis to get national day payrise as benefits not basic salary. *The National*. Available at www.thenational.ae/news/uae-news/emiratis-to-get-national-day-payrise-as-benefits-not-basic-salary

Salem, O. (2013a, May 7). Arab Spring will lead to teacher shortage for UAE private schools. *The National*. Available www.thenational.ae/news/uae-news/education/arab-spring-will-lead-to-teacher-shortage-for-uae-private-schools

Salem, O. (2013b, June 27). Emiratisation drive: HCT appoints five Emirati directors. *The National*. www.thenational.ae/news/uae-news/education/emiratisation-drive-hct-appoints-five-emirati-directors

Sasson, J. (1992). *Princess: A true story of life behind the veil in Saudi Arabia*. Atlanta, GA: William Morrow Press.

Saudi Arabia executes 7 for juvenile crime despite UN appeal. (2013, March 13). *RT.com*. Available at rt.com/news/saudi-arabia-execution-juveniles-188/

Saudi Aramco. (n.d.). Stop traffic accidents now! Available at www.saudiaramco.com/content/dam/Publications/Panorama/2012_Special/StopTrafficAccidents.pdf

Saudi women in private sector up by 330%. (2013, February 12). *Saudi Gazette*. Available at www.saudigazette.com.sa/index.cfm?method=home.regcon&contentid=20130212152881

Sayed, S. (2002). *Women, politics and development in the United Arab Emirates*. Abu Dhabi, UAE: Zayed University Special Emirates Collection.

Schacter, J., & Thum, Y. M. (2004). Paying for high- and low-quality teaching. *Economics of Education Review, 23*, 411–430. Available at citeseerx.ist.psu.edu/viewdoc/download?doi=10.1.1.3.9533&rep=rep1&type=pdf

Schafer, M. H., Wilkinson, L. R., & Ferraro, K. F. (2013). Childhood (mis)fortune, educational attainment, and adult health: Contingent benefits of a college degree? *Social Forces, 91*, 1007–1034.

Scholte, J. A. (2005). The sources of neoliberal globalization. *United Nations Research Institute for Social Development*. Available at www.unrisd.org/80256B3C005BCCF9/%28httpAuxPages%29/9E1C54CEEB19A314C12570B4004D0881/$file/scholte.pdf

Schriewer, J., & Martinez, C. (2004). Constructions and internationality in education. In G. Steiner-Khamsi (Ed.), *The global politics of educational borrowing and lending* (pp. 29–53). New York, NY: Teachers College Press.

Schultz, T. P. (1993). Returns to women's education. In E. M. King & M. A. Hill (Eds.), *Women's education in developing countries* (pp. 48–87). Baltimore, MD: Johns Hopkins University Press.

Schwalje, W. (2012). Measuring value for money in education system reform for knowledge-based development in Qatar. Available from dx.doi.org/10.2139/ssrn.2063825

Sending home the foreigners. (2013, July 8). *The Economist*. Available at www.economist.com/blogs/pomegranate/2013/07/united-arab-emirates

Shah, N. M. (2004). Arab migration patterns in the Gulf. *Migration in a Globalized World*, 91–113. Available at the International Organization for Migration website: publications.iom.int/bookstore/free/Arab_migration_globalized_world.pdf
Shaheen, K. (2009, November 11). Students prefer jobs in public sector. *The National*. Available at www.thenational.ae/news/uae-news/students-prefer-jobs-in-public-sector
Shaheen, K. (2010, January 29). Low wage teachers take on second jobs. *The National*. Available at www.thenational.ae/news/uae-news/education/low-wage-teachers-take-on-second-jobs
Shaheen, A. N. (2011, October 2). Three Saudi ministries meet to raise recruitment fees of expatriates. *Gulf News*. Available at gulfnews.com/news/gulf/saudi-arabia/three-saudi-ministries-meet-to-raise-recruitment-fees-of-expatriates-1.883361
Shediac, R., & Samman, H. (2010). *Meeting the employment challenge in the GCC: The need for a holistic strategy*. Booz & Company. Available at www.booz.com/media/file/Meeting_the_Employment_Challenge_in_the_GCC.pdf
Shehadi, R., Hoteit, L., Tarazi, K., & Lamaa, A. (2011). Educated, ambitious, essential: Women will drive the GCC's future. *Booz & Company*. Available at www.booz.com/media/file/BoozCo-Educated-Ambitious-Essential.pdf
Sheikh Saud bin Saqr Al Qasimi Foundation for Policy Research. (2013). *RAK Teacher's Network Analytics*. Unpublished internal document.
Sickles, R. C., & Taubman, P. (1986). An analysis of the health and retirement status of the elderly. *Econometrica, Econometric Society, 54*(6), 1339–1356.
Sicree, R., Shaw, J., & Baker, P. Z. (2011). The global burden. *International Diabetes Foundation*. Available at www.idf.org/sites/default/files/The_Global_Burden.pdf
Sidani, Y. (2005). Women, work, and Islam in Arab societies. *Women in Management Review, 20*(7), 498–512.
Silova, I. (2004). Adopting the language of new allies. In G. Steiner-Khamsi (Ed.), *The global politics of educational borrowing and lending*. New York, NY: Teachers College Press.
Simmons, R. (2010, December 6). Black male multiple choice: Unemployed, high school dropout or incarcerated. *Huffington Post*. Available at www.huffington-post.com/russell-simmons/black-male-multiple-choic_b_792737.html
Simpson, C. (2013a, April 15). Enter private sector 'for benefit of the UAE'. *The National*. Available at www.thenational.≥ae/news/uae-news/enter-private-sector-for-benefit-of-the-uae
Simpson, C. (2013b, June 12). Dubai's Princess Haya delivers stirring Expo 2020 speech in Paris. *The National*. Available at www.thenational.ae/news/uae-news/dubais-princess-haya-delivers-stirring-expo-2020-speech-in-paris#ixzz2c1zEVosO
Slackman, M. (2010, April 26). Privilege pulls Qatar toward unhealthy choices. *The New York Times*. Available at www.nytimes.com/2010/04/27/world/middleeast/27qatar.html?_r=1&
Slavin, B. (2011, January 7). Saudi Arabia faces new challenge from its restive youth. *Al-Monitor*. Available at www.al-monitor.com/pulse/originals/2013/01/saudi-arabia.html
Snyder, T. D., & Dillow, S. A. (2012). Digest of education statistics 2011. *National Institute for Statistics*. Available at nces.ed.gov/pubs2012/2012001.pdf
Soffan, L. U. (1980). *The women of the United Arab Emirates*. New York, NY: Barnes & Noble Books.

Soman, R. (2013, April 28). *Women's empowerment in Qatar.* Available at www.bqdoha.com/2013/04/women-empowerment-in-qatar

Sommers, C. H. (2013, September 13). How to make school better for boys. *The Atlantic.* Available at www.theatlantic.com/education/archive/2013/09/how-to-make-school-better-for-boys/279635/

Sonbol, A. (2006). Women, Islam and education. In R. Zia (Ed.), *Globalization, modernization and education in Muslim countries* (pp. 47–61). New York, NY: Nova Science.

Souad. (2003). *Burned alive: A victim of the law of men.* New York, NY: Warner Books.

Spreen, C. (2004). Appropriating borrowed policies: Outcomes-based education in South Africa. In G. Steiner-Khamsi (Ed.), *The global politics of educational borrowing and lending.* New York, NY: Teachers College Press.

Squalli, J. (2012). Expected returns to education and experience in the United Arab Emirates. *Review of Middle East Economics and Finance, 8*(2), 1–17.

SR5 billion spent on new Madinah school buildings. (2012, April 26). *Arab News.* Available at www.arabnews.com/node/411909

Stasz, C., Eide, E. R., & Martorell, F. (2007). *Post-secondary education in Qatar: Employer demand, student choice, and options for policy* [Google Books version]. Available at www.google.ae/books?hl=en&lr=&id=7Qn3pbRX8WMC&oi=fnd&pg=PP1&dq=the+development+of+education+in+qatar&ots=fRwy6Qc_ri&sig=Kj07nOj5RBEKJs2ZkCi-1isgFP4&redir_esc=y#v=onepage&q=the%20development%20of%20education%20in%20qatar&f=false

Statistical News. (2006). Government of Dubai Department of Health and Medical Services. Available at www.dha.gov.ae/EN/SectorsDirectorates/Sectors/HealthPolicy/Documents/Listing-Nov 6 2007 922AM-404.pdf

Steffensmeier, D., & Allan, E. (1996). Gender and crime: Toward a gendered theory of female offending. *Annual Review of Sociology, 22,* 459–487. Available from www.jstor.org/stable/2083439

Steiner-Khamsi, G. (Ed.). (2004). *The global politics of educational borrowing and lending.* New York, NY: Teachers College Press.

Stephenson, W. (2013, March 17). Are there more US black men in prison or college? *BBC News.* Available at www.bbc.co.uk/news/magazine-21791038

Stoet, G., & Geary, D. C. (2013). Sex differences in mathematics and reading achievement are inversely related: Within- and across-nation assessment of 10 years of PISA data. *PLoS ONE, 8*(3), e57988. doi:10.1371/journal.pone.0057988

Stott, K. 2012. Teachers', parents' and children's perceptions of child obesity in Ras Al Khaimah (Policy Paper No. 1). *Al Qasimi Foundation.* Available at alqasimi-foundation.com/Libraries/Publications/Pub2-paper_Kelly_Stott.sflb.ashx

Stromquist, N. (2012). Theory and ideology in the gender proposals of the World Bank's education strategy 2020, *16,* 133–149. doi: 10.1108/S1479-3679(2012)0000016011

Suliman, O. M., (2000). *A descriptive study of the educational system of the United Arab Emirates* (Unpublished doctoral dissertation, University of Southern California).

Sultanate of Oman Ministry of Education. (n.d.). A glance at the development of education in the sultanate of Oman. Available at www.moe.gov.om/portal/sitebuilder/sites/eps/english/ips/right_menu/edu_system/eduinoman1.aspx

Supreme Education Council. (2011). Education and training sector strategy 2011–2015. Available at www.sec.gov.qa/En/about/Documents/Stratgy2012E.pdf

Swan, M. (2013, March 14). New UAE minister of higher education to pick up the challenges. *The National.* Available at www.thenational.ae/news/uae-news/education/new-uae-minister-of-higher-education-to-pick-up-the-challenges

Taubman, P., & Rosen, S. (1982). Healthiness, education, and marital status. In V. R. Fuchs (Ed.), *Economic aspects of health* (pp. 121–142). Chicago, IL: University of Chicago Press.

Thomas, K. (2000). The new Arab women. *The Middle East*, 237, 43–45.

Topel, R. (1999). Labor markets and economic growth. *Handbooks in economics* (Vol. 5 [3 Part C], 2943–2984).

Torofdar, Y., & Yunngar, M. (2012). Nationalization of manpower resources in Saudi Arabia: A closer view at "Saudization." Conference Proceedings from 2nd Annual International Conference on Human Resource Management and Professional Development for the Digital Age.

Torr, R. (2011, March 2). Bahrain Training Institute (BTI) students and staff demand reforms. *Gulf Daily News*. Available at www.gulf-daily-news.com/NewsDetails.aspx?storyid=300882

Toumi, H. (2008, June 7). Rising living costs force expat teachers in Bahrain to quit. *Gulf News*. Available at gulfnews.com/news/gulf/bahrain/rising-living-costs-force-expat-teachers-in-bahrain-to-quit-1.110736

Toumi, H. (2010, October 21). Qatar independent schools boost staff salaries. *Gulf News*. Available at gulfnews.com/news/gulf/qatar/qatar-independent-schools-boost-staff-salaries-1.699782

Toumi. H. (2011, September 5). Report: Around one third of teachers in Qatar lack proper qualifications. *Gulf News*. Available at gulfnews.com/report-around-one-third-of-teachers-in-qatar-lack-proper-qualifications-1.861612

Toumi, H. (2012, September 16). Kuwait to appoint women as lawyers, judges. *Gulf News*. Available at gulfnews.com/news/gulf/kuwait/kuwait-to-appoint-women-as-lawyers-judges-1.1076722

Toumi, H. (2013a, January 17). Women banned from working in boys' schools. *Gulf News*. Retrieved April 2, 2013 from, gulfnews.com/news/gulf/qatar/women-banned-from-working-in-boys-schools-1.1133620

Toumi, H. (2013b, May 12). Women make up 72% of Kuwait teachers. *Gulf News*. Available at gulfnews.com/news/gulf/kuwait/women-make-up-72-of-kuwait-teachers-1.1182236

Toumi, H. (2013c, August 19). African mules used to smuggle cocaine through Qatar. *Gulf News*. Available at gulfnews.com/news/gulf/qatar/african-mules-used-to-smuggle-cocaine-through-qatar-1.1221944

Toumi, H. (2013d, September 16). Saudi guards foil attempts to smuggle people, weapons, drugs. *Gulf News*. Available at gulfnews.com/news/gulf/saudi-arabia/saudi-guards-foil-attempts-to-smuggle-people-weapons-drugs-1.1231518

Trading Economics. (2012). Primary education. Available at www.tradingeconomics.com/oman/primary-education-teachers-percent-female-wb-data.html

Trent, J. W., & Medskher, L. L. (1968). *Beyond high school*. San Francisco, CA: Joessy-Bass.

Tutton, M. (2010, July 23). Does Saudi have world's biggest amphetamine habit? *CNN*. Available at edition.cnn.com/2010/WORLD/meast/07/23/middle.east.drugs.amphetamine/index.html

Two youth sentenced to death for murder. (2013, August 12). *The Peninsula*. Available at thepeninsulaqatar.com/qatar/248520-two-youth-sentenced-to-death-for-murder.html

UAE Government. (2010). *Vision 2021: United in ambition and determination*. Available at www.vision2021.ae/downloads/UAE-Vision2021-Brochure-English.pdf

UIS (UNESCO Institute for Statistics). (2010). Education for all global monitoring report. Available at www.unesco.org/new/fileadmin/MULTIMEDIA/HQ/ED/GMR/pdf/gmr2010/gmr2010-annex-04-stat-tables.pdf

UIS (UNESCO Institute for Statistics). (2011). Global education digest 2011: Comparing education statistics across the world. Available at www.uis.unesco.org/Education/GED%20Documents%20C/GED-2011-Book-EN-web2.pdf

UIS (UNESCO Institute for Statistics). (2012). Opportunities lost: The impact of grade repetition and early school leaving. Available at www.uis.unesco.org/Education/GED%20Documents%20C/GED-2012-Complete-Web3.pdf

UIS (UNESCO Institute for Statistics). (2013). Custom data representation of gross enrollment ratio January 6, 2013. *UIS Data Centre*. Available at stats.uis.unesco.org/unesco/TableViewer/document.aspx?ReportId=136&IF_Language=eng&BR_Topic=0

United Arab Emirates index: Education. (n.d.). *Mongabay.com*. Available at www.mongabay.com/history/united_arab_emirates/united_arab_emirates-united_arab_emirateseducation.html

United Arab Emirates University (UAEU). (n.d.). About UAEU. Available at www.uaeu.ac.ae/about/

United Nations (UN). (2013). Millennium development goals: Goal 3. Available at www.un.org/millenniumgoals/gender.shtml

United Nations Children's Fund (UNICEF). (2004). State of the world's children. New York, NY: Author.

United Nations Children's Fund (UNICEF). (2008). Education statistics: Bahrain. Available at www.childinfo.org/files/MENA_Bahrain.pdf

United Nations Children's Fund (UNICEF). (2011). Kuwait MENA gender equality profile: Status of girls and women in the Middle East and North Africa. Available at www.unicef.org/gender/files/Kuwait-Gender-Eqaulity-Profile-2011.pdf

United Nations Children's Fund (UNICEF). (2013). Convention on the rights of the child: Fact sheet. Available at www.unicef.org/crc/index_30228.html

United Nations Commission on Sustainable Development (UNCSD). (1997). Social aspects of sustainable development in Bahrain. Available at www.un.org/esa/agenda21/natlinfo/countr/bahrain/social.htm

United Nations Development Programme (UNDP). (1995). Human development report, 1995. New York, NY: Oxford University Press. Available at hdr.undp.org/en/media/hdr_1995_en_complete_nostats.pdf

United Nations Development Programme (UNDP). (2006). The Arab human development report 2005: Towards the rise of women in the Arab world. New York, NY: United Nations Publications. Available at www.arab-hdr.org/publications/other/ahdr/ahdr2005e.pdf

United Nations Development Programme (UNDP). (2013). Arab statistics. Available at www.arabstats.org/group.asp?ind=124&gr=1&gid=0&sgid=0&yr=2003

United Nations Development Programme (UNDP) & Central Informatics Organisation (CIO). (2010). Review of the progress of the millennium development goals in the Kingdom of Bahrain: A national perspective. Available at www.undp.org.bh/Files/2010MDGProg/2010MDGBHRPROGRESS.pdf

United Nations Development Program (UNDP) & Ministry of Economy, UAE (2007). Millennium development goals: United Arab Emirates report. Available at ae.zawya.com/researchreports/p_2006_06_20_ 09_19_55/20070502_p_2006_06_20_09_19_55_112948.pdf

United Nations Development Programme (UNDP) & State of Kuwait. (2012). Paving the way for a sustainable future: Millennium development goals Kuwait progress report 2012. Available at www.scpd.gov.kw/arabic/DocLibl/MDG%20State%20of%20Kuwait%20Report%202012%20English.pdf

United Nations Educational Scientific and Cultural Organization (UNESCO). (2000). Dakar framework for action, education for all: Meeting our collective commitments. Available at unesdoc.unesco.org/images/0012/001211/ 121147e.pdf

United Nations Educational Scientific and Cultural Organization (UNESCO). (2002). Arab states regional report. *Quebec: UNESCO Institute for Statistics*. Available at www.uis.unesco.org

United Nations Educational, Scientific and Cultural Organization (UNESCO). (2008). *Education for all global monitoring report: Education for all by 2015: Will we make it?* Oxford, UK: Oxford University Press.

United Nations Educational, Scientific and Cultural Organization. (UNESCO). (2010). Regional literacy profile: Arab states. Available at stats.uis.unesco.org/unesco/TableViewer/document.aspx?ReportId=367&IF_Language=eng&BR_Region=40525

United Nations Educational, Scientific, and Cultural Organization (UNESCO). (2011). Education for all global monitoring report 2011. Available at www.unesco.org/new/fileadmin/MULTIMEDIA/HQ/ED/pdf/gmr2011-efa-development-index.pdf

United Nations Educational, Scientific and Cultural Organization (UNESCO). (2012). Education for all global monitoring report: Youth and skills: Putting education to work. Available at www.ungei.org/news/files/218569E.pdf

United Nations Educational, Scientific, and Cultural Organization (UNESCO) & International Bureau of Education (IBE). (2011). World data on education: Bahrain. Available at unesdoc.unesco.org/images/0021/002114/211438e.pdf

United Nations Office on Drugs and Crime (UNODC). (2010). World drug report 2010. Available at www.unodc.org/documents/wdr/WDR_2010/World_Drug_Report_2010_lo-res.pdf

United Nations Office on Drugs and Crime (UNODC). (2011). UNODC drug use statistics. In UNODC (Eds.), *World drug report 2011* (pp. 209–240). Available at www.unodc.org/documents/data-and-analysis/WDR2011/StatAnnex-consumption.pdf

United Nations Office on Drugs and Crime (UNODC). (2012). Recent statistics and trend analysis of illicit drug markets. Available at www.unodc.org/documents/data-and-analysis/WDR2012/WDR_2012_Chapter1.pdf

United Nations Office on Drugs and Crime (UNODC). (2013). UNODC homicide statistics. Available at www.unodc.org/unodc/en/data-and-analysis/homicide.html

United Nations Statistics Division. (2013). Official list of MDG indicators. Available at mdgs.un.org/unsd/mdg/host.aspx?Content=indicators/officiallist.htm

United States Agency for International Development (USAID). (2008). Education from a gender equality perspective. Available at www.ungei.org/resources/files/Education_from_a_Gender_Equality_Perspective.pdf

University of Bahrain (UoB). (2009). Brief history. Available at www.uob.edu.bh/english/pages.aspx?module=pages&id=1814&SID=312

Vaidya, S. K. (2010, August 26). Omani teachers stage protest demanding jobs. *Gulf News*. Available at gulfnews.com/news/gulf/oman/omani-teachers-stage-protest-demanding-jobs-1.673198

Vaidya, S. K. (2013, September 19). Armed drug peddler among four arrested in Oman. *Gulf News*. Available at gulfnews.com/news/gulf/oman/armed-drug-peddler-among-four-arrested-in-oman-1.1232953

Van Leijen, M. (2013, March 21). Why UAE mothers should be appreciated. *Emirates 24|7*. Available at www.emirates247.com/news/emirates/why-uae-mothers-should-be-appreciated-2013-03-21-1.499552

Verveer, M. (2010). Convention on the elimination of all forms of discrimination against women. Speech before the Senate Judiciary Committee, Subcommittee on Human Rights and the Law, Washington, DC. Available at www.state.gov/s/gwi/rls/rem/2010/151153.htm

Vreede-de Stuers, C. (1974). Girl students in Kuwait. *Bijdragen Tot De Taal-, Land- En Volkenkunde, 130*(1), 110.

Waiting list for admission crosses 15,000. (2011, April 22). *Emirates 24|7*. Available at www.emirates247.com/news/emirates/waiting-list-for-admission-crosses-15-000-2011-04-22-1.383908

Waljat College invites all students to career guidance session (2013, September 5). *AMEinfo*. www.ameinfo.com/waljat-college-invites-students-career-guidance-353435

Walker, M. (2011). Pisa 2009 Plus Results: Performance of 15-year-olds in reading, mathematics and science for 10 additional participants. *Australian Council for Educational Research*. Available at mypisa.acer.edu.au/images/mypisadoc/acer_pisa%202009%2B%20international.pdf

Wam. (2013, May 18). Majid launches 'Tejar Dubai' initiative for young entrepreneurs. *Emirates 24/7*. Available at www.emirates247.com/business/economy-finance/majid-launches-tejar-dubai-initiative-for-young-entrepreneurs-2013-05-18-1.506865

Washington, J. (2010, July 11). Blacks struggle with 72% unwed mothers rate. *NBC News*. Available at www.nbcnews.com/id/39993685/ns/health-womens_health/t/blacks-struggle-percent-unwed-mothers-rate/

Waters, A. M. (2013, December 2). Sharia law: Extremism the government ignores. *The Huffington Post*. Available at www.huffingtonpost.co.uk/anne-marie-waters/sharia-law-extremism-the-_b_2668212.html

Weaver-Hightower, M. (2003). The "boy turn" in research on gender and education. *Review of Education Research, 73*(4), 471–498. Available at www.engagingmen.net/files/resources/2011/Caroline/boy20turn20weaver-hightower_article.pdf

Wellcome Trust Sanger Institute. (2009, April 20). Learning disabilities in males: Nine new X chromosome genes linked to learning disabilities. *ScienceDaily*. Available at www.sciencedaily.com/releases/2009/04/090419133841.htm

Whitmire, R. (2010). Why boys fail: Saving our sons from an educational system that's leaving them behind [Google Books version]. Available at books.google.ae/books?id=5FE9hLvsv1kC&printsec=frontcover&source=gbs_ge_summary_r&cad=0#v=onepage&q&f=false

Who's who among Arab women. (n.d.). Fayza Al Khorafi. Available at www.whoswhoarabwomen.com/profiles.asp?a=307

Wilkins, S. (2001). Human resource development through vocational education in the United Arab Emirates: The case study of Dubai Polytechnic. *Journal of Vocational Education and Training, 54*(1), 5–26.

Wilkins, S. (2011). Who benefits from foreign universities in the Arab Gulf states? *Australian Universities' Review, 53*(1), 73–83. Available at www.academia.edu/1123652/Who_benefits_from_foreign_universities_in_the_Arab_Gulf_States

Wolfe, B. L., & Haveman, R. H. (2002). Social and nonmarket benefits from education in an advanced economy. *Federal Reserve Bank of Boston, 47*, 97–142.

World Bank. (2004). *Gender and development in the Middle East and North Africa: Women in the public sphere*. Washington, DC: The World Bank.

World Bank. (2008). *The road not traveled: Education reform in the Middle East and North Africa*. Washington, DC: The World Bank.

World Bank. (2009). *The status and progress of women in the Middle East and North Africa*. Available at siteresources.worldbank.org/INTMENA/Resources/MENA_Gender_Compendium-2009-1.pdf

World Bank. (2011). World development report 2012: Gender equality and development. Available at siteresources.worldbank.org/INTWDR2012/Resources/7778105-1299699968583/7786210-1315936222006/Complete-Report.pdf

World Bank. (2013). *Opening doors: Gender equality and development in the Middle East and North Africa*. Washington DC: The World Bank. doi:10.1596/978-0-8213-9763-3

World Bank. (2013a). Adjusted net enrollment rate, primary (% of primary school age children). Available at data.worldbank.org/indicator/SE.PRM.TENR

World Bank. (2013b). Public spending on education, total (% of government expenditure). Available at data.worldbank.org/indicator/SE.XPD.TOTL.GB.ZS

World Bank. (2013c). Education statistics—All indicators. Available at databank.worldbank.org/data/views/reports/tableview.aspx

World Bank. (2013d). Life expectancy at birth, female (years). Available at data.worldbank.org/indicator/SP.DYN.LE00.FE.IN/countries

World Bank. (2013e). Unemployment, female (% of female labor force). Available at data.worldbank.org/indicator/SL.UEM.TOTL.FE.ZS/countries

World Bank. (2013f). Education statistics—All indicators. Available at databank.worldbank.org/data/views/variableselection/selectvariables.aspx?source=education-statistics-~-all-indicators

World Bank. (2013g). Proportion of seats held by women in national parliaments (%). Available at data.worldbank.org/indicator/SG.GEN.PARL.ZS/countries

World Bank & Commonwealth Secretariat. (2009a). Regional Caribbean initiative on keeping boys out of risk. Available at lcr-results.net/PREM/BooR/files/Regional_Caribbean_Initiative_Keeping_Boys_OutofRisk.pdf

World Bank & Commonwealth Secretariat. (2009b). Regional Caribbean conference on keeping boys out of risk. Conference proceedings from Montego Bay, Jamaica. *UNICEF website*. Available at www.unicef.org/lac/regional_caribbean_Keeping_Boys_out_of_Risk_Report.pdf

World Economic Forum (WEF). (2013). The global gender gap report. Available at www.weforum.org/issues/global-gender-gap

World Economic Forum (WEF) & European Bank for Reconstruction and Development (EBRD). (2013). The Arab world competitiveness report 2013. Available at www3.weforum.org/docs/WEF_AWCR_Report_2013.pdf

World Health Organization (WHO). (2011). Mental health: Suicide rates per 100,000 by country, year and sex [Table]. Available at www.who.int/mental_health/prevention/suicide_rates/en/

Yaqoob, T. (2008). Female pilot flies solo into history. *The National*. Available at www.thenational.ae/news/uae-news/female-pilot-flies-solo-into-history

Young, S. (2013, June 2). Most Emirati students not motivated, says study. *Khaleej Times*. Available at www.khaleejtimes.com/nation/inside.asp?section=youthspecial&xfile=/data/youthspecial/2013/June/youthspecial_June2.xml

Zafeirakou, A. (2007). Teacher policies for underserved populations: A synthesis of lessons learned and best practices. United Nations Educational, Scientific and Cultural Organization (UNESCO). Available at unesdoc.unesco.org/images/0015/001555/155594e.pdf

Zaman, S. (2013a, July 30). 66% of private schools need improvement. *Gulf News*. Available at gulfnews.com/news/gulf/uae/education/66-of-private-schools-need-improvement-1.1215038

Zaman, S. (2013b, September 3). UAE teachers sought for public schools. *Gulf News*. Available at gulfnews.com/news/gulf/uae/education/uae-teachers-sought-for-public-schools-1.1227048

Zayed University (ZU). (2013). FAQs. Available at www.zu.ac.ae/main/en/colleges/graduate_studies/faqs.aspx

Index

Abdul Latif Jameel Company, 121–122
Abdulaziz, King, 29
Abdulla, F., 6, 49, 123
Abdullah, M. T., 15b
Abouchakra, R., 6, 30
Absal, R., 84
Abu Dhabi Education Council (ADEC), 13b, 20t, 21, 22, 23, 163
Abu Dhabi Indian School, 19b
Abu Dhabi National Oil Company, 40
Abu Dhabi, private schools in, 19b
Abudabbeh, N., 50, 110
AbuKhalil, A., 41, 81, 161
Abu-Lughod, L., 41, 81
Academia, women in, 43–44, 44t
ACER. *See* Australian Council for Education Research (ACER)
Achievement
 gender differences in, 3, 5; male academic retention, decline in, 5; male vs. female, 6
ADEC. *See* Abu Dhabi Education Council (ADEC)
Adely, F. J., 43
Afkhami, M., 41
AFP. *See* Agence France Press (AFP)
Agence France Press (AFP), 146
Aghaddir, A., 167
Agreements that focus on women and girls, 159
AGU. *See* Arabian Gulf University (AGU)

AHDR. *See* Arab Human Development Report (AHDR)
Ahlia University, 27
Ahmed, A., 57, 112, 113, 124, 144, 163
Ahmed, D. A., 57, 122
Akeel, M., 46t
Akhter, M. S., 25
Al Amir, S., 146
Al Banawi, N., 56, 121
Al Enezi, A. K., 119
Al Fahim, M., 68
Al Gharaibeh, F., 26, 47, 57, 122
Al Kadri, 144
Al Ketbi, M., 160
Al Khaduri, R., 46t, 48, 125
Al Khalifa, M., 57
Al Khan, M. N., 107t
Al Khateeb, H. M., 53
Al Khazraji, K., 106, 108, 114
Al Khoori, A., 146, 157, 167
Al Makaheleh, S., 123
Al Maktoum, R., 78, 105, 152
Al Marri, F., 140, 142
Al Masah Capital Limited, 49, 57, 88, 89t, 116, 116t
Al Mazroui, A., 115
Al Mohsen, M., 56
Al Munajjed, M., 6
 future of gender, education, and development, 158; modernity, 65, 66, 69; nationalization, 110, 113, 121; oil and expansion of education, 12b; rise of women in the Gulf, 47, 56; value of education beyond work, 141
Al Musalmy, S., 148, 150
Al Nabhani, M., 32, 33
Al Nahayan, Z., 48
Al Nahyan, Z., 18

Al Qasimi Foundation, 23
Al Qasimi, L., 59
Al Qudsi, S., 107, 109
Al Sabah, M., 10
Al Shamsi, F., 78
Al Sheikh, H., 78
Al Shmeli, S. B. H., 33, 34
Al Waqafi, M., 107, 114, 123
Al-Abdulkareem, S., 28, 29
Al-Adawi, S., 143
Alamri, M., 30, 32
Al-Asiri, S., 89
Al-Awadi, A. R., 11–12, 148
Aldosari, A., 28, 29, 30, 82
Al-Faruqi, L., 42
Al-Haddad, F., 144
Al-Hamad, N., 145
Al-Hidaya Al-Khalifa Boys School, 25
Al-Hourani, H., 144–145
Al-Hourani, H. M., 144
Al-Hussain, A. A., 148, 149
Ali, K., 81
Ali, K. A., 45
Ali, S. M., 25
Ali, Y., 41
Aljamal, A., 145
Al-katateeb education system, 17
Al-Kharafi, F., 57
Al-Kharafi, F. M., 15b
Alkhazim, M. A., 30, 31, 32
Al-Kinaei, Y., 10
Alkobaisi, S., 91
Allan, E., 150
Al-Matroushi, M. A., 144
Al-Mughni, 57
Al-Numaimi, Y., 144
Alpen Capital, 32
Alphonso, C., 86
Al-Rasheed, M., 28
Alromi, N., 29
al-Sabah, A. S., 17
Al-Sharaf, A., 88
Alsharif, A., 120
Al-Shehab, A. J., 15

Index   **205**

Al-Zuhayyan, A., 26
AME Info, 15
American Association of University Women, 2
Anbar, Z., 99
AP. *See* Associated Press (AP)
Arab Human Development Report (AHDR)
  modernity, 65, 66, 74, 75; rise of women in the Gulf, 42, 43, 44
Arabian Gulf University (AGU), 27
ARAMCO, 28
Arnold, T., 156t–157t
Aronson, G., 167
Arora, A., 7, 95t
Aslam, N., 32, 115, 122, 126
Assaad, R., 131
Assessment of education
  National Assessment Program (NAP), 84; OECD assessments, 7; in Oman, 34; in Qatar, 23; in UAE, 24t; UAENAP, 53
Associated Press (AP), 146
Asthana, A., 153
Astin, A. W., 138, 164
At-risk students, 164
Attainment, 50–54, 51t–53t
Australia, Boys' Education Lighthouse Schools, 154b
Australian Council for Education Research (ACER), 32
Autor, D., 1, 3, 5, 152, 153, 158
Avancena, J., 56
Ayntrazi, T., 12b–13b
Azzam, H., 120

Badih, S., 123
Bagnied, M., 145
Bahgat, G., 113
Bahrain
  education for women, 26; education mission in, 24–28; first girls' and boys' schools, 46t, 47; higher education, 27, 57; literacy rate, 26; Ministry of Education (MOE), 25, 27, 46t, 122; modernity, quest for, 75–76; nationalization, 111–112, 122–123; Vision 2030, 27, 110

Bahrain News Agency (BNA), 25
Bahrain Teachers College (BTC), 27
Bahrain Training Institute (BTI), 110
Baker, D., 5, 80
Baker, P. Z., 156t–157t
Baki, R., 113, 120, 121
Ball, S. J., 77
Bannon, I., 3, 5, 61, 62
Barback, J., 1
Barber, M., 69, 91
Barker, F., 143
Barrientos, A., 120
Barriteau, V., 64
Barro, R. J., 130, 136
Bassioni, Y., 78
Baxter, E., 108
BBC. *See* British Broadcasting Corporation (BBC)
Becker, H., 2, 130
Beeson, D., 47
Behrman, J., 49
Belfield, C., 80
BELS. *See* Boys' Education Lighthouse Schools (BELS)
Benard, C., 30
Berger, D. R., 93t, 94t
Berman, G., 153
Bieber, T., 63
Bin Ali, S. H., 28
Bin Said, Q., 32
Bin Zaal, A. A., 143
BNA. *See* Bahrain News Agency (BNA)
Boli-Bennett, J., 76
Bollag, B., 14b
Boonen, T., 154
Booz & Company, 64, 65, 66, 69, 77, 109
Bowen, H., 138
Boys, education for, 80–104
  conclusion, 103–104; difficulties in the Middle East, 81–82; English NAP score, 84, 84f; expatriate teachers, 91–103; falling behind in GCC schools, 82–88; female teachers in the GCC, 88–89, 89t; gender differential in assessment scores, 82, 84, 84t; higher education in Western countries,

80, 81t; male teacher shortage, 89–90; Oman grade 12 examination results, 84, 86t; Qatar senior school certificate scores, 84, 85f; secondary school dropouts and repeaters, 86, 87t; UAE boys' schools, 102b–103b
Boys' Education Lighthouse Schools (BELS), 154b
Boys' Reading Commission, 158b–159b
"Boy-turn," 5
Bradley, M., 96
Braga, M., 134
Brand, J. E., 138
Bratti, M., 134
Braxton, R. J., 109
Bremmer, I., 120
Breslin, J., 43, 57, 78
Brewer, D. J., 6
  future of gender, education, and development, 162; leaving the boys behind, 98; modernity, 68, 69; nationalization, 118b; oil and expansion of education, 36, 37, 38–39, 40; rise of women in the Gulf, 46, 46t
Brinkley, I., 108
British Broadcasting Corporation (BBC), 10, 28
British India Navigation Company, 24
Brooks-Gunn, J., 135
Broomhall, E., 123
Brown, R., 80
BTC. *See* Bahrain Teachers College (BTC)
BTI. *See* Bahrain Training Institute (BTI)
Buchmann, C., 1, 2, 3
Buckley, G., 125
Bullock, K., 41

CAA. *See* Commission for Academic Accreditation (CAA)
Calderwood, J., 16
Callister, P., 3
Cappon, P., 3
Card, D., 132
Career programs, 163
Carmichael, F., 110

Carnoy, M., 164
Castle, C. E., 95t
Center for Higher Education Data and Statistics (CHEDS), 19b, 20, 21
Center for Religious Freedom of the Hudson Institute, 30, 150
Centers for Disease Control and Prevention, 134, 144
Central Informatics Organization (CIO), 75, 76
Central Statistical Bureau, Kuwait, 116t
Centre for Social Justice (CSJ), 151, 153, 167
Centurino, V. A. S., 95t
Chabbott, C., 2, 61, 63
Change, barriers to, 159–161
Chansarkar, B., 123
Chase-Dunn, C., 76
Chatriwala, O., 59
CHEDS. *See* Center for Higher Education Data and Statistics (CHEDS)
The Chronicle of Higher Education, 16
CIA, 47
CIO. *See* Central Informatics Organization (CIO)
Clarke, M., 99
Cohen, J., 164
Coleman, J. S., 154
College of Education at Sultan Qaboos University, 163
College of Health Sciences, 27
Commission for Academic Accreditation (CAA), 19b
Commonwealth Secretariat, 165b
Connelly, P., 64
Constantine, Z., 148
Coomes, P., 132
Cooperative Institutional Research Program, 138
Copeland, W., 80
Correia, M. C., 3, 5, 61, 62
Costello, J. E., 80
Courington, K., 31

Criminal activity and education, 137, 146–150, 147t, 149f
Crookshank, F., vii
Crystal, J., 14b
CSJ. *See* Centre for Social Justice (CSJ)
Cunningham, C. D., 106
Curriculum in Qatar, 36–37; service component of, 164–165; of UAE, 18–19
Cutler, D. M., 134
Cuttance, P., 5, 154b
Cyclical benefits from education, 138–139

Dakar Framework for Action, 2, 61–62, 69
Damiano, K. M., 132
Dar, A., 153
Dasman Diabetes Institute, 145
Dave, C., 97, 101, 162
Davidson, C. M., 10, 12b, 16, 17–18, 19, 68
Davis-Kean, P. E., 135
De Laat, J., 90
Decent Work Country Programme, 122, 125
DEEWR. *See* Department of Education, Employment and Workplace Relations (DEEWR)
Del Castillo, D., 16, 75
Dennis, M., 3
Department of Education, Employment and Workplace Relations (DEEWR), 81t
Desjardins, B., 155
Dhal, S., 19b
DI. *See* Diplomatic Institute (DI)
Dickinson, E., 105, 110, 121
Dickson, M., 88
Dillow, S. A., 81t
Diplomatic Institute (DI), 7, 76, 117
DiPrete, T. A., 1, 2, 3
Dixon, M., 22
"Doha Rolls Out Private School Vouchers," 77
Doumato, E., 41
Drucker, K. T., 23, 52
Drugs and education, 148, 149f

D'Souza, R., 143
Dubai private schools, 19b; returns to education, 142; school administration, 21–22; school funding, 17
Duffy, M. J., 167
Duncan, G. J., 135
Dye, R. F., 138

EBRD. *See* European Bank of Reconstruction and Development (EBRD)
Economist Intelligence Unit, 44, 44t
EDI. *See* Education for All Development Index (EDI)
Education beyond work. *See* Value of education beyond work
Education for All Development Index (EDI), 26
Education for All (EFA), 1–2 Dakar Framework for Action, 2, 61, 62; *EFA Arab States Regional Report*, 42; *EFA Global Monitoring Report*, 44, 45, 45t; *2012 EFA Global Monitoring Report*, 5–6
Education for girls global policy for, 1–2; history of global policy for, 1–7
Education in Oman: The Drive for Quality, 35, 103
EFA. *See* Education for All (EFA)
EFA Arab States Regional Report, 42
EFA Global Monitoring Report, 44, 45, 45t
Egbert, A., 53
Egypt as education aid donor, 11, 12b–13b; Ministry of Education (MOE), 13b; portrayal of men as incapable, 81–82
Eide, E. R., 37
El-Sanabary, N., 46t, 47, 49
Else-Quest, N. M., 2
Elwood, J., 80

Emirates College of Advanced Education, 112
"Emiratis Throng Abu Dhabi Job Fair," 86
Employment, private-sector, 107–109, 107t
Engineering, women involved in, 44, 45t
English (writing) NAP score, 84f
English language teachers in RAK, 96, 97f
English writing scores, 84f
Engman, M., 12b, 13b, 17, 90, 91
Enrollment ratios, 3, 4t, 6
Epstein, D., 80
Erkanli, A., 80
Escobar, A., 64
European Bank of Reconstruction and Development (EBRD), 65
European Commission, 167
Ewing, K. P., 166
Eyler, J., 164

Fahad, King, 29
Fakkar, G., 13b
FAO. *See* Food and Agriculture Organization (FAO)
Farah, S., vii, 6, 18, 19, 100, 113, 151, 166
Fasial, King, 47
Fatima, S., 48
Faundez, J., 106
Federal Law No. 11 of 1972, 18
Felder, D., 114t, 117
Fenton, J., 37
Ferraro, K. F., 133
Fikry, M., 144
Financial Trend Forecaster, 13b
Foley, S., 41, 42, 68, 153
Follman, M., 167
Food and Agriculture Organization (FAO), 145, 146t
Forstenlechner, I., 69, 106, 107, 107t, 108, 109, 113, 114, 114t, 115, 119, 123
Foy, P., 7, 23, 52

Fractured Families: Why Stability Matters, 151, 153
Francis, S. M., 19b
Freeman, R. B., 138
"From Access to Academic," 86
Fryer, R. G., 1, 52

Gallagher, K., 69
Gara, T., 108
Gardner, A., 18, 24–25, 69
Gardner, W. E., 88, 99, 101
Garner, R., 154
GCC. *See* Gulf Cooperation Council (GCC)
GDI. *See* Gender-related development index (GDI)
Geary, D. C., 153
Gender
  gaps favoring females, 1;
  marginalization of, 1
Gender and Development in the Middle East and North Africa (MENA), 42
Gender gap in GCC countries, 155–159, 156t–157t
Gender parity index (GPI), 45, 55f
Gender-related development index (GDI), 2
General Secretariat for Development Planning (GSDP)
  gender gap measures, 156t–157t; leaving the boys behind, 84; modernity, 61; nationalization, 110, 117, 118b; oil and expansion of education, 37, 38, 39, 40; Qatar senior school certificate scores, 85f; rise of women in the Gulf, 49, 53, 55, 56; value of education beyond work, 139
Ghainaa Publications, 54t, 56
Giles, D. E., 164
"Girl Power," 156t–157t
Global Campaign for Education, 3
Global Gender Gap Report, 20t, 21, 62, 63

Goals of education for girls, 1–2
Godwin, S., 123
Gonzalez, E. J., 53
Gonzalez, G., 109, 113, 119, 122, 124
Gorssman, 130
Goulding, N., 78
Goveas, S., 32, 115, 122, 126
Government, women in, 43–44, 44t
GPI. *See* Gender parity index (GPI)
"Graduates Honoured," 57
Grant, M., 49
Grasgreen, A., 2
Gray, C., 164
Grossman, M., 133
GSDP. *See* General Secretariat for Development Planning (GSDP)
Gulf Cooperation Council (GCC), vii
  education for boys in. *See* Boys, education for;
  educational outcomes for girls, 49–54, 50t–53t;
  first girls' and boys' schools, 46t; oil and expansion of education, 9; secondary school dropouts and repeaters, 86, 87t
Gulf Technical College, 27
Gulf University, 27

Haddad, Y., 42
Hafner-Burton & Pollack, 78
Hagan, J., 150
Hall, R. L., 137
Hamdan, A., 47, 56, 156t–157t
Hamdan, S., 124
Hamilton, B. A., 143
Hannum, E., 79
Hanushek, E. A., 91, 136, 155
Harby, M. K., 36
Harding, D. J., 167
Harry, W., 114
Hartmann, S., 96
Hasib, N. I., 3
Hauser, S. M., 137
Hausmann, R., 20t, 21, 26, 55, 79, 81
Haveman, R., 130, 135, 142
Haveman, R. H., 136, 137
Haya, Princess, 78, 160

HCT. *See* Higher Colleges of Technology (HCT)
Health and education, 133–135, 143–146
Heard-Bey, F., 68
Hedin, D. P., 164
Helal, M., 140, 142
Helliwell, J. F., 137
Hendrixson, A., 166
Henry, J. K., 144–145
Heroin, 148, 149f
Hertog, S., 7, 106, 114, 119, 120, 123, 124
HESA. *See* Higher Education Statistics Agency Limited (HESA)
Hey, V., 80
Higher Colleges of Technology (HCT), 21, 112, 163
Higher Education Council, 27
Higher education for men in Western countries, 80, 81t
Higher Education Law No. 3, 27
Higher Education Statistics Agency Limited (HESA), 81t
Hilditch, L., 3
Hiltunen, J., 19b, 69
History of global policy for education of girls, 1–7
Hitomi, K., 155
Hodgkinson, V., 138
Hoffman, L., 78
Hong Kong & Shanghai Banking Corporation (HSBC), 19b
Hoteit, L., 19b, 69, 115
Hout, M., 132, 136–137, 138
How College Affects Students, 138
How Schools Shortchange Girls, 2
HRDF. *See* Human Resources Development Fund (HRDF)
HSBC. *See* Hong Kong & Shanghai Banking Corporation (HSBC)
Human Development Report, 2
Human Resources Development Fund (HRDF), 120
Hussain, T., 31

Husseini, R., 167
Hutton, W., 108
Hyde, J. S., 2

IASO. *See* International Association for the Study of Obesity (IASO)
IBE. *See* International Bureau of Education (IBE)
Ibn Saud, A., 28
ICPS. *See* International Centre for Prison Studies (ICPS)
IDF. *See* International Diabetes Federation (IDF)
IEA. *See* International Association for the Evaluation of Education Achievement (IEA)
ILO. *See* International Labour Organization (ILO)
Improving Education in the Gulf, 91
Info-Prod Research Ltd., 107t
Ingvarson, L., 91
Intergenerational benefits of education, 135
International, defined, 67
International Association for the Evaluation of Education Achievement (IEA), 23, 24t
International Association for the Study of Obesity (IASO), 143, 143t, 156t–157t
International Bureau of Education (IBE), 26, 28, 84
International Centre for Prison Studies (ICPS), 146, 147t, 151, 156t–157t
International Diabetes Federation (IDF), 145, 146t
International Labour Organization (ILO), 110t, 116t, 122, 125, 156t–157t
Islam, and Saudi Arabian education, 28–32
Islam, F., 120
Issa, W., 123, 124

Jacobson, L., 132
Jamal, A., 20t
Jamjoom, Y., 31
Janofksy, M., 78–79
Janofsky, M., 160
Jansen, J. D., 61, 63
Janssen, N., 75
Jepsen, C., 132
Jones, C. W., 126, 140, 150
Jones, T. C., 68

Kaestner, R., 133
Kaphle, A., 98
Karolak, M., 27, 57, 68, 69, 122, 123
Karoly, L. A., 117, 140–141
KCO. *See* Kuwait Cultural Office (KCO)
Kelly, S., 43, 57, 78
Kenkel, D. S., 133
Kennedy, A., 53
Kennedy, A. M., 53
Kenya, returns from education, 132
Kerr, R., 164
Khalaf, S., 91
Khalifa, Sheikh, 25
Khatri, S. S., 37, 77, 118b
KHDA. *See* Knowledge and Human Development Authority (KHDA)
Kherfi, S., 86
Kilpatrick, J., 149
Kimenyi, M. S., 132
Kimko, D. D., 136
King Abdullah University of Science and Technology, 32
King Saud University, 29
Kingdom of Saudi Arabia Ministry of Education, 32
Kinsey, D. F., 164
Kippels, S., vii
Kirdar, S., 115
Kirk, D., 69
Klasen, S., 109
Klebanov, P. K., 135
Knickmeyer, E., 120
Knowledge and Human Development Authority (KHDA), 20t, 21–22, 23, 77, 158, 161
Krause, W., 15, 57, 78
Kuwait
 education as development priority, 10–16; first girls' and boys' schools, 46t,

47; formal schooling, 10; gender and education, 16; health and education, 145; higher education, 56–57; Kuwait University, 14–15, 14b–15b, 16; levels of national education system, 11; literacy rate, 15; Ministry of Education (MOE), 10, 46t; modernity, 75; nationalization, 119; oil and expansion of education in, 9–16; public school challenges, 15–16; regional competition, 11–12
Kuwait Cultural Office (KCO), 10, 47
"Kuwaiti Jobs for Bahraini Teachers," 112

Labor force, women in the, 43–44, 44t
Labour Fund, 122
"Labour Market Problems Threaten Relations," 114, 124
Labour Market Regulatory Authority, Bahrain, 116t, 122
Laessing, U., 120
LaLonde, R. J., 132
Lamaa, A., 115
Lamanna, F., 109
Lavy, V., 155
Layarda, P., vii
Le Roux, J., 22, 88
Lee, J. W., 136
Leigh, J. P., 134
LeTendre, G., 5, 80
Lev Ari, L., 79
Levin, H. M., 80
Levins, C., 106
Levitt, S. D., 1, 52
Lewin-Epstein, N., 132
Lewis, K., 109
Lewis, M. A., 5
Lietz, P., 154
Lifestyle diseases, 145, 146t
Lightfoot, L., 154
Lightowler, H. L., 144–145
Linder, C., 167
Lindsey, U., 37, 110, 118b
Linn, M. C., 2
Literacy
in Bahrain, 26; in Kuwait, 15; National Literacy Trust, 5, 158b–159b; Progress in International Reading Literacy Study (PIRLS), 23, 53t; in Qatar, 30; in UAE, 20
Little, B. B., 144
Lleras-Muney, A., 134
Lochner, L., 130, 137
Lockheed, M. E., 5
Looney, R., 114t, 120
Lynch, C., 164

Madany, I. M., 25, 27, 68
Madhi, S., 120
Madi, M. T., 107
Mahmoody, B., 41
Malek, C., 86, 126
Mann-Whitney U test, 100
Manpower and Government Restructuring Program (MGRP), 119
Markaz Research, 114t
Maroun, N., 6, 30, 69
Martens, K., 63
Martin, M. O., 7, 23, 52, 53, 93t, 94t, 95t, 156t–157t
Martinez, C., 63
Martorell, F., 37
Masdar Institute, 59
Mashood, N., 123, 124
Mathematics
Omani performance in, 34; teacher requirements for teaching, 92, 93t, 95t
Maw, J., 80
Mazawi, A. E., 106
McKinsey & Company, 69, 77, 91
McMahon, W., 133, 134
McMeans, A., 105
MDGs. See Millennium Development Goals (MDGs)
Medsker, L. L., 137
Meenaghan, G., 148
Meleis, A. I., 47, 56–57
Mellahi, K., 121
MENA. See Middle East and North Africa (MENA)
MENA Development Report, 45
Mettle-Nunoo, R., 3
Metz, H. C., 10, 14, 15, 28, 29–30, 110
Meyer, J. W., 76
MGRP. See Manpower and Government Restructuring Program (MGRP)
Michigan State University (MSU), 10
Middle East and North Africa (MENA)
development report, 66–67; diabetes and obesity, 145; *Gender and Development in the Middle East and North Africa (MENA)*, 42; MENA Development Report, 45; *Opening Doors: Gender Equality and Development in the Middle East and North Africa (MENA)*, 2, 65; tradition as hindrance to modern society, 65–66
Millennium Development Goals (MDGs)
for girls, 7; to promote gender equality and empower women, 2; targeting females, 61–62
Millennium Development Goals: United Arab Emirates Report, 74
Mills, A., 121
Milne, D., 93t, 94t
Mincer, J., 134–135
Ministry of Business and Trade, 36
Ministry of Economy, UAE, 74
Ministry of Education and Higher Education, 112
Ministry of Education (MOE), 1
Bahrain, 25, 27, 46t, 122; Egypt, 13b; English writing scores, 84f; Kuwait, 10, 46t; Oman, 6, 33, 34, 35, 46t, 53, 58, 58t, 69, 75, 84, 86, 86t, 89, 90, 103, 104, 112, 113, 125, 126, 156t–157t; Qatar, 91; Saudi Arabia, 29, 30, 31, 32; Sharjah Educational Council, 22; United Arab Emirates, 17, 18, 97f, 144
Ministry of Higher Education and Scientific Research (MOHESR), 19b, 20, 21, 84

210 Index

Ministry of Justice, UK, 153
Ministry of Scientific Research, 112
Minnich, C. A., 95t
Minnis, J. R., 106
Mittleberg, D., 79
Modernity, quest for, 61–79
 boys' education as illogical, 63; casualties of discourse, 77–79; current discourses, 70–77; discourse linking gender, education, and modernity, 64–68; global policies, 63–64; goals targeting females, 61–62; history and trajectory of project, 68–70; male disadvantage, 72, 73t; Millennium Development Goals, 61; modern, defined, 67; policy documents, 70, 71t; for trade and influence, 160; word frequency cloud, 70–72, 72f
Modernization project in education, 68–70
Moghadam, V., 41
MOHESR. *See* Ministry of Higher Education and Scientific Research (MOHESR)
Monetary returns to education, 131–133, 139–141
Monkman, K., 78
Morada, H., 105
Moretti, E., 130, 137
Morreti, E., 136
Moujaes, C. N., 6, 19b, 30, 69
Mourshe, M., 69
MSU. *See* Michigan State University (MSU)
Muennig, P., 80
Mullis, I. V., 7, 53
Mullis, I. V. S., 7, 23, 24t, 52, 83t, 93t, 94t, 95t, 156t–157t
Muralidharan, K., 90
Murdock, S., 136
Musaiger, A. O., 143
Muslim Brotherhood, 13b
Muslim Culture Hypothesis, 52
Mwabu, G., 132

Nagel, I. H., 150
Nagy, S., 156t–157t
NAP. *See* National Assessment Program (NAP)
National Assessment Program (NAP), 84, 84f
National Center for Education Statistics (NCES), 81t
National Curriculum Project, 18
National Employment Project, 122
National Health Service (NHS), 155
National Literacy Trust, 5, 158b–159b
National Media Council, 141
National Qualifications Authority (NQA), 18, 20, 21
Nationalization, 105–128
 age structures of national GCC populations, 109, 109t; in Bahrain, 122–123; characteristics and challenges of policies, 113–116; early programs, 114, 114t; education sector implications, 110–113; in Kuwait, 119; in Oman, 124–125; origination of, 106; private sector employment, 115, 116t; private sector employment of GCC citizens, 107, 107t; in Qatar, 117, 118b; reason for, 105; rentier state and rise of initiatives, 106–110; in Saudi Arabia, 119–122; unintended outcomes, 125–128; in United Arab Emirates, 123–124; workforce participation, 125, 125t; youth unemployment, 109, 110t
NationMaster, 47
NCES. *See* National Center for Education Statistics (NCES)
Nelson, C., 114, 123
New School Model (NSM), 22
New York Institute of Technology, 27

Newell, J., 3
NHS. *See* National Health Service (NHS)
Nonpecuniary returns to education, 133–135, 141–150
NQA. *See* National Qualifications Authority (NQA)
NSM. *See* New School Model (NSM)

Obesity rates, 143, 143t
OBG. *See* Oxford Business Group (OBG)
OECD. *See* Organisation for Economic Co-operation and Development (OECD)
Oil and the expansion of education, 9–40
 Bahrain, education mission in, 24–28; Kuwait, education as development priority in, 10–16; oil discoveries and the first formal schools, 9t; Oman, education quality in, 32–36; overview, 40; private education, 19b; public spending on education, 22f; Qatar, education in, 36–40; Saudi Arabia, Islam and education in, 28–32; trucial states, formal schooling in, 16–24; UAE education system, 20t; UAE performance assessments, 24t
Olarte, O., 59, 162
Olarte-Ulherr, O., 163
Olson, J. R., 93t, 94t
Oman
 crime and education, 150; education quality in, 32–36; female participation in the university, 58, 58t; first girls' and boys' schools, 46t, 48; gender gap in favor of girls, 35, 84, 86t; grade 12 examination results, 84, 86t; Ministry of Education (MOE), 6, 33, 34, 35, 46t, 53, 58, 58t, 69, 75, 84, 86, 86t,

89, 90, 103, 104, 112, 113, 125, 126, 156t–157t; nationalization, 112, 124–125; number of schools and enrollment figures, 33t; Vision 2020, 33
Onghena, P., 154
OPEC. *See* Organization of Petroleum Exporting Countries (OPEC)
Opening Doors: Gender Equality and Development in the Middle East and North Africa (MENA), 2, 65
Opportunity for students, 161–165
  at-risk students, 164; career programs, 163; improve teaching quality in preparatory and secondary boys' schools, 162; introduce practical curricular subjects, 162–163; service component in curricula, 164–165
Oppression of Arab women, 43–44
Oreopoulos, P., 130–131, 135
Organisation for Economic Co-operation and Development (OECD), 5
  assessments, 7; future of gender, education, and development, 158; leaving the boys behind, 83t; modernity, 62–63; oil and expansion of education, 23, 24t; Program on International Student Achievement, 3; rise of women in the Gulf, 44, 51t; Trends in International Mathematics and Science Study (TIMSS), 3
Organization of Petroleum Exporting Countries (OPEC), 28
Osell, 1
O'Sullivan, P., 78
Outcomes for girls, 49–54
  attainment, 50–54, 51t–53t; school life expectancy, 49–50, 50t

Oxford Business Group (OBG), 15, 124

Pan, D., 167
Park, A., 79
Parpart, J., 64
Pascarella, E. T., 138
"Pearson Helping UAE," 23
Perry, M., 3
Peterson, J. E., 6, 16, 68
Petroleum Company, 11
Phillips, D., 63
Pipher, M., 2
PIRLS. *See* Progress in International Reading Literacy Study (PIRLS)
PISA. *See* Program on International Student Achievement (PISA)
Policy documents, 70, 71t
Political expediency of education, 160
Poole, G., 153
Posusney, M., 41
Powell, J., 153
Private monetary returns to education, 131–133
Private nonpecuniary returns to education, 133–135
Private schools
  as alternative or only option, 19b; availability of, 161; vouchers for, 77
Private Schools Landscape in Dubai, 2012–2013, 20t
Private Tutoring Trends in the UAE, 100
Private-sector employment, 107–109, 107t
Prodromidis, K., 131
Prodromidis, P., 131
Program on International Student Achievement (PISA), 3, 23, 51t, 83t, 156t–157t
Progress in International Reading Literacy Study (PIRLS), 23, 53t, 83t
Psacharopoulos, G., 130, 131, 140
Psychological benefits of education, 135
Public welfare savings of education, 136–137
Putnam, R. D., 137

QAAET Annual Report, 53
Qatar
  education reform, 36–40; literacy rate, 30; Ministry of Education (MOE), 91; National Development Strategy, 110; nationalization, 111, 117, 118b; performance assessments, 23; Qatar University, 37–38, 54t; returns to education, 139–140; school enrollment, 46; school funding shortage, 39; senior school certificate scores, 84, 85f; student lack of motivation, 39; teacher quality, 38–39; women vs. men studying math and science, 55
Qatar Information Exchange, 116t
Qatar National Research Fund, 38
Qatar News Agency, 36
Qatar Statistics Authority (QSA), 7, 55–56, 76, 107, 107t, 117
Qatari, A. T., 143
Qatari National Human Development Report, 39
Qatar's Science and Technology Park, 117
QSA. *See* Qatar Statistics Authority (QSA)
Quality Assurance Authority for Education and Training, 28

Raanan, Y. L., 49
RAK Teachers' Network, 23
RAKFTZ, 20t
Ramazani, N., 115
RAND Corporation, 38, 77
Randall, M., 113
Randeree, K., 6, 7, 105, 106, 107, 107t, 114, 117, 119, 120, 122, 124, 126
Ras Al Khaimah (RAK)
  English language teacher, 96, 97f; male educators, 91, 92f; student achievement, 100, 101f
Rassekh, S., 32, 33, 33t, 34, 35, 48, 90

References to modernity and gender in GCC countries, 72, 73t
Regional Caribbean Initiative on Keeping Boys Out of Risk, 165b
Reimagining gender and education in the Gulf states, 166–168
Rendall, M., 152
Rentier state, 106–110
Returns to education, 130–150
  cyclical benefits, 138–139; in GCC countries, 139–150; monetary returns, 139–141; nonpecuniary returns, 141–150; private monetary returns, 131–133; private nonpecuniary returns, 133–135; social returns, 135–138, 141–150
Review of the Progress of the Millennium Development Goals in the Kingdom of Bahrain, 74–75
Reviving Ophelia: Saving the Selves of Adolescent Girls, 2
Reynolds, K., 3
Reynolds, L., vii
Riddell, C. W., 136
Ridge, N.
  future of gender, education, and development, 154, 158, 162, 164; gender gap measures, 156t–157t; Gulf stereotype, 6; leaving the boys behind, 86, 87t, 88, 89, 91, 92f, 93t, 96, 97, 98, 99, 100, 101, 101f, 102b–103b, 103, 104; modernity, 69, 79; nationalization, 110, 113; oil and expansion of education, 18, 19, 39; progress of girls vs. boys, 3; rise of women in the Gulf, 49, 50; value of education beyond work, 141, 142, 148, 151
Rivkin, S. G., 91
The Road Not Traveled: Education Reform in the Middle East and Africa, 45, 65, 77

Rodeghier, M., 137
Rosen, S., 133
Rouse, C., 80
Rousseau, R., 75
Rowe, K., 91
Royston, S., 77
Rumberger, R. W., 155
Rutledge, E.
  modernity, 69, 78; nationalization, 106, 107, 107t, 108, 109, 113, 114t, 115, 119, 127
Rutledge, E. J., 107
Rynhart, G., 125

Saadouli, N., 119
Sabbagh, K., 6, 12b, 65, 66, 69, 113, 141
Sabbagh, S., 6, 41, 42, 46t, 47, 49
Sabry, S., 123
Sahlberg, P., 69
Salama, S., 161
Salehi-Isfahani, D., 131
Salem, O., 108, 112
Salvanes, K. G., 131, 135
SAMA. *See* Saudi Arabian Monetary Agency (SAMA)
Samman, H., 6, 30, 79, 109, 119, 121–122, 124
Sasson, J., 41
Saudi Arabia
  crime and education, 149–150; first girls' and boys' schools, 46t, 47; Islam and education, 28–32; Ministry of Economy and Planning, 110; Ministry of Education (MOE), 29, 30, 31, 32; nationalization, 111, 119–122; returns to education, 140–141; teaching force, 31; tertiary institutions, 56; Vision 2020, 110
Saudi Arabian Monetary Agency (SAMA), 149
"Saudi Women in Private Sector Up by 330%," 116t
Sax, L. J., 164
Sayed, S., 115
Schafer, M. H., 133
Schneider, P., 108
Scholte, J. A., 78

School life expectancy, 49–50, 50t
Schriewer, J., 63
Schultz, T., 2, 130
Schultz, T. P., 3
Schwab, K., 62
Schwalje, W., 69
Science
  Omani performance in, 34; teacher requirements for teaching, 92, 94t, 95t; women involved in, 44–45, 45t
Scott, D., 3
Secondary school
  male dropouts, 86, 87t; math teacher requirements, 92, 93t; net enrollment, 48t; science teacher requirements, 92, 94t
Selim, H. M., 107
Semyonov, M., 132
"Sending Home the Foreigners," 98
Shah, N. M., 57
Shaheen, A. N., 110
Shaheen, K., 86, 100
Shami, S., vii, 6, 151
Sharjah Educational Council, 22
Shaw, J., 156t–157t
Shediac, R., 79, 109, 119, 121–122, 124
Shehadi, R., 115, 127
Sheikh Saud Bin Saqr Al Qasimi Foundation for Policy Research, vii, 23
Sickles, R. C., 133
Sicree, R., 156t–157t
Sidani, Y., 41, 42, 43
Silova, I., 63, 69
Simpson, C., 78, 124, 160
Slackman, M., 143
Slavin, B., 121
Smith, A., 130
Snyder, T. D., 81t
Social returns to education, 135–138, 141–150
Soffan, L. U., 47
Soman, R., 166
Sommers, C. H., 5
Sonbol, A., 41
Souad, 41
Spending on education, 21, 22f
Spreen, C., 63

Index

SQU. *See* Sultan Qaboos University (SQU)
Squalli, J., 140
"SR5 Billion Spent," 32
Stanco, G. M., 7, 93t, 94t, 95t
Stasz, C., 37, 38, 115
Statistical News, 144
Status and Progress of Women in the Middle East and North Africa, 42
Steffensmeier, D., 150
Steiner-Khamsi, G., vii, 63, 69, 76
Stephenson, W., 151
Stereotype
 of Arabian women, 41–42; higher education for women, 80; literature and media coverage of, 6
Stoet, G., 153
Stott, K., 143, 144, 145, 151
Stromquist, N., 6, 78
Suliman, O. M., 18, 19
Sullivan, S., 132
Sultan Qaboos University (SQU), 34, 54t, 58, 163
Sundararaman, V., 90
Supreme Education Council, 163
Swan, M., 21

Tarazi, K., 115
Taubman, P., 133
Teachers
 background characteristics, 91–97; for boys' schools in the GCC, 88–91; expatriate teachers and boys' education, 91–103; impact on boys' education, 99–103; improve teaching quality in preparatory and secondary boys' schools, 162; middle/lower-level math or science requirements, 92, 95t; national, 111–112; national male teacher shortage, 89–90; percentage of female teachers, 88, 89t; in Qatar, 38–39; secondary-level math teacher requirements, 92, 93t; secondary-level science teacher requirements, 92, 94t; working conditions, 98–99
Tejar Dubai, 126
Ten-Year Plan, 31
Terenzini, P. T., 138
Tertiary education, 54–59, 54t, 55f, 58t
Thabit, M., 144
Thomas, K., 123
Thunayan, I. A., 47
TIMSS. *See* Trends in International Mathematics and Science Study (TIMSS)
Topel, R., 135
Torofdar, Y., 119, 120
Torr, R., 110, 112, 123
Total Quality Management (TQM), 33
Toumi, H., 27, 39, 59, 89, 110, 146, 148
Trade, modernity for, 160
Trading Economics, 115
Treaties that focus on women and girls, 159
Trends in International Mathematics and Science Study (TIMSS), 3, 23, 51t, 52t, 83t
Trends of gender, education and development, 152–168
 barriers to change, 159–161; Boys' Reading Commission, 158b–159b; gender gap in GCC countries, 155–158, 156t–157t; high-quality private education, 161; modernity for trade and influence, 160; opportunity for all students, 161–165; overview, 152–155; political expediency, 160; Regional Caribbean Initiative on Keeping Boys Out of Risk, 165b; reimagining gender and education in the Gulf states, 166–168; treaties and agreements that focus on women and girls, 159
Trent, J. W., 137
Troske, K., 132
Trucial States
 formal schooling system, 16–24; independence of, 18; school funding, 17–18; shift from Islamic education to secular and vocational education, 17
Tunali, I., 131
Tutton, M., 146
2005 Arab Human Development Report: Toward the Rise of Women in the Arab World, 65
2008 World Bank Middle East and North Africa (MENA) Development Report, 65
2012 EFA Global Monitoring Report, 5–6
2013 MENA Development Report, 66–67
Tyson, L. D., 20t, 79

UAE. *See* United Arab Emirates (UAE)
UAE National Assessment Program (UAENAP), 53
UAENAP. *See* UAE National Assessment Program (UAENAP)
UAEU. *See* United Arab Emirates University (UAEU)
UIS. *See* UNESCO Institute for Statistics (UIS)
Ulrichson, K. C., 108
UNCSD. *See* United Nations Commission on Sustainable Development (UNCSD)
UNDP. *See* United Nations Development Programme (UNDP)
Unemployment of youth, 109–110, 110t
UNESCO. *See* United Nations Educational, Scientific, and Cultural Organization (UNESCO)
UNESCO Institute for Statistics (UIS), 7
 enrollment ratios, 4t; gender gap measures, 156t–157t; leaving the boys behind, 81t, 87t; rise of women in the Gulf, 44t, 46, 47, 48, 48t, 50t, 54

UNICEF. *See* United Nations Children's Fund (UNICEF)
United Arab Emirates (UAE)
  adult literacy rates, 20; boys' schools in, 102b–103b; education system, 20–24, 20t; first girls' and boys' schools, 46t, 47–48; health and education, 143–144; male retention and achievement, 6; Ministry of Education (MOE), 17, 18, 97f, 144; national curriculum, 18–19; nationalization, 112–113, 123–124; nationalization programs, 114t; oil and expansion of education, 22; performance in international assessments, 24t; private sector employment, 22–23; public spending on education, 21, 22f; returns to education, 140, 142; rise of women in the Gulf, 53; teacher quality, 162; Trucial States independence, 18; Vision 2021, 110
United Arab Emirates University (UAEU), 21, 54t
United Kingdom, 153, 158b–159b
United Nations Children's Fund (UNICEF)
  future of gender, education, and development, 159; gender gap measures, 156t–157t; leaving the boys behind, 80, 87t; nationalization, 119; World Summit on Children, 1
United Nations Commission on Sustainable Development (UNCSD), 25
United Nations Development Programme (UNDP)
  discourse focused on girls, 5; enrollment ratios,

4t; *Human Development Report*, 2; modernity, 64, 65, 66, 74, 76; oil and expansion of education, 21; rise of women in the Gulf, 45
United Nations Educational, Scientific, and Cultural Organization (UNESCO), 7
  Dakar Framework for Action, 2; education goals, 62; *EFA Arab States Regional Report*, 42; *EFA Global Monitoring Report*, 45, 45t; leaving the boys behind, 84, 88; modernity, 65; oil and expansion of education, 26, 27, 28, 30, 32; rise of women in the Gulf, 44, 48; *2012 EFA Global Monitoring Report*, 5–6; World Conference on Education for All, 1–2
United Nations, Millennium Development Goals, 2. *See also* Millennium Development Goals (MDGs)
United Nations Office on Drugs and Crime (UNODC), 147t, 148, 149f
United States Agency for International Development (USAID), 5, 81
University College of Arts, Science and Education, 27
University education timeline, 54t
University of Bahrain (UoB), 27, 49
UNODC. *See* United Nations Office on Drugs and Crime (UNODC)
UoB. *See* University of Bahrain (UoB)
Uros, P., 130
USAID. *See* United States Agency for International Development (USAID)
U.S.–British Kuwait Oil Company, 10
Useem, B., 137

Vaidya, S. K., 112, 146
Value of education beyond work, 129–151
  cyclical benefits, 138–139; gender implications, 150–151; monetary returns, 139–141; nonpecuniary returns, 141–150; overview, 129–130; private monetary returns, 131–133; private nonpecuniary returns, 133–135; returns to education, 130–139; returns to education in GCC countries, 139–150; social returns, 135–138, 141–150
Van Damme, J., 154
Van Leijen, M., 59
Vegas, E., 90
Verhoeven, H., 123
Verveer, M., 159
Vision 2020, 33, 110
Vision 2021, 110
Vision 2030, 15, 27, 110
Vreede-de Stuers, C., 49, 54t, 56
Vuollo, M., 114t, 117

"Waiting List for Admission Crosses 15,000," 19b
"Waljat College Invites All Students to Career Guidance Session," 163
Walker, M., 51t, 156t–157t
Wam, 126
Ward, R., 110
Wasserman, M., 1, 5, 152, 153, 158
Waters, A. M., 41
The Wealth of Nations, 130
Weaver-Hightower, M., 5
WEF. *See* World Economic Forum (WEF)
Weitzman, M., 138
Welcome Trust Sanger Institute, 153
Whelan, F., 69
Whitmire, R., 5
WHO. *See* World Health Organization (WHO)
Wilkins, S., 123, 142
Wilkinson, L. R., 133
Wizarat Al-Maarfa, 36
Wolfe, B., 130, 135, 142
Wolfe, B. L., 136, 137

Women in the Gulf, rise of, 41–60 attainment, 50–54, 51t–53t; conclusion, 59–60; educational outcomes for girls, 49–54; enrollment of girls vs. boys, 44–45; expansion of schooling opportunities for girls, 46–49; oppression of women, 42–43; school life expectancy, 49–50, 50t; science and engineering fields, 44, 45t; secondary school net enrollment, 48t; stereotypes, 41–42; tertiary education, 54–59, 54t, 55f, 58t; timeline of first schools, 46t; women in the labor force, government, and academia, 43–44, 44t

Women's Rights in the Middle East and North Africa: Progress Amid Resistance, 43

Word frequency cloud, 70–72, 72f

Working conditions for teachers, 98–99

World Bank benefits of gender equality, 2; *Education in Oman: The Drive for Quality*, 35; future of gender, education, and development, 165b; *Gender and Development in the Middle East and North Africa*, 44; gender gap measures, 156t–157t; gender gaps favoring females, 1; leadership development, 6; leaving the boys behind, 84, 86, 86t, 89–90, 103, 104; Millennium Development Goals, 5; modernity, 64, 65, 66, 67, 69, 75, 77; nationalization, 109, 109t, 110t, 112, 113, 115, 123, 125, 125t, 126; oil and expansion of education, 21, 22f, 31, 33, 34, 35; rise of women in the Gulf, 42, 44t, 45, 53, 55f, 57, 58, 58t

World Development Report 2012: Gender Equality and Development, 2

World Economic Forum (WEF), 21, 62–63, 64, 65

World Expo 2020, 160

World Health Organization (WHO), 144, 156t–157t

Worthman, C. M., 80

Xie, Y., 138

Yaqoob, T., 59
Young, S., 6, 160
Youth in the GCC: Meeting the Challenge, 65, 66
Youth unemployment, 109–110, 110t
Yunngar, M., 119, 120
Yusuf, N., 56, 121

Zafeirakou, A., 89, 90
Zahidi, S., 20t, 79
Zaman, S., 13b, 123, 163
Zayed University (ZU), 21
ZU. *See* Zayed University (ZU)
Zuabi, V., 31

About the Author

Natasha Ridge is the executive director of the Sheikh Saud Bin Saqr Al Qasimi Foundation for Policy Research based in Ras Al Khaimah (RAK), United Arab Emirates (a quasi-governmental organization that serves as a bridge between the research and policymaking communities). Natasha holds a doctorate of education in international education policy studies from Teachers College, Columbia University, and a master's degree in international and community development from Deakin University, Australia. Her research focuses on gender, education quality, and teachers in the GCC countries. Natasha has published a number of book chapters, working papers, and policy briefs. She has also consulted on curricula, assessment, training, and other aspects of educational policy for the World Bank, UNICEF, and USAID in Kyrgyzstan, Tajikistan, and Uzbekistan. Prior to this, Natasha worked in senior administrative and teaching positions in schools in the United Arab Emirates, Singapore, and Australia.